C000001951

'*Psychoanalysis and Ethics* aims to overcome a split training that arose, as David M. Black puts it, from lacked a philosophical base on which to consider t of ethics. In fact, human life is ethical life, and it ess_____, _____ _____ _____, frustrations, furies and tremendous joys of putting ethical life into words. Through subtle readings of Dante, as well as Melanie Klein, Hans Loewald, Donald Winnicott and many others, *Psychoanalysis and Ethics* revives our understanding of allegorical thinking and its power. This book is passionate and thought-provoking, rigorous and imaginative.'

Jonathan Lear, *Committee on Social Thought, the University of Chicago*

'Few books so generously provide a rich and nuanced conceptual scaffolding to help us to push open new doors in our thinking. This is one of those rare books. Masterful in his integration of philosophy, theology, psychoanalysis and literature, David M. Black has instantiated the "necessity of perspective" through his interdisciplinary approach to ethics. In the morally challenging times we live in, this book is essential and rewarding reading, not only for psychoanalytic clinicians and academics, but also for anyone interested in ethics – it is a book that I am sure I will return to many times.'

Alessandra Lemma, *fellow, British Psychoanalytic Society and visiting professor, Psychoanalysis Unit, University College London; author of* First Principles: Applied Ethics for Psychoanalytic Practice

'David M. Black has made an extraordinary individual contribution to psychoanalytic writing over many years. He approaches psychoanalysis from a unique combination of experiences and trainings in which he has been deeply immersed: religion, philosophy, ethics, psychoanalysis, literature – most recently the mammoth project of translating and writing commentaries on Dante. His voice is very much his own, and he approaches any subject with this very broad set of references, which infuses his writing with a particular quality of contemplation and vitality. I always look forward hungrily to receiving his latest psychoanalytic contribution.'

Francis Grier, *editor-in-chief,* International Journal of Psychoanalysis; *training analyst and supervisor of the British Society of Psychoanalysis*

Psychoanalysis and Ethics

Psychoanalysis and Ethics: The Necessity of Perspective is an attempt to look deeply into the relationship between psychoanalysis and ethics, and in particular into the failure of traditional psychoanalytic thinking to recognise the foundational character of ethical values.

In recent years, partly because of the climate crisis, the need for an "ethical turn" in our thinking has been recognised with increasing urgency. Using different historical lenses, and with special reference to the thought of the philosopher Emmanuel Levinas and pioneering American psychoanalysts such as Hans Loewald and Stephen Mitchell, the author discusses the perspectives needed in addition to those of science if the facts of "psychic reality" are to be more adequately recognised. In particular, this book emphasises the importance of a coherent account of the role of ethics in shaping the development both of the individual and of society.

Psychoanalysis and Ethics is essential reading for those concerned for the importance of ethics in psychoanalytic practice and theory, and more widely for those seeking to understand the place of ethics and religion in psychological development.

David M. Black is a Scottish writer and psychoanalyst, author of *Why Things Matter: The Place of Values in Science, Psychoanalysis and Religion* and editor of *Psychoanalysis and Religion in the 21st Century: Competitors or Collaborators*? In 2022, his translation and commentary on Dante's *Purgatorio* received the American National Translation Award for Poetry.

The New Library of Psychoanalysis

General Editor: Anne Patterson

The *New Library of Psychoanalysis* is published by Routledge Mental Health in association with the *Institute of Psychoanalysis*, London.

The purpose of the book series is:

- to advance and disseminate ideas in psychoanalysis amongst those working in psychoanalysis, psychotherapy and related fields
- to facilitate a greater and more widespread appreciation of psychoanalysis in the general book-reading public
- to provide a forum for increasing mutual understanding between psychoanalysts and those in other disciplines
- to facilitate communication between different traditions and cultures within psychoanalysis, making some of the work of continental and other non-English speaking analysts more readily available to English-speaking readers, and increasing the interchange of ideas between British and American analysts.

The *New Library of Psychoanalysis* published its first book in 1987 under the editorship of David Tuckett, who was followed by Elizabeth Bott Spillius, Susan Budd, Dana Birksted-Breen and Alessandra Lemma. The Editors, including the current Editor, Anne Patterson, have been assisted by a considerable number of Associate Editors and readers from a range of countries and psychoanalytic traditions. The present Associate Editors are Susanne Calice, Katalin Lanczi and Anna Streeruwitz.

Under the guidance of Foreign Rights Editors, a considerable number of the *New Library* books have been published abroad, particularly in Brazil, Germany, France, Italy, Peru, Spain and Japan. The *New Library of Psychoanalysis* has also translated and published several books by continental psychoanalysts and plans to continue the policy of publishing books that express as clearly as possible a variety of psychoanalytic points of view. The *New Library of Psychoanalysis* has published books representing all three schools of thought in British psychoanalysis, including a particularly important work edited by Pearl King and Riccardo Steiner, *'The Freud-Klein Controversies 1941-45'*, expounding the intellectual and organisational controversies that developed in the British psychoanalytical Society between Kleinian, Viennese and 'middle group' analysts during the Second World War.

The *New Library of Psychoanalysis* aims for excellence in psychoanalytic publishing. Submitted manuscripts are rigorously peer-reviewed in order to ensure high standards of scholarship, clinical communications, and writing.

For a full list of all the titles in the New Library of Psychoanalysis main series as well as both the New Library of Psychoanalysis 'Teaching Series' and 'Beyond the Couch' subseries, please visit the Routledge website.

Psychoanalysis and Ethics

The Necessity of Perspective

David M. Black

Routledge
Taylor & Francis Group

LONDON AND NEW YORK

Designed cover image: Saint Jerome in His Study, Antonello da Messina © The National Gallery, London

First published 2024
by Routledge
4 Park Square, Milton Park, Abingdon, Oxon OX14 4RN

and by Routledge
605 Third Avenue, New York, NY 10158

Routledge is an imprint of the Taylor & Francis Group, an informa business

© 2024 David M. Black

The right of David M. Black to be identified as author of this work has been asserted in accordance with sections 77 and 78 of the Copyright, Designs and Patents Act 1988.

All rights reserved. No part of this book may be reprinted or reproduced or utilised in any form or by any electronic, mechanical, or other means, now known or hereafter invented, including photocopying and recording, or in any information storage or retrieval system, without permission in writing from the publishers.

Trademark notice: Product or corporate names may be trademarks or registered trademarks, and are used only for identification and explanation without intent to infringe.

British Library Cataloguing-in-Publication Data
A catalogue record for this book is available from the British Library

ISBN: 978-1-032-58834-6 (hbk)
ISBN: 978-1-032-58835-3 (pbk)
ISBN: 978-1-003-45167-9 (ebk)

DOI: 10.4324/9781003451679

Typeset in Times New Roman
by KnowledgeWorks Global Ltd.

Contents

Acknowledgements

Almost all of the chapters in this book appeared first as papers in journals. I am grateful to the editors and publishers of the following journals for permission to reprint revised versions of the papers listed:

The *International Journal of Psychoanalysis*: for permission to reprint Chapter 2, The Working of Values in Ethics and Religion; Chapter 4, Who Founded Buddhism? and Chapter 5, Dante's Two Suns;

Psychoanalytic Inquiry: for permission to reprint Chapter 8, The Transcendent in Everyday Life;

the *British Journal of Psychotherapy*: for permission to reprint Chapter 3, Jonathan Lear; Chapter 7, Freud and Idealization; and Chapter 9, Religion as the Affirmation of Values;

Raritan: for permission to reprint Chapter 6, Dante, Duality, and the Function of Allegory;

Earlier versions of several papers were first given as lectures. Chapter 9 was first presented at a conference on Psychoanalysis and Philosophy at Senate House, University of London in October 2014. Chapter 6 was presented at the "Psychology and the Other" Conference in Boston in September 2021. Chapters 4, 6 and 8 were first presented at Scientific or Applied Section meetings of the British Psychoanalytic Society. All these chapters have been influenced by the ensuing discussions.

I owe more debts than I can remember to friends and colleagues, who read these chapters or with whom I discussed these issues. I think in particular of David Bell, Michael Brearley, Robert Chandler, Bob Chisholm, Elizabeth Cook, Francis Grier, John Herdman, Martha Kapos, Richard Rusbridger, Jerry Sokol, Harvey Taylor and Sally Weintrobe. Some of the chapters are interdisciplinary, requiring a reaching out to adjacent intellectual territory. Richard Gombrich and Kemmyo Taira Sato were both kind enough to read and comment on Chapter 4, which examines a particular thread in the history of Buddhist thought (though I take sole responsibility of course for its conclusions). With Giovanna di Ceglie, Matt Hoffman and my wife, Juliet Newbigin, I spent many hours reading and discussing Dante's

Divine Comedy, often from a psychoanalytic angle. And I owe a special debt to Sarah Richmond, who commented very helpfully on several of the chapters that engage with larger philosophical themes.

I dedicate the book to the memory of June Broadhurst, who died while it was in preparation. A friend and later a colleague for over half a century, her honesty, attentiveness and total lack of pretension contributed much to convincing me of the importance and efficacious reality of ethical seriousness.

DMB
September 2022.

Chapter 1

Introduction

The essays in this collection are probably best thought of as free-standing, but they circle somewhat obsessively around a few related themes. Central to them all is the thought that psychoanalysis, when Freud founded it, had no adequate philosophical base from which to consider the hugely important questions of ethics.

This, in the late nineteenth century, was unremarkable. The triumphs of science, including Darwin's account of the evolution of species, and the formulation by Helmholtz and others of the law of the conservation of energy, seemed at the time to carry all before them. It seemed as if Descartes' dream was about to be fulfilled: that the dominance of the thinking mind could render humankind "the masters and possessors of Nature" (Descartes 1997, 111). Unnerving as that formula sounds to many of us today, this was the dream of Enlightenment thinking; its echoes are present in many of Freud's early formulations of psychoanalysis. The hypersensitive Nietzsche, so alert to ethical issues that in retrospect he seems a sort of philosophical litmus paper, both recognised the power of the scientific vision and recoiled from the ethical void that accompanied it. He first embraced the idea of a Superman, whose exuberant self-assertion would "laugh above abysses," untouched by the suffering of others, unappalled by life's total absence of meaning in a merely mechanistic universe; shortly afterwards, he embraced a beaten horse, burst into tears and went quietly mad. The sociologist Max Weber, psychologically more robust but aware of similar issues, spoke of the effects of capitalism, of what he called the "tremendous cosmos of the modern economic order;" it was bound, he said, to "the technical and economic conditions of machine production which today determine the lives of all the individuals who are born into this mechanism." In a famous image, he said that concern for external goods should lie on the shoulders "like a light cloak;" under capitalism, however, it had become an "iron cage" (2003, 187). He spoke of nature becoming "disenchanted" as the understandings of science prevailed over all others.

Both these thinkers in their different ways were responding to the loss of a vision of the world and human life derived from the stories told by religions – humanly meaningful, however mythological – and their replacement by a mechanistic picture of the world based on rational science: one in which the existence of the world and of life were ultimately "random" and without purpose, and in which, when

DOI: 10.4324/9781003451679-1

things were not random, they were governed implacably by the laws of cause and effect: a "heartless world," as Marx succinctly summarised it, and a purely mechanical one.

Viewed from the first quarter of the twenty-first century, and with awareness of the gathering dangers of populism and the ever-enlarging threats to the Earth's climate and biodiversity, the ethical failures of the past century and a half are all too apparent. Even Communism, benign in its initial formulation, where it became powerful became dominated by class-hatred and the love of power. Fascism was well described by Walter Benjamin as representing the triumph of a false "aesthetics" over ethical and human values; neo-liberalism represented the triumph of a similar aesthetic fantasy, this time one of power and unrestrained free markets – unrestrained competition, perhaps modelled on a Hobbesian misreading of Darwin. As the British philosopher Elizabeth Anscombe recognised in the 1950s (Anscombe 1958), followed by Alasdair MacIntyre in the 1980s (MacIntyre 1981, 1988), the ordinary language of ethics remained in use, but it was becoming increasingly hollowed out by the inability of science to give meaning to the idea of intrinsic value: we retained the traditional vocabulary of ethics, but the words were becoming empty shells. Why should we be "good" or concerned for justice, kindness or truth-telling? What force have these requirements? And in psychoanalysis, the superego, someone else's values imported into the psyche, could offer no route to a true "conscience," whereby a person recognises in his or her own right the commanding power of ethical values.

This ethical failure, accompanied by the ever more dazzling achievements of technology, now threatens humanity and the Earth's ecosystems with catastrophe. At the same time, in the past few decades, there has been an increased awakening to the problem. As far back as 1959, Erik Erikson wrote: "In some periods of his history, and in some phases of his life-cycle, man needs ... a new ideological orientation as surely and as sorely as he must have air and food" (Erikson 1959, 20). I believe the present is such a period. Donna Orange (2020, 120) has spoken of an "ethical turn" in the work of intersubjective and relational psychoanalysts in the United States. Such a development necessarily demands a re-thinking, a radical new dialogue of psychoanalysis with philosophy. Among philosophers I have mentioned Anscombe and MacIntyre, two well-respected figures in Anglo-American philosophy; many others have contributed valuably to new ethical thinking, including Thomas Nagel, Charles Taylor, Mary Midgley and Ronald Dworkin (whom I discuss at more length in Chapter 10); these have not in general been much discussed in psychoanalytic contexts. Most valuable of all, I think, is the French philosopher Emmanuel Levinas, a Jew and Holocaust survivor, whose profound insights have increasingly been recognised in the English-speaking world, and very clearly, more recently, by Donna Orange and some of the analysts she refers to.

Levinas stands in the tradition of Husserl and Heidegger, with both of whom he studied. I give a summary account of his life in Chapter 10. His phenomenology, the prioritising of direct experience over theoretical understanding, allowed him to make an important move: he declared that ethics was "first philosophy," that ethical insight, derived from a perception of "the other" in all his or her alterity, recognised something that was prior to "ontologies" such as those that underpin the natural sciences. Levinas rarely mentions psychoanalysis explicitly, but he was surely contrasting his own view with the goal of Freudian psychoanalysis when he wrote (in his characteristically difficult and idiosyncratic prose): "The I endowed with personal life, the atheist I whose atheism is without wants and is integrated in no destiny, surpasses itself in the Desire that comes to it from the presence of the other" (1969, 62). When we experience that Desire, when we recognise the command of ethics, when, seeing "the face of the Other," we become aware of our obligation of responsibility, we are seeing, he said, a truth that is primary and not to be argued with. Throughout his career, Levinas returned again and again to this crucial insight, forever deepening, enlarging and strengthening it.

It was the discovery of Levinas' thought that enabled me to move on from my own earlier writings on these matters (Black, 2011), which were still impeded by the over-valuation of science in the Freudian tradition (virtually unquestioned when I trained in London in the 1980s). I think now that that tradition needs to be stood on a different philosophical foundation, a phenomenological base, as the American psychoanalyst Hans Loewald showed a path to doing, and as has increasingly been recognised since by recent psychoanalysts, in America especially. This is not a repudiation of science, but a recontextualising of it in relation to ethics. I discuss Loewald at more length in Chapter 2: a profoundly respectful and careful psycho-analytic thinker, with a background in philosophy, his influence has increasingly penetrated the world of American psychoanalysis through the work of, among others, Stephen Mitchell, Jonathan Lear and Joel Whitebook.

In addition to ethics, these essays return repeatedly to themes of religion: how to understand it and how to conceive its importance, despite the fact that many of the stories that religions tell are undoubtedly, to use Freud's word, "illusion." Levinas used to say, jokingly, that his goal in philosophy was to translate the Bible into Greek. He meant that his goal was to translate the profound, idiosyncrati-cally phrased, local insights of a particular religion – in his case, Judaism – into the universal language of philosophy. ("At no moment," he said, "did the Western philosophical tradition in my eyes lose its right to the last word" [1985, 24].) This "translation" continues to be a project of great importance, and my discussion here of religious themes – in my case usually Christian or Buddhist – is intended as a contribution to it. The full implication of such a translation remains to be seen, but it is likely to be very far-reaching: it implies that religious objects can be under-stood as ultimately "allegorical" in nature – that far from being merely "illusion" they have a perfectly recognisable function, from a social and ethical point of view, which is educational. Emotional and ethical education has traditionally been one of the central functions of religions; the discrediting of religion, in the eyes of so many educated people in our society, has resulted in an enormous void in our think-ing which, until recently, has gone almost unnoticed. "Allegory," as I discuss the term in two essays here, Chapters 5 and 6, does not imply "illusory;" it implies that what is being spoken of cannot be wholly encompassed by the language used to refer to it. It holds open a door to deeper and further meaning – ultimately to what Levinas called "infinity."

By the same token, the scope of ethics is enlarged. What Levinas meant by ethics is something rather different from what concerned Aristotle. Levinas is concerned with something deeper, which provides the necessary perspective from which "Aristotelian" virtues and ethical decisions can be addressed. In Chapter 5, discussing Dante's *Divine Comedy*, I suggest that Dante, when he felt the need to introduce two very different guides, Virgil and Beatrice, as he negotiated the three realms of the afterlife, was grappling, probably quite consciously, with this issue. As the philosophers Ronald Dworkin and Peter Singer also argue (quoted here in Chapters 9 and 10), it is not ultimately possible to separate from ethics the issue of "meaningfulness," which is so profoundly important when one seeks to assess one's own or another person's history and life-choices.

The individual essays

Franz Rosenzweig disliked introductions, which he described as the hen's clucking after she has laid her egg. I shall try to keep my comments brief therefore as I indicate in a little more detail the specific content of the individual essays included here.

Chapter 2: *The Working of Values in Ethics and Religion*. This essay sets out the basic shape of the issues by reviewing the history of internal objects in British and American psychoanalysis. It attempts to show how the initial standpoint of psychoanalysis on the base of natural science (as understood at the end of the nineteenth century) rendered the nature of internal objects, their power to organise the psyche and the question of the commandingness of the values they represent, impossible to address adequately. More recently, a more phenomenological approach and, particularly, the thinking of American psychoanalysts such as Loewald, Roy Schafer, Stephen Mitchell and Jonathan Lear have opened up new possibilities. The fact that different ethical values may be incommensurable, and that some are more commanding than others, requires a recognition of hierarchy within the psyche. The notion of "allegorical objects" is briefly introduced.

Subheadings: Introduction
"Internal objects": Freud to Winnicott
Hans Loewald
Some implications of the phenomenological nature of internal objects
Organisation implies hierarchy
Ethical values and allegorical objects
Conclusion

Chapter 3: *Jonathan Lear: heir to a different legacy*. This chapter is a review essay on a collection of papers by the philosopher and psychoanalyst Jonathan Lear, *Wisdom won from Illness* (Lear 2017). It focuses on some of Lear's central themes, in particular on the role of interpretation and the question of what *really* makes for psychological development in an analysand. Also, linking with the themes of the previous chapter, it discusses the "different legacy" for psychoanalysis that Lear describes, deriving from the thought of Hans Loewald and enabling psychoanalysis to be set on a more secure philosophical basis than that of Freud's understanding of science.

Subheadings: Introduction
What makes a developmental difference?
Irony
The thought of Hans Loewald

Chapter 4: *Who Founded Buddhism?*. This chapter considers the psychological pressures shaping the development of a religion. Taking Buddhist history as an example, it considers what were the psychological pressures that shaped the very remarkable development of Buddhist thought from the initial Enlightenment of the historical Buddha, Gautama Siddhartha, as he sat under a peepul tree, to the apparently very different vision of the Japanese Pure Land Buddhist schools in the twelfth century CE. The explicit recognition by Buddhism that its religious objects are always "mental constructs" is shown to have had a central place in making this development possible. The emphasis is on the psychoanalytically understandable pressures which shaped the evolution of the religion, and which increasingly pushed for a "silent" (unformulated) part of Buddhist experience to be foregrounded and formulated explicitly.

Subheadings: Introduction
The Buddha's Enlightenment
The Mahāyāna
The Buddha Amitābha
The effectiveness of religious objects
Allegorical objects
Conclusion

Chapter 5: *Dante's Two Suns*. This essay looks further into the notion of allegory and attempts to understand its working by way of one of its most famous examples. It discusses a central idea in Dante's *Divine Comedy:* that human life requires two very different value systems, spoken of by Dante in *Purgatorio* using the metaphor of "two suns," both of which are sources of light or sources of authority in their own right. This idea is allegorised further in the role of Dante's two guides, Virgil and Beatrice, and is present very directly in his preoccupation with the dualities of Christianity and classical thought, Pope and Emperor, contemplation and activity (and many others). In this essay, it is illustrated in some detail by reference to Dante's account of his meeting in Purgatory with the poet Statius. The picture of Statius is an elaborate fiction: Dante presents Statius, a pagan Roman epic poet, as having secretly become a Christian convert, and moreover claims that he did so inspired by elementary misreadings of the non-Christian poet, Virgil. This surprising and seemingly arbitrary fiction opens a door to reflection on some of the psychological subtleties of Dante's thought.

Subheadings: Introduction
The meeting with Statius
The attraction of classicism to Dante
Dante's personal qualities
The larger project
Discussion

Chapter 6: *Dante, Duality and the Function of Allegory.* This essay is a further discussion of the dualities in Dante's thought, particularly in relation to Virgil's meeting the limit of his understanding at the top of the Terraces of Purgatory, and Dante's very carefully described re-meeting with Beatrice in the Earthly Paradise. It suggests that one of the functions of the two guides is to represent two different sorts of love which it is necessary in a fulfilled human life to encounter; these had become problematic for Dante himself following the death of his mother in his early childhood.

Subheadings: Introduction
The structure of Purgatory
A second world of values
Allegory and the logic of Incarnation
Conclusion: wider implications

Chapter 7: *Freud and Idealisation.* A review essay of a book by Joel Whitebook: *Freud: an intellectual biography* (Harvard UP, 2017). This chapter discusses the persistent problem of idealisation in the psychoanalytic world, and its relation in particular to the "legend" of Freud's life, deriving partly from Freud himself and partly from disciples such as Ernest Jones. This tendency to idealisation has often made it difficult to think clearly about psychoanalytic ideas and has inhibited the freedom of psychoanalytic thinkers to move into new territory. Whitebook's biography shows clearly the roots of this idealisation in Freud's personal history.

Subheadings: Introduction
The originality of Whitebook's biography
Freud and women
Freud and science
Jewishness and religion
Conclusion

Chapter 8: *The Transcendent in Everyday Life.* This chapter, the first of three offering a discussion of the thought of Emmanuel Levinas, relates in particular to the use of his thought by the psychoanalysts Viviane Chetrit-Vatine and Eyal Rozmarin. Levinas typically presents his ethical thinking in a way that makes no mention of the subject's personal history: this essay attempts to show how from a psychoanalytic point of view ethical sensitivity and personal history necessarily form part of a single picture. It suggests too that the "transcendent" values of obligation and responsibility, which Levinas recognises with so much subtlety, far from being exotic, are a familiar if rarely acknowledged part of everyday experience, both in ordinary life and in the consulting room.

Subheadings: Introduction
The notion of value
Emmanuel Levinas
Matricial space
Case example: Emily
Discussion
Conclusion

Chapter 9: *Religion as the Affirmation of Values.* This chapter attempts to answer the question: what is the social importance of religion? Why is it facile to suppose that "growing out of religion" (Winnicott's phrase), and replacing religion by rational thought and the "reality principle," the alleged achievement of Freudian psychoanalysis, is a development that entails no significant social or psychological cost? Using in particular the thought of Martin Buber, Levinas and Ronald Dworkin, this essay suggests that a crucial social function of religions has been educational: to provide ways to single out, to remember and to affirm (though not to create) the foundational ethical values that are recognised in the "epiphanic" direct experience that Levinas describes.

Subheadings: Introduction
Background: psychoanalysts on religion
Emmanuel Levinas
Developments in analytic philosophy: objectivity of values
The function of religions

Chapter 10: *Levinas' Re-basing of Religion.* Emmanuel Levinas described his understanding of religion in one of his two principal books, *Totality and Infinity* (1961). This essay attempts to follow his account in some detail and to compare it with Freud's picture of religion in *The Future of an Illusion* (1927). Freud's picture, like that of most subsequent psychoanalytic theorists, emphasised the role of religious "objects," figures such as gods, angels or bodhisattvas, or purported spiritual realities such as the career of the soul in the afterlife, which are different in different religions. Such "objects" are notably absent from Levinas' account. The essay goes on to consider the significance of this absence. It suggests that Levinas' account opens up a deeper perspective in which to perceive the true importance religions may have for the life of the individual, and for society more largely, which may be hard to recognise when the emphasis is on their "objects."

Subheadings: Introduction
Emmanuel Levinas: a brief outline of his life
Levinas' account of religion
Discussion
Conclusion

References

Anscombe, G.E.M. (1958). Modern moral philosophy. *Philosophy* 33: 124.

Black, D.M. (2011). *Why Things Matter: the Place of Values in Science, Psychoanalysis and Religion*. New York, NY and London: Routledge.

Descartes, R. (1997). Discourse on the Method (1637). In E.S. Haldane and G.R.T. Ross (trans) *Key Philosophical Writings*. Ware: Wordsworth Editions.

Erikson, E. (1959). *Young Man Luther: A Study in Psychoanalysis and History*. London: Faber and Faber.

Lear, J. (2017). *Wisdom* Won from Illness. Cambridge, MA: Harvard UP.

Levinas, E. (1969). *Totality and Infinity: An Essay on Exteriority*. Trs. A. Lingis. Pittsburgh, PA: Duquesne UP.

Levinas, E. (1985). *Ethics and Infinity*. Trs. R.A. Cohen. Pittsburgh, PA: Duquesne UP.

MacIntyre, A. (1981). *After Virtue*. London and New York, NY: Bloomsbury.

MacIntyre, A. (1988). *Whose Justice? Which Rationality?* London: Duckworth and Co.

Orange, D. (2020). Radical Ethics. In *Psychoanalysis, History, and Radical Ethics: Learning to Hear* 120. New York, NY and London: Routledge.

Weber, M. (2003). *The Protestant Ethic and the Spirit of Capitalism (1904)*. Trs Talcott Parsons. New York, NY: Dover Publications.

Chapter 2

The working of values in ethics and religion

Introduction

The triumphs of science in the nineteenth century (of which Darwin's theory of evolution and Helmholtz's law of the conservation of energy may stand as iconic instances) created a profound division within philosophy. Was its task to become the loyal servant of all-conquering science, pointing out the implications of what science discerned, and policing the frontiers of sound science and rational argument, or did it still have a separate and more fundamental role in creating a "worldview" within which the sciences would have, of course, a respected place, but in which they would not be the dominant partner?

To accept the first of these paths was to accept "positivism," a word meaning broadly the belief that only science and what can logically be derived from scientific findings can be the ground of truth: it involved accepting materialism and rationality, and rejecting metaphysics, idealism and religion. Darwin implicitly, and Helmholtz and Freud's teacher Ernst Brücke explicitly, accepted this position; it became the basis of Viennese "logical positivism" in the 1920s, and though it then lost prestige in the world of analytic and ordinary language philosophy, it remains the default assumption, probably, of most scientists and many ordinary educated people in the West. When Freud spoke of the scientific *Weltanschauung*, in his view the *Weltanschauung* of psychoanalysis, positivism was what he had in mind. Joel Whitebook (2004, 106) has said that it is "simplistic" to describe Freud as a positivist, and it's true that Freud's writings are hugely rich, often metaphorical, and frequently speculative. Nevertheless, the nineteenth century materialist conception of science was the authority to which Freud returned, and to which he made his ultimate appeal. When, writing on religion, he concluded resonantly: "Our science is no illusion. But an illusion it would be to suppose that what science cannot give us we can get elsewhere" (1927, 56), he gave virtually a definition of positivism.

For thinkers concerned for subjectivity, values and "meaningfulness," positivism was problematic. Nietzsche's madman's perceptive and alarmed response (1882) ("Do we not feel the breath of empty space? Has it not become colder? ... God is dead") influenced a generation; the pioneering sociologist Max Weber lamented the "iron cage" in which rationality would increasingly encase us (1904).

DOI: 10.4324/9781003451679-2

A creative counter-argument came from the phenomenologists: Brentano, Husserl and Heidegger, each the pupil of his predecessor, built on the fundamental Kantian insight that knowledge is dependent, not only on "what is the case" but also on the nature of the receptive capacities of the knower.[1] What could be known about these capacities was, of course, also subject to the same restriction. Subjectivity, a puzzle to the positivist, could in the phenomenological picture be given a central role as the terrain in which all experience, including scientific research and logical reflection on its implications, takes place and is encountered.

If the philosophical precursor of the phenomenologists was Kant, the precursor of positivism was Descartes. Descartes' division of reality into mind and matter authorised, as he said, the project of "rendering ourselves the masters and possessors of Nature" (1637, 111), nature now being conceived as mindless *res extensa*, extended stuff. By the end of the nineteenth century, this project looked to many to be well along on the road to completion (Peat 2002, x). The American physicist Albert Michelson wrote: "The more important fundamental laws and facts of physical science have all been discovered, and these are so firmly established that the possibility of their ever being supplanted ... is exceedingly remote" (1903, 25). (His remark reads ironically nowadays: as we now know, the revolutions of relativity and quantum physics were about to contradict it emphatically.)

But Descartes' argument also made the notion of "ourselves" problematic. The *cogito*, in the first person singular, authorises only a single person to be the subject: "I" think, therefore "my" existence as a thinking subject is assured – but if this is my one certainty then, as the philosopher John Macmurray (2004) pointed out, others, including "you," can only be on the far side of a dividing line. The Cartesian universe can only be a solipsism (or perhaps, puzzlingly, a plurality of solipsisms). Descartes glimpsed this difficulty, and he brought in God as a good demon to guarantee the truth of our perceptions; but if one takes the logic of the *cogito* seriously it can only leave God in the same position as "you" – outside the magic space of the unique thinker.

On the whole, the nineteenth century scientists, such as Darwin, Helmholtz and Charles Lyell, didn't feel a need to concern themselves with such issues; their findings could be plausibly presented in the everyday language of a shared external reality. But when we arrive at psychoanalysis, the lurking problem in Descartes' formulation emerges to haunt us. I, the thinking scientist, may look out on a mindless material world, governed by the laws of a mechanical Nature; and while you, standing beside me, do the same, we speak in harmony. But if I turn to look at you, our tune fails. If "I" am the unique thinker of whose existence I can be certain – and nature is only mindless mechanism – "you," who have clearly as Darwin has shown emerged as part of nature, can only be perceived by me as mindless mechanism; I am returned, either to solipsism, or, if I am sufficiently resolute in my pursuit of logical consistency, to the heroic declaration that I too, *really*, am mindless mechanism, and my subjectivity is illusion: ultimately, there can be no subjects. The gates of Weber's "iron cage" clang shut behind me. (I'm not certain that it's actually possible to believe this last position, but consistent behaviourists, for example, are compelled to think they do.)

This then was the ambiguous intellectual weather into which Freud launched the ship of psychoanalysis, which to the end of his life he declared to be a science.

This present chapter reflects on the fact that, in the modern era, neither philosophy nor psychoanalysis has been able to furnish an adequate account of a basis for the compelling power of ethics to motivate decision, or to recognise the values without which humanity is unlikely to survive. Psychoanalysis itself, as a therapy, is necessarily an ethical activity, but along with the other sciences it has lacked a base in its theory from which the importance of ethics could be understood. Its ethical seriousness, always present, derived from elsewhere, from medical ethics, the wider culture, implicit religious values and so forth.

This lack of a proper base has been true as well of much recent Western philosophical thinking about ethics. It's not that we lack the names for the necessary values, but we can give no account of what grounds them, and they have to a large extent lost their "efficacy" or power to command. The philosopher Alasdair MacIntyre went so far as to compare our current use of ethical language to the use of the word *taboo* in eighteenth century Polynesia: people remembered that certain things were taboo, and they acted accordingly, but they no longer had any story to tell of *why* they were taboo, and their traditions were easily overthrown (MacIntyre 1981, 129–31). Something similar presumably was the case with the "ordinary decent Germans" in the 1930s who succumbed so readily to the allure of Hitlerism. MacIntyre's own solution was to turn back to what he saw as the founding tradition, the Catholic Christianity of Aquinas. I shall argue here that, for most of us, the intellectual discrediting of traditional religions, inevitable when religion is construed as a matter of "beliefs," has deprived values of this grounding; there remains, however, another sort of thinking which may give more access to the necessary quality of efficacy. This thinking I shall call "allegorical." It has deep roots, and it can be found in certain modern thinkers – I am especially aware of Martin Buber and Emmanuel Levinas – but it has been weakening in the West ever since the rise of individualism and "nominalism" in about the fourteenth century. So I shall attempt to describe it as well by referencing the work of an explicitly allegorical thinker, namely, Dante.

Psychoanalysis has the potential to contribute importantly to this discussion, which calls for both philosophical and psychological input. This is particularly because of its notion of "internal objects", and its increasing recognition of their role in organising the psyche. I shall begin this essay therefore with a brief sketch of their history, suggesting that the understanding of them has tended to change from a notion of "internalised others" (as in Freud's account of the superego) to a more phenomenological picture in which they work to organise the mind in the moment of their occurrence and any relation they may have to external "others" is secondary. I am influenced in this account by the theories of Hans Loewald, Roy Schafer and Stephen Mitchell in particular.

"Internal objects": Freud to Winnicott

The word *object* has been over-used in psychoanalytic history. As far back as 1891, in his monograph *On the Conception of the Aphasias*, Freud described a version of an internal object. He wrote: "A word ... acquires its meaning by being linked to an 'object-presentation' ... [which is] a complex of associations made up of the greatest variety of visual, acoustic, kinaesthetic and other presentations" (Freud 1891, 213). This "object-presentation" is very close to what he would later call a "thing-presentation," the unconscious content which is made conscious when linked to a word-presentation ("hyper-cathected") (1915, 201–2). A great deal of psychoanalysis is foreshadowed in this conception alone.

Soon after, the word *object* acquired another use in Freud's theory of drives, which have both an *aim* (the "removal of excitation") and an *object*, the person or thing by which that aim can be attained (1933, 96). Freud took as given a one-person starting point: "primary narcissism" was our natural state, from which our drives impelled us, and on which society impinged; we sought to rid ourselves of the resulting excitations. In such a picture, a person's goals can only be the satisfaction of the aims of his or her drives; other people are of value, positive or negative, insofar as they are objects of, or objects impeding, that satisfaction. For this reason, it became habitual in psychoanalysis to refer not to "self and others" but to "ego and its objects."

Later, when Freud wrestled to understand the emotions involved in such complex matters as mourning, conscience, "civilisation" and religion, the one-person standpoint became increasingly difficult to maintain. "Identification" (internalisation of the external "object") allowed for increasing complexity. The ego "as altered by the object" could then itself become an object for the ego "as critical agency" (Freud 1917, 249). In *The Ego and the Id*, he said he hadn't realised how "common and typical" such identifications were: he suggested that the whole character of the ego was built up from them (1923, 28–9).

This account of a part of the ego, "altered by the object," developed into one sort of internal object, the intrapsychic representative of a real, external other. The critical agency too, later named the superego, was recognised as created also by identifications; it came to be understood as another sort of internal object, formed by identification with what was called a "part-object," in this case the "voice" and valuations of another person, and adopted to avoid the penalties and painful guilt-feelings that would otherwise afflict the individual. Education and personal development came to be seen as a complex sequence of identifications and rejections of identification, with the result if all went well of creating a rich and relatively stable "inner world" of internal objects.

If we ask what sort of a thing an internal object is, however, we are left with several puzzles. For example, an internal object (whether whole object or part object) exists only as what it is to the subject. No one else has access to it. Whatever its origins, unlike an ordinary object in the physical world, it has in the moment of its occurrence no other reality by reference to which the subject's experience can be contradicted or corrected. It has no independent substrate of which continuity can be predicated.

If, through experience with a parallel external ("real") object, the internal object is changed, there is then a different internal object. The paradoxicality of this formulation is I think an inescapable consequence of using the language of "internal objects." It has to do with the fact that nouns ("substantives") are suited to the nature of external objects but not to internal ones. Roy Schafer once suggested that, if we are not to continue "to subordinate new ideas to old solutions" (1976, 7), psychoanalysis needed to develop an "action language" for the inner world in which substantives were replaced by verbs and adverbs. He was recognising the confusion created by speaking of internal objects in language appropriate to external objects, which do indeed have persisting "substance" independent of their phenomenal appearance to the subject. But, alas, there is no such action language, and we are left with a problem that has deep roots in philosophical history: what is the relation of continuity to what is subjective? Faced with this problem, both Buddhism and David Hume quite independently concluded that ultimately there was no enduring "self" at all. But this too is unsatisfactory. Ethical activity – for example, promising – and psychoanalysis, with its account of personal development, cannot dispense with the notion of a continuing subject. I think at present we have no good solution to this difficulty. In this paper, I shall refer to this quality of internal objects – that they don't endure but can only be replaced by, so to speak, different editions – as their "phenomenological nature."

Freud, always marching to more than one drummer, never wholly gave himself up to the picture of "internal objects" (he never let go of the "drives," and beyond them some prospective material foundation in neurobiology), but some of his followers, particularly those influenced by Melanie Klein, took it very much further. Klein, an extraordinarily gifted intuitive thinker, without formal scientific training (she had trained as a nursery-school teacher) adopted many of Freud's hypotheses – Oedipus complex, death drive, superego, internal objects – as if they were givens. She went further than any previous analyst in imagining the experience of the baby, pushing Freud's concepts back to very early stages of development, but also boldly departing from Freud's thought in important ways. In particular, she thought that babies were object-related from birth (there was no primary narcissism). For her, the fundamental form of unconscious mentation was phantasy involving internal objects, and this was the case from birth and even pre-natally.

When her ideas were challenged from within the British Society in the 1940s, Marjorie Brierley, one of the acutest thinkers in the Society, criticised Klein's use of internal objects as failing to clearly distinguish concepts from percepts. Work with patients, said Brierley, is rightly "done with percepts," in the language of immediate experience, including the language of internal objects; but theory should be done in the different language of generalisation and abstraction:

> Melanie Klein lays herself open to misunderstanding in her generalizations by a choice of terms too close to her specific source material. Thus, in the expression 'whole object' she uses the word 'whole' to distinguish a person-object from an organ- or part-object. But she also uses the term 'whole' in the sense of undamaged or intact to distinguish it from the object which a child in a certain state of anxiety feels to be in pieces. Now it is quite possible to think of a person being dismembered but it is not possible to conceive of a mental object being literally shattered – one cannot take a hammer to a mental object.
>
> (Brierley 1942, 109)

This is a perceptive criticism, and it comes from the scientific side of the argument. But Klein, theoretically less sophisticated than Brierley, and working more spontaneously and often with child patients, was moving almost unawares away from Freud's world of nineteenth century science, and in particular away from the automatic assumption that "the body" was the prime foundational reality of "the person." The abandonment of primary narcissism had profound philosophical consequences: it meant that "persons" could begin to be thought of as essentially social beings, and not primarily, as in Descartes' model, as solitary egos in separate bodies looking out onto the world. Brierley could see that Klein was moving away from "science," as understood by Freud; what neither she nor Klein could see was that Klein was moving in a potentially coherent direction, towards the more phenomenological world in which personal life is lived.

Klein's segue away from Freud stimulated other thinkers, notably Ronald Fairbairn and Donald Winnicott, to go further. The British scholar Kate Forbes-Pitt discusses an early unpublished paper by Fairbairn (1930) in which he examined the repeated dualisms in Freud's drive theory, and suggested, very boldly at the time, that they sprang from Freud's allegiance to theory rather than to observation. Freud always needed two sets of drives, said Fairbairn, because he needed to account for his theory of repression (Forbes-Pitt 2018). Attempting to find a more coherent theory of drives, Fairbairn moved on to an account of libido as having as its central goal relationship with others rather than drive-satisfaction.

Fairbairn was an unusual figure in psychoanalysis. A Scot who had studied Divinity at Edinburgh, and then fought throughout the First World War, he remained a lifelong Christian. Following the war, he retrained as a psychiatrist and then as a psychoanalyst, remaining in Edinburgh and outside the formal structures of the British Psychoanalytic Society. He became a notably independent thinker. Relational psychoanalysts (Greenberg & Mitchell 1983, Grotstein & Rinsley 1994; Mitchell 2000) have recently brought him centre-stage in psychoanalytic history by recognising that he was the pioneer of "a radically different, relational theory of mind" (Mitchell 2000, 104), central both to attachment theory and to the American relational schools.

Strongly influenced by Klein, and wanting to simplify the complexities of Freud's thinking, Fairbairn postulated one drive, libido, and one goal, human relationship. He conceived growth in terms not of genitality but of the move from infantile to mature dependency (Scharff 2005). Pleasure and avoidance of unpleasure remained important but were no longer primary. Mitchell saw this picture as still struggling with past formulations but spoke with admiration of its originality. "Fairbairn, Sullivan, and other architects of the relational model were redefining the nature of the human psyche as fundamentally social and interactive. Fairbairn was suggesting that object-seeking is not the vehicle for the satisfaction of a specific need, but is the expression of our very nature, the form through which we become specifically *human* beings" (Mitchell 2000, 106). He was "among the first to intuit that the establishment and maintenance of relationships with others is as fundamental to the nature of the human organism as breathing oxygen" (107).

That is well put and captures Fairbairn's crucial insight. He was perhaps the first major psychoanalytic thinker to identify explicitly the key weaknesses in Freud's theory, the elimination of subjecthood in favour of objectivities (which followed from Freud's adoption of the standpoint of reductive materialism), and the separation of drive from "object" in the psychoanalytic sense. Fairbairn himself wanted to base his theory on the newer scientific developments, in relativity and quantum physics, which had succeeded the mechanistic physics of Helmholtz; he thought that psychoanalysis had failed to keep abreast of the implications of these developments. He was impressed by the inseparability of energy and structure in the quantum conception of matter and proposed that the psyche is similarly a "dynamic structure," "oriented towards outer reality, and thus determined by a reality principle from the first" (1946, 140).

Fairbairn took an important step towards central issues, but by taking physics as his model, he continued to objectify the subject. He failed to address the central problem of post-Cartesian thought, described by John Macmurray as a confusion of the *logical* dualism of subject and object – the fact that "experience" logically implies an "experiencer" – with the *metaphysical* dualism of mind and matter, in which both terms name objective "things" (in Descartes' language, material *res extensa* and immaterial *res cogitans*) (Macmurray 2004).

This distinction, between logical and metaphysical dualism, which may at first sight look off-puttingly technical, is in fact the avenue to something extremely far-reaching. It allows us to say that though our fundamental nature may be subjective, this need not imply the existence of a distinct "soul" (*Seele* in Freud's language) or "mind" (in the language of anglophone psychoanalysis). It is perhaps what Buddhism recognises with its no-self teaching, and it sheds light on what Roy Schafer was seeing when he suggested (1976) that psychoanalysis should be done in a language of verbs rather than nouns. But ordinary grammar and ordinary language compel us to speak in ways that imply metaphysical dualism – that the mind is a separate entity – and to use non-ordinary language, like Heidegger, inevitably introduces a whole new raft of alternative misleading assumptions. So I think the best solution is to continue to use ordinary words and grammatical structures, but warily, and occasionally drawing attention to the traps they set for us. That is what I shall attempt to do in this book.

For the sake of brevity, I shall mention only in passing the hugely important contribution of Donald Winnicott. His recognition that "there is no such thing as an infant" (1960), expressed a truth that directly contradicts the notion of primary narcissism; it implies the crucial, inescapable importance of the reciprocity of relationship with another subject – not "object" – in our earliest experience. At the same time, by wording it as a paradox, almost as a joke, Winnicott avoided having to face the full implication of his departure from Freudian orthodoxy. When, speaking of his idea of the "transitional object," he said that the child has an "illusion" that is not to be questioned, he continued to speak, like Freud, as if the truth of objective observation is the final truth: as if the external "fact" is the real truth, and the "internal object" of experience is "illusion," with the overtones that that word inescapably carries of unreality or deceptiveness. He had adopted the word "illusion" from Freud, but it failed to catch his true meaning; using another paradoxical phrase, he once spoke of "the substance of illusion" (1951, 230) in an attempt to escape the trap he had set for himself.

By using the word "substance," Winnicott was gesturing towards the fact that, to the subject, the internal object is a true object, a phenomenological object in the moment of its occurrence; this is true regardless of how the object may appear in other recensions of its reality. But by saying "illusion," he simultaneously expressed a prejudice in favour of the scientific, objective viewpoint. This prejudice prevented him from claiming the full significance of what he was recognising. Perceptions, if "illusions," are by definition unreliable and should be subordinated to their other recensions (objective description, others' viewpoints): they are rightly dealt with by recognising them as illusion and by conforming to the perception of others. But "substance," of course, implies reality. By using the phrase, "the substance of illusion," Winnicott was using a paradox to hold on to a fact for which he didn't have a sufficiently developed vocabulary.

Winnicott's paradoxes are very important. They were ways of holding on to insights that couldn't be clearly formulated in the existing vocabulary of psychoanalysis. In many ways, they were like the "anomalous observations" that Thomas Kuhn described (1962), which accumulate when an established scientific paradigm is approaching its end, but the new paradigm has not yet found its own formulations.

Hans Loewald

The British analysts I have mentioned all with varying degrees of discomfort accepted the scientific assumption that there is one sort of truth and one reality principle, and therefore anything that seems to conflict with it can only belong in a subordinate position as "illusion," "phantasy," "projection" and so forth. The American psychoanalyst Hans Loewald, who had studied in Freiburg with Heidegger before undertaking medical and psychoanalytic training, brought a more philosophical approach to the phenomenological nature of internal objects. At the start of his paper "On Internalization" (1973), he repeatedly emphasises how changing one's "viewpoint" shows one a different world: a viewpoint that starts from evolutionary biology sees a different world from one that starts with Buddhist introspection. (He is too subtle to label his viewpoints, which I am crudely doing here for the sake of brevity.) "Objects are not givens," he says very clearly (1971, 127): no one viewpoint has a monopoly on truth. Roy Schafer's emphasis that narrative is "inevitably" the "mode in which truth and reality are presented" is an important enlargement of this thought (1992, xiv–v).

Heidegger came out of the second response of philosophy to the challenge of science at the end of the nineteenth century. He was and remains a controversial figure. By joining himself to the phenomenological tradition of Husserl, and giving the central place not to scientific "knowledge" but to "experience," Heidegger kept open the possibility for philosophy of giving a more adequate account of subjectivity. Lawrence Friedman in an excellent essay has asked: "Is there a use-able Heidegger for psychoanalysts?" He identified a central failure in Heidegger's extraordinary and virtuosic attempt to create a new language appropriate to a phenomenological stance, namely, that Heidegger portrays "world" as "something subjective," but without the subjectivistic concept of 'subject' which the state of "being in the world" erases …. "the ambiguous term *Dasein* finesses this question by serving as the carrier of human meaning while being neither subject nor object" (Friedman 2016, 619).

Heidegger trained first as a theologian. George Steiner (1991, 63) remarked that one can often make surprising sense of Heidegger's difficult statements about "being" if one substitutes the word "God." But by using *Sein* (being) and *Dasein* (existence), Heidegger avoided the more personal words: "God" and "I"; Friedman captures well the resulting ambiguity and air of evasion. No approach that remembers to take seriously the personal nature of psychological development can dispense with an account of subjects and objects; our personal development depends on interaction with others, and we apprehend others both as subjects "like ourselves" and as "objects" whom we treat instrumentally. How we conceive, and how we handle, this complicated ethical fact is difficult, but the fact itself is irreducible.

Nevertheless, Loewald's background in Heidegger studies was helpful to him when he became a psychoanalyst and addressed the issues of the internal world. His picture of childhood development, influenced by Margaret Mahler, has much in common with Winnicott's, and he shared Winnicott's recognition that the adult social world of culture, politics, art and religion – Freud's "civilisation" – could not be adequately accounted for in terms solely of drives and the management of drive anxieties. Towards the end of his life, Loewald reformulated Freud's drive theory in a way that avoids metaphysical dualism. Instead of speaking of biological stimuli impinging on a pre-existing "psychic apparatus," he spoke of "interactional biological processes that find higher organisation on levels which we have come to call psychic life" (Loewald 1978, 208).

Loewald recognised that what was truly original in *Beyond the Pleasure Principle* (Freud 1920) was not the introduction of the death drive, a variant of the constancy principle that Freud had derived from Fechner, and that had been a component of Freud's thought ever since his early days as a neurologist (Sulloway 1979, 66–7), but was the introduction of Eros, a force making for integration. Joel Whitebook writes: "This means that, rather than 'getting closer to a state of rest', with 'higher ego organisation' … there is more life"(Whitebook 2004, 105 – the quotations are from Loewald). (We may note the important idea of "higher organisation", a phrase frequently used by Loewald.) Jonathan Lear writes:

> Loewald is a hedgehog, not a fox. Although he takes up many aspects of the psychoanalytic experience, it seems to me that he is always trying to answer a single question: 'what would it be to take seriously the thought that within the human realm love is a developmental force?'
>
> (Lear 2017a, 178)

With Loewald, more than with any previous psychoanalytic thinker, psychoanalysis became able to step away from its initial base in medicine and the natural sciences, and to stand on a richer and more complex base in philosophy. This is the paradigm shift that Winnicott's use of paradox prefigured. To say this is in no way to disrespect science, but to recognise that the "phenomenological" nature of the internal world makes it a different sort of thing from the shared objective world that science describes so successfully – not a replacement of it, as Heidegger perhaps thought, but different from it and requiring a different approach to language if we are to grasp it appropriately. Stephen Mitchell says:

> In his quiet, undramatic fashion, Loewald … transformed the basic values guiding the analytic process, substituting meaning for rationality, imagination for objectivity, vitalization for control.
>
> (Mitchell 2000, 25)

And Jonathan Lear writes: "… one of the joys of Loewald's writings is that he offers a different choice of inheritance."

> (2017b, 193)

It would be interesting to detail the ways in which Loewald's thought went on to permeate the new thinking in the American relational schools, and also in independent thinkers such as Lear himself. But the crucial point of this summary history of internal objects is now made: that, at least in some corners of the psychoanalytic field, their nature had gradually changed, under pressure of clinical and other experience, from Freud's initial picture of internalised external objects to one of phenomenological objects with a distinctive reality of their own.

Some implications of the phenomenological nature of internal objects

One problem with the psychoanalytic notion of a "reality principle" is that it assumes that we, or *someone*, is in a position to say what reality is. And it isn't easy to put into words the complexity of the world that is implied by saying that the nature of internal objects is phenomenological. For the subject, the internal object is its phenomenological presence; but there are many sorts of internal object, and many of them correspond to objects in the shared external world, and many correspond to phenomenological objects known to other subjects. (I use the vague word "correspond" to imply "not identical with but to a certain degree resembling.") And all these different realities are apprehended by the subject "phenomenologically." Science by its techniques of measurement and repeated observation, and by subordinating the so-called secondary qualities (those dependent on the nature of the human senses) to the primary ones (those that can be measured), attempts to get as close as it can to an objective impersonal account of the object; this is useful for "mastery," as Descartes saw, but has only a variable relationship to the world the subject inhabits, the world of experience.

Because the subject by direct experience knows only a phenomenological world, he/she may also know "objects" that are without material correlates: abstract, remembered and fictitious objects are examples. Abstract objects such as numbers are hugely important but are not particularly the concern of the psychoanalyst. Objects of memory may have had a material correlate in the past; fictitious objects may never have had a material correlate and may be private to the individual or may be shared with others. Sherlock Holmes would be an example of a shared fictitious object. In which category an internal object belongs is often very unclear and its importance is not dependent on its category. As Donnel Stern writes: "imagined witnesses can be as effective as real ones" (2010, 114).

These different sorts of internal objects have different functions, but essentially their function is that they act to organise or give shape to the psyche. It's a commonplace observation that people are different in conversation with different others, a formula we might rephrase to say that relating to a different object causes the psyche spontaneously to reorganise itself to adapt to the new situation. Of course, this reorganisation may be resisted (but that then gives rise to another reorganisation), or the object may be misperceived because of projections, which we call transference; or it may come to be perceived differently as a result of experience; in each case a different "internal object" reorganises the psyche.

(I am aware that in speaking of "the psyche" I am falling back into the language of Cartesian metaphysical dualism; it might be better to say not "I *become* different" but "I *am* different" in the presence of different internal objects.)

The ordinary work of psychoanalysis is to bring consciousness to the impacts of the internal objects that are influencing the subject, so that they can be thought about and brought into relation with the subject's values and more general estimate of his/her reality situation. In psychoanalytic writings, most often interest focuses on the origin and history of the internal objects that distort the subject's perception of his/her present situation – their source in the subject's history of love, loss, trauma, parental character etc. In the early days of psychoanalysis, interpretation of childhood history was possibly over-valued, but it remains extremely helpful in revealing more accurately the nature and tenacity of the current internal objects and the affects that allow them to exert their grip on the subject. The nature of the change that psychoanalysis aspires to cause is a new orientation towards the internal objects that most deeply shape the psyche. This change, and the introduction of greater conscious awareness to the relation of subject and internal object, is the essence of what is described by Loewald's brilliant metaphor (1960, 248–9) when he said that psychoanalysis allows one's "ghosts" to become "ancestors" – enables one's internal objects to acquire definition both as deriving from understandable events and persons, and as locatable in and relevant to particular moments in time and place.

In this chapter, however, I want to focus on something different, on organisational hierarchy and the functioning of certain sorts of internal object that have been a puzzle for psychoanalysis, in particular those that give rise to, or affirm, ethical values. Freud's account of conscience, in terms of a "superego," is one of the least satisfactory parts of psychoanalytic theory, and much remains to be thought in relation to it.

It is not only psychoanalysis that has had difficulty in thinking about values. The tradition within philosophy that gives "science" the central place as our model for knowledge and for the process of acquiring knowledge has valorised certain philosophical modes – ontology, epistemology – at the expense of ethics. It has typically diminished the claim of ethics upon us either to personal or aesthetic preference, or to instrumental usefulness, as in utilitarianism, where the value of the good aimed for is either treated as self-evident – "the greatest happiness of the greatest number" – or is again described in terms of personal preference. Such philosophy resembles Freud's account of the superego in an important way. Both speak of the claim of ethics from the position of the detached onlooker, seeking to account for something from the outside, rather than from a position that includes the subject, aware of the power of the claim from direct personal experience. This detachment is echoed in Freud's response in *Civilization and its Discontents* to Romain Rolland's attempt to describe mystical feeling: "I cannot discover this 'oceanic' feeling in myself" (1930, 65). Elsewhere and rather similarly, he describes the state of being in love as one in which "a considerable amount of narcissistic libido overflows on to the object" (1921, 112).

Whether there is something theatrical in speaking with such "objectivity" about these crucial areas of experience, in which the sense in the individual of sovereign autonomy is put in question, we need not enquire at this point. But it's clear that such a detached stance makes it hard to recognise any situation in which an ethical claim could have authority over inclination; the cynic has only to say: "that is not *my* preference" or "why should I care about *that*?" and he or she is released from ethical obligation. The power of the superego, as described by Freud, is the power of the remembered or fantasised stick or carrot; once recognised in these terms, there can be no good reason to be governed by it. Similarly the ego ideal, conceived as the projection into the future of primary narcissism (Freud 1914; Chasseguet-Smirgel 1985), can only lose its power once it's perceived as such.

So we need to look first at the organisational structure of the subject, to see if there can be a basis for hierarchy, before we go on to consider ways in which we might understand the power of ethical obligation to occupy a commanding position in such a hierarchy.

Organisation implies hierarchy

Internal objects act by "organising" the psyche. For example, when listening to a patient, the mind of the analyst is typically organised by the presence of the patient to exercise a "containing" function: to listen, to reflect empathically on what is said, to notice features of the communication such as hesitations, emphases, divergences, inconsistences and so forth. It is organised also by an awareness of responsibility for boundaries, both of the duration of the session and of appropriate styles of response. At the same time, every analyst has been a patient, and is aware of what it's like to have one's psyche organised in relation to such a person as a psychoanalyst, with freedom to be, so to speak, shapeless – inconsistent, rambling, free-associating as one chooses; forgetful, though only up to a point, of boundaries and the ordinary restraints of politeness, etc.

Maturing as an analyst is not to leave these roles behind, but to come to feel that they are less incompatible: one occupies the role of analyst but remains aware of the reactions one might have if one were in the other role: a "counter-transference" is not so very unlike a "transference," but it is thought about, if possible, rather than enacted. And to mature as a patient, correspondingly, is to develop a capacity to think more understandingly about one's reactions, rather than be governed by them. As we know, "enactments" by the analyst happen, even in the best analyses, and the skill of the analyst then is to find ways to acknowledge honestly what has happened and to return to the task of thinking about it. And the challenge to the patient is to endure such dislocations and return, also, to the task of thinking. If the work is to continue, appropriate psychic organisation has to be retrievable.

"Thinking" and "reactions" in such a story can only be conceived in a hierarchical relation. In enactment, reaction has governed thinking; when the enactment is honestly recognised, thinking can regain the higher position. The peculiar genius of psychoanalysis is that it doesn't demand suppression of wayward impulses – it doesn't, like some traditional ethical systems, declare certain impulses "bad" or sinful by definition – but it suggests that the subject will be put on a firmer base by becoming conscious of the impulse and in some way, including it – integrating it – in a larger structure. This is what Loewald meant by a "higher organisation."

What follows "becoming conscious" is, from the strictly psychoanalytic point of view, only further becoming conscious, but the responsible practitioner is bound to have misgivings about possible repercussions, if the impulse concerned turns out to be, say, suicidal, or paedophiliac, or murderous. In the early days, it was said that patients should not make important life-decisions while in analysis; I recall a colleague who worked with great skill with a very disturbed adolescent, but then expressed concern at having uncovered in him terrifying impulses of cruelty.

So the question of what governs what in the psyche is not one about which we can afford to be casual. It points to an inescapable hierarchy in psychic organisation, a vertical structure. This is in part a logical necessity. If I desire to commit suicide, and desire also to live, I must, logically, make a choice – but logic alone can't guide me to a choice. What guides my choice, in the absence of coercion, is my psychic organisation, which is ultimately shaped, consciously or unconsciously, by my internal objects. Any significant life-choice can therefore also be described as taking responsibility for accepting a certain psychic organisation. We describe those who are unable to make life-choices securely as "split," meaning that they are unable to arrive at such responsibility and acceptance: they are torn, so to speak, between the claims of competing, and incompatible, internal objects. The following case example illustrates the way in which an internal object can organise a person's decision.

A patient, Vicky, a doctor in her early 30s, had lived for several years with her partner, Richard, a civil servant. He was offered an interesting appointment which involved living overseas for several months. Vicky was angry and felt abandoned when he decided to accept it. During his absence, an older colleague, Gareth, made it clear to Vicky that he was attracted to her; he asked her out. She came to a session, saying that she was sorely tempted. Gareth was an attractive man; she was angry with Richard; she was lonely and sexually frustrated with living alone; what should she do?

She came to the following session, however, saying she had decided to turn down the possibility with Gareth. "I am angry with Richard," she said, "and I'd like to get my own back by having an affair. But the person I want to be wants to make it work" (i.e. the relationship with Richard) – she decided not to imperil that relationship.

Vicky's mother had left her father for another man when Vicky was aged seven. Vicky had become for a time a violent and uncontrollable child. Her father had suffered bewildered grief, and then fallen into a long depression. To use the language of internal objects, from these experiences Vicky had derived an "ego ideal," an ideal internal object, a person who remained steady and could be trusted; she was choosing to identify with this figure: "the person I want to be." Such an object embodies an important value, derived from experience; it is not well described as a "projection of primary narcissism."

Ethical values and allegorical objects

If the discussion so far has been coherent, it has supported two notions: firstly, that internal objects are "phenomenological" in nature, and secondly, that the psyche has a "vertical structure," that's to say that its structure is organised more powerfully by some internal objects than by others. Traditional psychoanalysis accepts this idea in the notion of a "superego"; it accounts for moral behaviour by seeing the ego as obedient to the internalised voices and attitudes of parents and educators; the superiority and authority of such voices is ultimately based on a memory of having been small when those others were large.

Such superiority is undoubtedly very real, but our task in relation to it can only be to "emancipate" ourselves from it (Britton 2003) – to discern what is of value in those early teachings, and discard the rest. But the phrase "of value" takes us beyond what the theory of the superego can tell us. What can it mean to say that something is "of value"?

The word *value* (cognate with *valency, valour, prevail,* etc.) is to do with having strength: what gives values, in particular ethical values, their strength? If ultimately it is based on the physical size and strength of others, then the idea of the value of ethics as such, of *intrinsic* ethical value, is a masquerade. This view has always been held by some. Classically, it was called cynicism; it was the view of Nietzsche in some moods, and it has been widespread, in fascism and elsewhere, since the rise of the belief in materialism in the nineteenth century.

The most psychologically convincing account of intrinsic ethical value comes not from a psychoanalyst but from a philosopher, Emmanuel Levinas. He had an impressive fore-runner in Kant. In addition to his better known discussion of the categorical imperative, Kant gives a picture of the spontaneous affective response to ethical virtue, which he calls *Achtung*, generally translated *respect*. He writes:

> Fontenelle says: 'I bow before a great man, but my mind does not bow'. I would add, before an humble plain man, in whom I perceive uprightness of character in a higher degree than I am conscious of in myself, my mind bows whether I choose it or not, and though I bear my head never so high that he may not forget my superior rank. Why is this? Because his example exhibits to me a law that humbles my self-conceit when I compare it with my conduct: a law, the practicability of obedience to which I see proved by fact before my eyes ... Respect is a tribute which we cannot refuse to merit, whether we will or not; we may indeed outwardly withhold it, but we cannot help feeling it inwardly.
>
> (Kant 1788, 48)

I have discussed this passage elsewhere (Black 2011, 170) and linked it with Charles Taylor's discussion (1989, 341) of "making sense of one's own moral horizon." What unites them is the recognition that, if ethical value is intrinsic, it must itself evoke an affective response in the subject. There is no other route by which its power can make itself felt. This claim Levinas brings sharply into focus when he writes of perceiving "the face of the other."

Emmanuel Levinas (1906–1995) was influenced by Martin Buber, and Buber's account of a "Thou," the unique, singling-out, second person singular, stands behind Levinas' account of the other. Like Loewald, Levinas had studied under Heidegger; he had been appalled by Heidegger's espousal of Nazism. As a Jew, he was fortunate to survive the Second World War as a prisoner-of-war in a German military camp (other members of his family were not so lucky).[2] Both a Talmud scholar and a philosopher, he devoted his philosophical energy to understanding, above all, the nature of responsibility and ethical obligation.

The crucial experience for Levinas is what he describes as seeing "the face of the other." This does not mean the physical face – he gives an example from a novel by Vasily Grossman in which what is seen is the person's back (Morgan 2007, 1–20) – but something more like the vulnerability, the human reality of the other as a subject like oneself. Such a perception gives rise to the awareness of responsibility, which he phrases in the language of the biblical commandment: "Thou shalt not kill." He speaks of this obligation using Heidegger's word, "being": it comes from beyond being; it is "transcendent." He writes:

> There is a paradox in responsibility, in that I am obliged without this obligation having begun in me, as though an order were slipped into my consciousness like a thief .... But this is impossible in a consciousness, and clearly indicates that we are no longer in the element of consciousness.
>
> (1998, 13)

Levinas emphasises that, when we speak of obligation and responsibility, the "subjects" involved – I, you, he, she – are uniquenesses: "… it is no longer a question of the ego, but of me. The subject which is not an ego, but which I am … is not a subject in general: we have moved from the ego to me who am me and no one else" (13–4). The encounter with transcendence, so central to Levinas' thought, is characterised by the absolute uniqueness of the ethically significant situation: "the identity of the subject comes from the impossibility of escaping responsibility" (14). In my quotation, the word "order" (*ordre* in French) has "command" as its primary meaning, but carries also the implication of "organising," creating order: it is as if an organising principle "slipped into my consciousness like a thief."

He goes on to say that responsibility lies deeper than freedom: "the subjectivity of a subject come late into a world which has not issued from his projects does not consist in treating this world as one's project. The 'lateness' is not insignificant" (1998, 122). Levinas' vision implies a decisive rejection of materialism and of Descartes' project of becoming "the masters … of Nature". My responsibility for my neighbour, for "the stranger and sojourner", is one "to which nothing in the rigorously ontological order binds me – nothing in the order of the thing, of the something, of number or causality" (1984, 84). This is what Levinas means by saying that the power of obligation is transcendent. And it's on this that he bases his claim that ethics is "first philosophy" and is "prior to ontology."

Levinas' description of the "epiphany" of ethical responsibility is of a compelling psychological event – "like a shot 'at point-blank range'" (83). From the psychoanalytic point of view, it invites us to ask what sort of object the "face of the other" is. Though it appears to reference a physical object, it is not that physical object, and it isn't a metaphor, since it is part of its nature that it can't be translated into literal statement: any attempt to state it literally would be to take it back into ontology, would make it part of "totality" and not of "infinity" (1969), would destroy its transcendence.

I think, in using this phrase, Levinas is presenting the other to us as what I shall call an "allegorical object." The characteristic of allegory is that it presents a value directly in the form of the object; unlike the characters created by a novelist, these objects may (or may not) be fictitious, but they are not attempts to imagine a convincing whole-person; allegory conceives objects that embody a single motive or group of motives. In the hands of a master, like Dante, allegory can be used with great subtlety as an instrument with which to think about events in the internal world, and in particular tensions and conflict among values.

As, to many readers nowadays, "allegory" may seem the name merely of an outmoded literary device, I shall say a few words to introduce it. Allegory in medieval times made possible a carefully thought-out attempt to grasp the structure of the internal world; it was discussed with great subtlety in medieval philosophy, not least because it was the model on which the Scriptures were understood. In particular – as becomes very apparent in Dante's *Purgatorio* – it was a way of thinking that could conceive of Christ's double nature, both God and man. Two fundamental forms of allegory were distinguished: one, which came to be known as "theological," in which an actual historical event, such as the Israelites' Exodus from Egypt, was perceived to have a spiritual meaning, and a second, called "poetic," in which a fable or mythic story was interpreted as having moral or psychological significance.

I borrow the example of the Exodus from Dante; following the Exodus, he said, "Judea became holy and free"; similarly, following its exodus from sin, the soul "is made holy and free in its power." His example of a "poetic" allegory is Orpheus' calming of wild beasts by his music, meaning, Dante suggested, that the voice of the wise man calms those who are governed by passions (Dante 1304/2018, 59). He references the medieval notion of four levels of meaning in a written text: the literal, the "allegorical" (meaning emotional or psychological), the moral and the anagogical or spiritual.

Dante's own practice is freer than this suggests, but he emphasised that there must always be a "literal" level, if any of the other meanings are to be conveyed, just as "it is impossible to reach the interior without first reaching an exterior," or as it is impossible to build a house without first laying a foundation. This literal level is comparable to the use of the case example in a psychoanalytic clinical paper. It reminds us that whatever generality we may be dealing with, it is encountered first in a unique particular. And compared with the abstract discourse that is our favoured mode for presenting theory, in certain respects, if our concern is with "subjects" rather than "objects," allegory has an advantage: abstract discourse, unless very carefully handled, is always at risk of converting its ethical subjects into objects – in Levinas' language, converting unique and situated "me," a person, into a generalised object, an "ego." The allegorical object, by contrast, is always encountered also as a subject; to properly encounter the allegorical object is to feel the power of the value the allegorical subject embodies. To properly perceive the heraldic lion *is* to experience the appeal of nobility and courage. To see "the face of the other" *is* to experience the commandingness of ethical obligation. In allegory, to see the perception unaccompanied by the affective dynamism is not to see it at all. In Dante's *Comedy*, the Emperor Trajan, speaking with the widow in Purgatorio X, embodies authority-influenced-by-compassion: we see him changing his mind in response to the appeal of suffering. That's who he is: he is an "allegorical object," (a subject), without the complexity of an actual person, but nevertheless entirely individual, in a specific historical context, meeting someone in a specific predicament.

Kant's "humble plain man" of upright character is similarly an allegorical object: he represents his uprightness, without further complexity, and it's to this that Kant responded with *Achtung*: he "couldn't help" doing so. If we assume that Kant was remembering an actual experience, we might say that he met a complex real person, but the phenomenological internal object he perceived was the allegorical object he described. Many of the "shades" Dante encounters in the *Comedy* are of this sort: real people Dante had met or heard of, but present now as internal objects, as the vivid allegorical figures he describes. He uses them to create a rich and encyclopaedic picture of human motives.

Developmentally, it's likely that our first perception of an ethical value happens when we encounter an "object," an other who seems to us to embody the value. Melanie Klein's account of the infant internalising the mother's care, kindness, playfulness and giving to create a "good internal object" is a story of this sort. A developmental account of conscience (different from "superego") might speak of a memory of persons or teachers, not "who were big when we were small," but who embodied important values for us – and who now inhabit us as "allegorical internal objects." In such a case, the external object has been perceived empirically, like any other external object – but has also, on a specific occasion, been perceived "allegorically," as embodying a value that has power for "me," a unique subject. If it is to be effective, this experience needs to make a certain impact on the subject. In the moment of its occurrence, I may ignore or reject its claim, or I may "forget" it by moving on briskly to other considerations. Scientific training may encourage such ignoring or forgetting. The ethical function of religions by contrast has been to offer systems of thought in which perceptions of particular values are remembered, affirmed and inter-subjectively validated. (I discuss this further in Chapter 9.)

If we define an "allegorical object" as one that embodies an important value and is also encountered as a unique "subject" that awakens his/her/its motive in "me," then religious objects are best understood as a species or class of allegorical objects. In Christianity, the issue has been confused by the intense preoccupation with *believing* in religious objects, "believing" being construed (in the Nicene creed for example) as refusing to distinguish between objects in the external and internal worlds. ("Suffered under Pontius Pilate," for example – plausibly a historical fact – is set alongside "ascended into heaven," clearly an allegorical image.) To be required to "believe" as historically factual things that are incompatible with one's rational understanding of how the world works is intimidating and infantilising, and bound to create psychic incoherence. This emphasis on "believing" is less present in other religions, for example Judaism (where what is emphasised is more the observance of certain requirements of behaviour – Levinas used to say: "belief is not a primary issue": see Malka 2006, 241), and hardly at all in Buddhism, where mythological entities are regularly described as "mental constructs."

Dante contrived largely to avoid this confusion of allegorical objects with empirical reality by putting his historical figures into an internal psychological framework, symbolised as the "afterlife." In this setting, each can be portrayed as governed by a single dominating passion or conflict and can function therefore allegorically. When Freud wrote about religious objects as "illusory" and in conflict with science (1927), he was influenced by the distracting insistence on "belief" and failed to recognise that science and religion are dealing with quite different sorts of object.

To speak of religious objects as allegorical is liberating in several sorts of ways. It allows them, as Levinas says, to have real and even commanding importance in the internal world, while dispensing them from needing to compete with science in accounting for the material universe. It also opens up the possibility of mutual respect and tolerance among the religions. The theologian Raimon Panikkar used to say that different religions are like different languages: you can tell the truth in every language, he said, but the truths you can tell in one language are slightly different from those you can tell in another (personal communication). Such an understanding is not possible if stories involving religious objects are insisted on as literally true.

Some will object that in speaking of the power of ethical and religious values, I am ignoring the many cases in which such values appear to have no power. This is a huge topic, but to comment very briefly: it should be acknowledged that to rec-ognise the power of an ethical value is already an ethical achievement – it requires a particular "orientation" (to borrow a term from di Ceglie [2013]) towards the internal object. But if it is to result in ethically appropriate action in the real world, then there must in addition be a practical reading of the complex external real object or situation. In the case of my patient Vicky, the relation of the ideal object to her dilemma was comparatively straightforward, but very often the situation is much more complicated and ambiguous. And often stances of self-preoccupation will block access to ethical concern altogether.

I suggest in Chapter 4 that the development of religious objects in one strand of Buddhist history, leading to the creation of the Japanese Pure Land schools, was governed by a need to see ever more explicitly stated the crucial importance of a certain value, namely, love or compassion. With Levinas it is possible to sense a similar evolution in the history of European phenomenology: Levinas said what Heidegger had rather spectacularly failed to say. If we wish to extend the idea of encountering "the face of the other" into the language of affect, we would need to speak first I think of "sympathy," the spontaneous capacity by which we recognise another as a subject and which makes compassion possible (Black 2004). And then we would also need to speak of the desire for justice.

Levinas would object that such an extension risks undermining his conception: it re-entangles ethics with ontology and may divert one's gaze from what is essen-tial, the command, to something contingent, the affect, which may or may not be present, and may or may not be fully conscious. Granting this objection, it remains true that if perception of the "face" gives rise to obligation, it must involve an affective component. Eyal Rozmarin, who writes well of Levinas from a psycho-analytic standpoint, has objected to the extremity of Levinas' ethics, by which he means the fact that "for Levinas, the basic truth of ethics is that *the other comes first* in all senses of the word" (2007, 355). Psychoanalysis, says Rozmarin, "can-not put me ahead of the other, or the other ahead of me," because it essentially sees healthy relating as a matter of "the continuous establishment of a basis where both can live" (359), characterised by equality and reciprocal ambivalence.

Rozmarin sees as "extremity" what Levinas would see as foundational. Ethics for Levinas cannot be founded on ambivalence, nor on reciprocity, although it can of course find expression only in a world of complex and competing values. But if it is to be the ultimately important thing, then it needs its transcendence and also its simplicity (see Chapter 7). Melanie Klein with intuitive brilliance recognised this, in her account of the need of the baby to have an unambiguously good object, even at the price of splitting both itself and its object to exclude awareness of the limitations in the real object, the mother, and in the baby's experience (1946, 1952; see also the discussion in Chapter 4 here). Her developmental account has no parallel in Levinas, but it opens a path to thinking why, psychoanalytically, some people may have access to the sort of experience Levinas describes, and others may be closed to it. Similarly, Levinas' awareness of a second, more ordinary viewpoint, that of "ontology," may have a parallel in Klein's account of the "depressive position."

Dante's allegory does contain a parallel to Levinas' insight. At a crucial moment in the *Purgatorio*, on the Terrace of the gluttonous, Dante meets the poet Bonagiunta da Lucca. Bonagiunta asks him who he is. Dante responds with a self-description:

.... I am one who, when Love
breathes in me, I take note, and as I go
mark down in signs what he dictates within.
(Pg XXIV, 52–4)

The parallel is that, in response to attention given to an experience of external encounter (with Beatrice, perhaps), a command comes from within, not from without. Obedience to the command, for Dante, causes him to write poetry; for Levinas, it results in awakening to "the human dimension" (1984, 86), an achievement as Levinas understands it and not the mere characteristic of a species. "The human," he writes, "is the return ... to the capacity to fear injustice more than death, to prefer to suffer rather than to commit injustice" (85). (He is quoting phrases from Socrates in the *Gorgias*.)

Dante also contrived to describe two viewpoints on reality, similar to though not identical with the two viewpoints of Levinas and Rozmarin, or Klein's paranoid-schizoid and depressive positions. He did so in the two guides, Virgil and Beatrice, whom he found necessary for negotiating the different realms of Inferno/Purgatory and Paradise (Black 2017). Virgil represents the classical virtues of rationality and courage, Beatrice the Christian revelation of divine or "transcendent" love. Allegory at this level of sophistication is able to comment on itself, and it does so in Dante's depiction of the relationship between Virgil and Beatrice, and her unmistakably senior position in the hierarchy. (It is she who sends Virgil to Dante's help; it is Virgil who guides Dante through many perils to reunite with her.)

As a species of allegorical objects, religious objects are those that embody the "extreme" or transcendent values. In Dante, ultimately a monotheist, we find a number of subordinate religious figures, for example Saint Lucy, the patron saint of eyesight, who embodies clarity of vision (*lux* = light); Lucy carries Dante bodily to the gate of Purgatory when he is in confusion after escaping from Hell. Lucy represents the clarity of ethical vision that enables Dante to recognise which of his motives are damaging to his long-term welfare ("sins"). It is this recognition that makes possible the repentance of souls in Purgatory. The fact that she carries him sleeping suggests that this clarity is still unconscious, is still potential, but it will become conscious as he journeys through the thought-evoking structure of Purgatory itself. Beatrice too, though (at one level) an ordinary woman, is also an avenue to, and avatar of, divine love, and in this she is an allegorical figure like Christ himself, both god and man.

The ultimate religious allegorical object – "God" – is mentioned many times in the poem, but as he comes closer, so to speak, the inadequacy of any allegorical object to represent him becomes clearer, and finally Dante presents him only by the name of his fundamental energy, love, the source of all valuations. For Dante, all motives are ultimately versions or perversions of love (Purgatorio XVII) – there is nothing resembling a death drive – and so the final monotheistic vision is of an integrated cosmos: the scattered pages of all the universe "bound by love into a single volume," and then the supreme concluding vision: "the love that moves the sun and the other stars" (Paradiso XXXIII, 145).

Conclusion

I shall attempt now to summarise the thesis of this essay. If we speak of internal objects as "phenomenological" in nature, we are enabled to lessen the vividness of the distinction between those derived from the material world (everyday "reality") and those derived from elsewhere. To the subject, the power of an internal object has no necessary correlation with correspondence to a material counterpart.

The thesis of this essay is that there is a species of internal objects, described as "allegorical," which represent ethical values to the subject. Internal objects tend to organise the psyche; allegorical objects tend to organise it in a vertical dimension, in accordance with the value they represent, which is recognised by the subject when he or she experiences the appeal, the power, of an ethical motive. Allegorical objects act so as to change, or to tend to change, the subject's structure of motivation, something that is never entirely settled, although the gradual process of psychic integration helps it towards a degree of stability.

Certain allegorical objects, like Levinas' "face of the other," embody values felt to be of transcendent (commanding) importance. When such objects are affirmed and validated in a specific cultural tradition, they are described as "religious." At this point, the language of positivist science ceases to be illuminating. If a reductive nineteenth century materialism is our metaphysics, there can be no "transcendent" values: the compelling power of such objects can only be attributed to "illusion," to some fantasy derivable from sex or power (or, for those who accept the death drive, to some derivative of aggression). Any "transcendent" ethical claim can only be illusion; conscience can only be a superego; seeing "the face of the other" may give rise to affect but cannot give rise to command.

Loewald (and Levinas) offer an alternative vision. But if we are to follow it, it will not just be a matter of agreeing with one argument rather than another, as one might decide to be a Kohutian rather than a Kleinian. It will be to recognise that ethical and religious values raise issues that go beyond the scope of our present thinking, and that to explore their implications with full seriousness psychoanalysis will need to enter much further into dialogue with philosophy.

Notes

1 Husserl's indebtedness to Kant is interestingly discussed by Morgan (2007, 550–2).
2 I give a brief outline of Levinas' life in Chapter 10.

References

Black, D.M. (2004). Sympathy reconfigured: Some reflections on sympathy, empathy and the discovery of values. *Int. J Psychoanal.* 85: 3, 579–96.

Black, D.M. (2011). *Why Things Matter: The Place of Values in Science, Psychoanalysis and Religion.* London and New York, NY: Routledge.

Black, D.M. (2017). Dante's "Two Suns": Reflections on the psychological sources of the *divine comedy. Int. J. Psychoanal.* 98: 6, 1699–717.

Brierley, M. (1942). "Internal Objects" and theory. *Int.J. Psychoanal.* 23: 107–12.

Britton, R. (2003). Emancipation from the Superego. In *Sex, Death, and the Superego.* London: Karnac.

Chasseguet-Smirgel, J. (1985). *The Ego Ideal: A Psychoanalytic Essay on the Malady of the Ideal.* Trs. P. Barrows. London: Free Association Books.

Dante (1304/2018). *Convivio.* Trs. A. Frisardi. Cambridge: Cambridge UP.

Descartes, R. (1637/1997). Discourse on the Method. Trs. E.S. Haldane & G.R.T. Ross. In E. Chavez-Arvizo (ed) *Descartes: Key Philosophical Writings* (1997) 71–122. Ware: Wordsworth Editions.

Di Ceglie, G.R. (2013). Orientation, containment and the emergence of symbolic thinking. *Int. J. Psychoanal.* 94, 1077–91.

Fairbairn, R. (1946). Object-Relationships and Dynamic Structure. In *Psychoanalytic Studies of the Personality* (1952). London: Tavistock/Routledge.

Forbes-Pitt, K. (2018). From dualism to dynamism: Fairbairn's critique of libido theory 1930–1950. *British J. of Psychotherapy* 34: 1, 95–113.

Freud, S. (1891). Appendix C, The Unconscious (1915) 209–215. SE XIV.

Freud, S. (1914). On Narcissism: An Introduction. SE XIV.

Freud, S. (1915). The Unconscious. SE XIV.

Freud, S. (1917). Mourning and Melancholia. SE XIV.

Freud, S. (1920). *Beyond the Pleasure Principle.* SE XVIII.

Freud, S. (1921). Group Psychology and the Analysis of the Ego. SE XVIII.

Freud, S. (1923). *The Ego and the Id.* SE XIX.

Freud, S. (1927). *The Future of an Illusion.* SE XXI.

Freud, S. (1930). *Civilization and Its Discontents.* SE XXI.

Freud, S. (1933). Anxiety and Instinctual Life. Lecture XXXII of *New Introductory Lectures on Psychoanalysis.* SE XXII.

Friedman, L. (2016). Is there a useable Heidegger for psychoanalysts? *Journal of the American Psychoanalytic Association* 64, 3.

Greenberg, J. R., & Mitchell, S. (1983). *Object Relations in Psychoanalytic Theory.* Cambridge, MA and London: Harvard UP.

Grotstein, J. & Rinsley, D.B. (1994). *Fairbairn and the Origins of Object Relations.* London: Free Association Books.

Kant, I. (1788/2005). *The Critique of Practical Reason*. Trs. T Kingsmill Abbot (2005). Digireads.com.

Klein, M. (1946). Notes on Some Schizoid Mechanisms. In *Envy and Gratitude and Other Works, 1946–1963* 1–24. London: Hogarth Press.

Klein, M. (1952). Some Theoretical Conclusions Regarding the Emotional Life of the Infant. In *Envy and Gratitude and Other Works, 1946–1963* 61–93. London: Hogarth Press.

Kuhn, T. (1962). *The Structure of Scientific Revolutions*. Chicago, IL: Univ. of Chicago Press.

Lear, J. (2017a). Eros and Development. In *Wisdom Won from Illness*. Cambridge, MA and London: Harvard UP

Lear, J. (2017b). Mourning and Moral Psychology. In *Wisdom Won from Illness*. Cambridge, MA and London: Harvard UP.

Levinas, E. (1969). *Totality and Infinity*. Trs. A. Lingis. The Hague: Martinus Nijhoff.

Levinas, E. (1984). Ethics as First Philosophy. In S. Hand (ed) *The Levinas Reader*. Oxford: Blackwell Publishing.

Levinas, E. (1998). *Otherwise than Being, or Beyond Essence*. Trs. A. Lingis. Pittsburgh, PA: Duquesne UP.

Loewald, H. (1960). On the Therapeutic Action of Psychoanalysis. In *Papers on Psychoanalysis* (1980) 221–56. New Haven, CT and London: Yale UP.

Loewald, H. (1971). On Motivation and Instinct Theory. In (eds) *Papers on Psychoanalysis* (1980) 102–137. New Haven, CT and London: Yale UP.

Loewald, H. (1973). On Internalization. In *Papers on Psychoanalysis* (1980) 69–86. New Haven, CT and London: Yale UP.

Loewald, H. (1978). Instinct Theory, Object Relations, and Psychic Structure Formation. In *Papers on Psychoanalysis* (1980) 207–18. New Haven, CT and London: Yale UP.

MacIntyre, A. (1981). *After Virtue* (3rd ed. 2007). London: Bloomsbury.

Macmurray, J. (2004) The Dualism of Mind and Matter. In E. McIntosh (ed) *Selected Philosophical Writings* 13–29. Exeter: Imprint Academic.

Malka, S. (2006) *Emmanuel Levinas: His Life and Legacy*. Trs. M. Kigel & S.M. Embree. (French original, 2002). Pittsburgh, PA: Duquesne UP.

Michelson, A.A. (1903). *Light Waves and Their Uses*. Chicago, IL: Chicago UP.

Mitchell, S. (2000). *Relationality: From Attachment to Intersubjectivity*. Hove and New York, NY: Routledge.

Morgan, M.L. (2007). *Discovering Levinas*. Cambridge: Cambridge UP.

Nietzsche, F.W. (1882/1974). *The Gay Science*. Trs. W. Kaufmann. New York, NY Vintage.

Peat, F.D. (2002). *From Certainty to Uncertainty: The Story of Science and Ideas in the Twentieth Century*. Washington, DC: Joseph Henry Press.

Rozmarin, E. (2007). An other in psychoanalysis: Emmanuel Levinas's critique of knowledge and analytic sense. *Contemporary Psychoanalysis*3: 327–60.

Schafer, R. (1976). *A New Language for Psychoanalysis*. New Haven, CT and London: Yale UP.

Schafer, R. (1992). *Retelling a Life*. New York, NY: Basic Books.

Scharff, J. S., & Scharff, D.E. (2005). The Development of Fairbairn's Theory. In Scharff & Scharff (eds) *The Legacy of Fairbairn and Sutherland*. London and New York, NY: Routledge.

Steiner, G. (1991). *Martin Heidegger*. Chicago, IL: University of Chicago Press.

Stern, D.B. (2010). *Partners in Thought: Working with Unformulated thought, Dissociation, and Enactment*. New York, NY and Hove: Routledge.

Sulloway, F. (1979). *Freud, Biologist of the Mind.* Basic Books.

Taylor, C. (1989). *Sources of the Self: The Making of the Modern Identity.* Cambridge: Cambridge UP.

Weber, M. (1904/2009). *The Protestant Ethic and the Spirit of Capitalism.* Trs. T. Parsons, ed. R. Swedberg. New York, NY and London: Norton.

Whitebook, J. (2004). Hans Loewald: A radical conservative. *Int. J. Psychoanal* 85: 1, 97–116.

Winnicott, D.W. (1951). Transitional Objects and Transitional Phenomena. In *From Paediatrics to Psychoanalysis* 229–42. London: Hogarth Press.

Winnicott, D.W. (1960). The Theory of the Parent-Infant Relationship. In *The Maturational Processes and the Facilitating Environment* 37–55. London: Hogarth Press.

Chapter 3

Jonathan Lear

Heir to a different legacy[1]

Introduction

At one point in his collection of essays, *Wisdom won from Illness*, Jonathan Lear tells a story from Plato's *Phaedrus* (Lear, 2017). The Egyptian god Theuth, having invented writing, is boasting of his invention. King Thamus rebukes him. Your invention, he says, will create forgetfulness in your hearers' souls: "they will be the hearers of many things and will have learned nothing"; they will "have the show of wisdom without the reality" (*Phaedrus* 275, Jowett trs).

Jonathan Lear shares King Thamus' anxiety. His central question, which he addresses from many angles, is: how do our words become truly meaningful to us, so that they "make a difference" and help us with our development; and, correspondingly, what happens when nothing happens, when we go through a performance of words or actions and nothing is changed? He is haunted by the comment of the Crow (Native American) chief, Plenty Coups, who told the history of his people until 1884, the year they were compelled to abandon their nomadic way of life as buffalo-hunters and adopt a settled life on a reservation. "After that," said Plenty Coups, "nothing happened." The Crow survived. What does "happened" mean, in that sentence?

Lear has written a whole book about the crisis of the Crow (Lear 2006), and he returns to it in one of the essays in *Wisdom won from Illness*. It is hard not to hear the plight of the Crow as a parable with profound resonances for the modern world: what happens to our sense that life is meaningful, when we lose the deep embodied metaphors in which meaningfulness has traditionally been conveyed in our culture?

Lear is unusual among psychoanalytic writers in that he trained first as a philosopher, with a speciality in classical Greek philosophy. He continues to be fully immersed in both disciplines and is currently both a practising psychoanalyst and a Professor of Philosophy at the University of Chicago. He occupies therefore an interdisciplinary position that is particularly relevant to our current needs, when psychoanalysis has proliferated into so many schools and vocabularies, with so many underlying assumptions and models, that it is often hard for one part of the profession to understand and respect another. In particular, it can be hard to know when an apparently new discovery is genuinely of something new, or is a "rediscovery of the

DOI: 10.4324/9781003451679-3

wheel," made in some new silo of the profession. (Although, of course, "the same thing" in another vocabulary is never quite the same thing, as all translators know.)

What makes a developmental difference?

These essays are of several different kinds. Some are psychoanalytic and appeared first in psychoanalytic journals, others are philosophical and appeared in philosophy journals. Several could well come under the heading of literary criticism. I shall attempt to deal with this mass of various material by singling out four themes that are, I think, central to Lear's current thought. These are the question of how a psychological event, such as understanding a psychoanalytic interpretation or hearing a story, can make a real developmental difference to a person; the role in particular of "irony" in producing such change; the contribution of Hans Loewald's thought, and specifically the central importance Loewald gave to love and mourning in psychological development; and, fourthly, the question I am tempted to summarise, imitating one of Lear's earlier book-titles, as "ethics and its place in nature." These are all far-reaching themes and each makes an appearance in several of the chapters in this collection.

Philosophers have always attempted to describe psychic structure. Both Plato and Aristotle taught that *nous* (reason, "the intellect") should govern *psyche*, a word Lear often translates as soul (a better word than the ubiquitous "mind" of anglophone psychoanalysis). For Aristotle, the soul is the principle of unity in living creatures. But in man the soul is often not unified. How can reason "govern," and therefore unify, the non-rational parts of the soul, to which reason is by definition alien, without simply becoming a tyrant, in psychoanalytic language a superego? Aristotle says the different parts need to learn to speak in harmony – "with the same voice." Lear agrees; but, he asks, how is this to be achieved?

It's here that classical philosophy has no detailed account to give, and psychoanalysis can make a contribution to the discussion. Lear puts particular emphasis on the "fundamental rule," which Freud didn't properly formulate until 1912, and is less impressed by the sort of psychoanalytic theorising that purports to know what is "in the unconscious" of the analysand. This is not the sort of knowledge we can actually have, he says, and psychoanalysis has often gone astray – has become, perhaps, the sort of thing King Thamus might have feared – when psychoanalysts have claimed such knowledge and patients have submitted to their claims. The patient then accepts a third-person account of him- or herself – perhaps believes it, perhaps repeats it – and words may be used with an appearance of depth but without the quality of inner connectedness that makes for real psychic change, by which I don't merely parrot some "insight" but "I" become different.

Giving central place to the fundamental rule points to a different sort of functioning for the analyst. The analyst becomes someone who listens attentively to the flow of the patient's discourse and notes impediments – interruptions, breaks, non-sequiturs, mistakes, repetitions. The analyst doesn't claim to know what these things mean, but she senses that they do mean something, and she draws the patient's attention to them. As Lear says, very often a patient will be aware, when he hesitates, that his thoughts are drawing him in a direction to which he doesn't want to turn; directing the patient's attention to the hesitation – taking the interruption to the flow seriously – may cause the patient (not the analyst) to recognise something of how his mind is working, and what his "defences" are defending him against. To actually experience one's defences at work is a very different thing from being told about them by an expert. A psychic development made on this basis has an unmistakable authenticity. And in time the patient may begin to be in a position "to bring about her own psychic change … *via the efficacy of her own self-conscious understanding*" (25, Lear's emphasis).

Any theorisation of technique is bound to highlight and to some extent idealise one or some of the aspects of the multitude of things every analyst inevitably does in an analytic session, but Lear's account is of great interest. It points to a picture of what psychic health, in his view, consists in: a free flow of communication within the psyche – he calls it the "free flow of self-consciousness" (7) – in which all the elements are in contact with one another. The idea that such a soul might "speak with one voice," harmoniously, begins to make at least intuitive sense.

Discussing Plato's use of "myth and allegory" in the *Republic*, Lear approaches another aspect of the same issue. The non-rational parts of the soul are not going spontaneously to be impressed by the sorts of argument that impress the rational part – the sorts of argument that impress philosophers. Plato, Lear suggests, was recognising this when he came to write the *Republic*. Socrates first has an argument with the cynical Thrasymachus, whom Socrates defeats at a rational level but fails to persuade. In other words, Thrasymachus embodies an emotional mood, a "nonrational part of the soul" (2), that doesn't recognise the government of reason. Socrates moves on to a different interlocutor, the honest and thoughtful Glaucon, but equally significantly he moves on to a different mode of discourse, a succession of "stories," including the allegory of the Cave and the myth of Er, designed to engage the imagination and not only the "reason," the conscious thinking, of his hearers.[2] Images involve the non-rational parts of the psyche in a way that fits with their nature, as rational argument does not. Lear spells this out in careful detail; he suggests that using the imagination to follow a story, or a complex image like that of Plato's Cave, can cause something to *really* happen in the soul, quite differently from the use of argument and rational thinking.

With this in mind, one detail of the *Republic*, the expulsion of the poets from the ideal *polis*, which has often puzzled Plato's commentators – more especially as it's advocated in a work, the *Republic*, in which Plato's own poetic gifts are so impressively on display – may seem less surprising. The "poets" are the ones who produce images and stories, and the psychological effectiveness of stories may turn out to be very powerful, not only in guiding the soul towards virtue, but also in leading the soul astray. As we might put it nowadays, Plato is recognising the enormous power, and the enormous danger, of "fake news," distorting stories, which may lead the soul into seriously wrong and self-harming directions. (Replace "poets" with "tabloids" and you might see good reason to banish them from a responsible commonwealth.)

This discussion could continue rather naturally into a consideration of religion, and the stories religions tell, which Freud so unceremoniously dismissed as "fairytales" (1927, 29). Plato's myth of Er is itself a step in this direction. Lear doesn't go there, directly. But in another essay he discusses Marilynne Robinson's novels *Gilead* and *Home*. He again touches on some of his central themes. He suggests that the town of Gilead (rather like, though he doesn't say this, the Crow on their reservation) is a community that has lost its *raison d'être*; when it was founded, it was, very heroically, a centre for abolitionists on the "Underground Railroad," offering help and shelter to escaping slaves. Now, it is just a village with all the unthought-out prejudices of rural Iowa, paying lip-service to a Christianity that no longer governs anyone's behaviour – scarcely even that of the Rev. Ames.

This leads on to a most interesting discussion of Jack, the central figure – it's hard to say "hero," and yet perhaps in spite of everything the hero – of the second novel, *Home*. Lear sees Jack, in his baffling combination of petty criminality and earnest truth-telling, as somehow the truest Christian in the story, someone who refuses to go along with the hypocrisy of his family and his community, and who embodies specifically the profoundest Christian value of care for the outcast. After extended and thoughtful reflection on "true" Christian values – in which Lear is careful to tell us that he himself is not a Christian – he ends with a moment at which suddenly he himself seems unsure about what our best values may look like. Robinson, he says, has taught him "that there are serious costs attached to living as I do" (285). He is not more specific, but it's as if Lear's theme has been suddenly and disconcertingly enacted in his own person: that imagining with his impressive capacity for insight the story created by Robinson's profoundly Christian imagination has "caused something to happen," has opened up some unexpected and vertiginous perspective in his own world of values.

Irony

Several of these essays have the form of literary studies: two are of novels by the South African writer J.M. Coetzee, one is of *As You Like It*, and another is of Plato's *Symposium*. It makes no sense to ask which hat Lear is wearing when he writes these studies: they are literary criticism, philosophy *and* psychoanalysis, and they work admirably as examples of all three.

A key-term in his discussion of how the use of words can enable psychological development is *irony*, a word to which he gives a very particular significance. (He was preceded in this by Kierkegaard, whose usage he follows closely.) Irony is a difficult word. In a perfectly conventional sense, *As You Like It* is often cited as an example of Shakespeare's "dramatic irony," in which the audience are privy to information the characters don't possess. In it, the character Rosalind, a girl acted in Elizabethan drama by a boy, adopts the role of a youth, Ganymede, who befriends the love-struck Orlando and offers to help "cure" him of his sickness of love. The object of Orlando's love, as it happens, is Rosalind. Ganymede's remedy for Orlando's trouble is to invite Orlando to treat him, Ganymede, as if he were Rosalind (as of course in reality he is), whereupon he, Ganymede, speaking as Rosalind, will give

Orlando wise advice. Meanwhile the audience already knows that the "real" Rosalind, near the bottom of this little heap of gender-identities, is herself in love with Orlando, and so the advice given to "cure" Orlando's love will in fact be tailored to foster and educate it. And since this is comedy, we may be confident it will succeed.

No lack of scope for irony in this situation! But Lear wants us to discover the concept of irony in a deeper dimension. He suggests that although apparently the story is of Rosalind educating the clumsy Orlando in how to love her more skilfully, in reality Rosalind herself is learning how to love in the course of the play. The Rosalind who sets up the action is very different from the Rosalind who accepts to marry Orlando at the end of it. For all the comedy and absurdity of the plot, the central narrative is powerful because it is one of psychological development – of Rosalind coming to integrate her splendid satirical intelligence and her acute perception of social reality with her "love-sick" longings, her tears and her sexuality. "My affection hath an unknown bottom," she says to her friend Celia, "like the bay of Portugal" (*As You Like It*, IV: i, 220). Funny, sexy, and poignant all at once, her words embody the whole predicament of adolescent love.

Kierkegaard took as a central example of irony the question: "Among all these Christians, is there a Christian?" (quoted, 66). Lear asks many variants of this question – "Among all the Crow, is there a Crow?" (65), "among all our lovers, are there any lovers?" (133) – as a touchstone for irony and its potential to recognise new degrees of depth. Among all the Christians in Gilead, is there a Christian? Well, yes and no. It's far from clear. But in thinking about the question, we deepen our understanding and our imagination of what it means to be a Christian. We can't seriously consider the question without altering our relation to the words we use so fluently. Irony brings us, says Lear, "to the core of our finite existence: we are creatures who, for our very existence, depend on concepts that depend on us" (135).

It may be a little problematic to put such weight on the notion of irony. I am tempted to say that transformative power is only present in such "ironies" if we refuse to be ironic about them, that "irony" in at least one of its common usages is what *prevents* us from engaging in transformative thinking, or from recognising the true significance of allegorical objects. Chronically depressed patients are sometimes past masters in the use of irony. When Lear asks his "litmus-test" question about the Crow ("among all the Crow, is there a Crow?"), I fear that to describe the Crow's tragic plight as "ironic" may be to diminish it and assimilate it to far less terrible scenarios. Nevertheless, whether or not "irony" is fully up to playing the heavyweight role Lear demands of it, he undoubtedly manages to use it to identify a very important vector of psychic experience, and one that makes for creative and disorienting destabilising of our habitual mental postures.

The thought of Hans Loewald

Irony links too of course with Lear's background in classical Greek philosophy, where he studied above all not only Aristotle, but also Plato; he is always aware of the so-called Socratic irony by which Socrates claimed to know only that he knew nothing. Again, irony is what this is called, but I'm not sure it's the right word for it. Surely Socrates' posture is similar to that of the psychoanalyst who deliberately distances himself from his own "knowings" in order to listen as carefully as possible to his patient. This is to adopt a posture appropriate to a task; it's only "ironic" to the onlooker who doesn't understand what's happening. There's also a sense in which Socrates' claim represents the literal truth: he was questioning the working of language, and therefore necessarily doubting the validity of all statements he might make in it.

Be that as it may, Lear makes a persuasive case for the fundamental good sense of Aristotle's account of "ethical virtue" as an "excellence of the nonrational part of the soul," desire-and-emotion, when it "listens to reason" and "speaks with the same voice" as reason (30). But, as we have seen, Lear also points to the insufficiency of Aristotle's account of how this excellence can be achieved. There is a need for something more. The fundamental rule of psychoanalysis shows us in the abstract how psychoanalysis can act to promote the integration of the psyche, but to suggest that integration will have a bearing on "ethical virtue" requires us to think in more concrete detail. And if poets are excluded from the *polis* because their stories might lead people astray, we are left with a need for a close-textured, psychoanalytic account of a way in which desires and emotions may safely be identified, communicated with, and found a non-destructive place, both in the larger context of the psyche with its goals and motives, and, of course, also in the *polis*, in society.

Refreshingly, Lear directly contradicts Freud's famous claim to have effected the "third Copernican revolution," the "third and most wounding blow" to human megalomania, by demonstrating that the ego is not master in its own house (5). Lear shows both that this issue was abundantly familiar in classical Greece, and also, and creatively, that it has always been seen as an issue about which something needed, in principle, to be done. We can't understand what is genuinely new, says Lear, if we stick with "fantasies of revolution" (6).

This leads directly to the importance for Lear of the thought of Hans Loewald, the senior American psychoanalyst whom Lear initially hoped to have as his training analyst. When Loewald said he was too old, Lear made a counter-suggestion that they should meet once a week to discuss philosophical issues. This arrangement continued for six years and was clearly of enormous importance, no doubt to both parties, but certainly to Lear.

Hans Loewald (1906–1993) was born in Germany and studied philosophy under Martin Heidegger before training as a doctor. He emigrated to the United States in 1939 where he trained as a psychoanalyst and became well-known as an exceptionally sensitive and thoughtful theorist. In two very beautiful and appreciative essays here, Jonathan Lear reveals the quietly transformative power Loewald's thought had for him and for many others. "One of the joys of Loewald's writing," he says, "is that he offers a different choice of inheritance" from that of Freud (193).

Lear describes Loewald as a hedgehog and not a fox. The hedgehog knows "one big thing"; in Loewald's case, the thing that preoccupied him was the question, in Lear's words, "what would it be to take seriously the thought that within the human realm love is a developmental force?" (178). Loewald thought that Freud had failed to understand the power of his own concept of Eros, becoming distracted instead by the less interesting notion of the death drive. Partly influenced by Klein, Loewald also emphasised the enormous importance of the related concept of mourning, and the internalisations and reintegration that can derive from it.

With the notion of a "different choice of inheritance," and with a most moving story of his own father's devastation after the death of his (the father's) mother, Lear gives us pointers to the importance of Loewald to himself personally. At the end of the second of these two essays, "Mourning and Moral Psychology," he comments on Loewald's caution in speaking about religion. He says that Freud's dismissal of it "had a chilling effect on the psychoanalytic profession as a whole" (203). Whereas Freud claimed that modern man had become estranged from himself, Loewald commented that "Freud's critique of religious belief unnecessarily *contributes* to that estrangement" (204, Lear's emphasis). Lear speaks of an "intense privacy" lying at the heart of Loewald's commitment and suggests that it was "a private and personal relation to God" (205). As with the discussion of Marilynne Robinson, one has the sense of coming upon a boundary that Lear is recognising with increasing clarity, that between psychoanalysis and religion, but has not yet allowed himself to go beyond.

The necessarily ethical direction of psychoanalytic change

The final theme I want to focus on links all the others and is foundational. It follows from Aristotle's notion of "ethical virtue." It is that the changes that develop in psychoanalysis have a necessarily ethical tendency. This is not the result of "moralistic" intentions on the part of the analyst but is the necessary result of the nature of psychic integration. Psychoanalysis moves us towards increased recognition of the reality of others and towards a broadening of the range of our understanding and sympathy. I am inclined to think that this is a secret hidden in plain sight in our profession, but it has been concealed, or scotomised, ever since Freud (1912, 115) used his metaphor of the impartial surgeon to describe the psychoanalyst. It has left psychoanalysts with a wish to assure us they have no "goals for the patient," or no "wish to do anything but analyse the patient." It is rather like saying, "I have a mill, so I grind corn; don't ask me what I grind corn for."

Most of the essays in this collection have a bearing on this question, but Lear addresses it most directly in his most technical paper, "Technique and final cause in psychoanalysis." By "final cause," Lear means Aristotle's fourth category of causation (efficient, material, formal and final) – the *telos* or goal that could also, said Aristotle, be regarded as exerting a causal influence on a thing, a person or an event. Lear approaches this idea by way of a very interesting thought-experiment. He quotes a clinical vignette from a paper by Lawrence Levenson and then proceeds to imagine four ways of responding to the material, one that of Levenson himself, the others by Loewald, by a Contemporary Kleinian, and by a Lacanian. Lear considers that each response has validity – but how can that be, if each is a response to the same clinical material, and if there were nothing but "efficient causes" at work (i.e. causes running from past to present)?

His answer is that, despite their diversity, all four of these analysts share a "final cause" with the others. This final cause is the patient's "freedom": "freedom is the kind of health that psychoanalysis aims to facilitate" (150). "We can evaluate an approach not only in terms of how well it discloses what is already going on in the analysand's psyche, but also how well it facilitates the analysand's movement in the direction of psychic well-being" (151), that's to say, his or her psychic freedom.

He then unpacks the notion of freedom under several headings: freedom of mind (which includes freedom of reflection, freedom from attacks on the mind's own functioning, freedom to symbolise, freedom to mourn one's haunting "ghosts" and allow them to take their place as "ancestors" [Loewald's brilliant metaphor], and so on). There is also freedom "to speak one's mind" and not only to speak from parts of it (we remember the development of Rosalind in this connection), and freedom "to be and to let be."

This last is extremely interesting and causes Lear to touch on a fundamental issue: in what terms do we spontaneously make sense of our own lives, when we reflect on them unconstrained by theory? Lear suggests several questions we may ask ourselves: are we someone who can love and be loved? Are we capable of creative engagement with the world? Can we be a friend? These are the sorts of categories in terms of which people spontaneously gauge the success or failure of their own lives; they are hugely important, and they need to be understood subjectively: they can't usefully be affirmed, or contradicted, by third parties.

The notion of "freedom" is very general, perhaps too much so to be entirely convincing as the "final cause" of psychoanalysis. But Lear has in mind in particular the sort of freedom that he calls "the free flow of self-consciousness" (7), and this is a freedom with complex implications, including the need for impulse control and affect regulation, which may at first glance not look like "freedom" at all. Via the Kleinian emphasis on envy, Lear segues from it into something more specific. The analyst doesn't, he says, facilitate every sort of freedom. The analyst can't say: "I should facilitate the patient's freedom to enviously attack her objects." Psychoanalysis "is constitutionally directed away from envy…" and he goes on: "This is basically an ethical dimension to psychoanalysis. It recognises that freedom to be inherently involves freedom to let be" (155).

One of Lear's early books was entitled *Love and its Place in Nature* (1990). In his present essays, he is risking the thought that ethics too has its place in nature. This is a very profound and very important idea. For the moment, we can only state it with caution. But the recognition of an inherently ethical dimension to psychoanalysis, and the suggestion that Hans Loewald's thought represents the possibility of a different legacy from Freud's, one in which the irrationality of love is given its full redemptive power, opens up the possibility that psychoanalysis could in the future found itself on a more coherent and stronger philosophical base than Freud himself, product of the late nineteenth century's fascination with natural science, was able to give it. It opens the door, as Lear puts it, referencing

Bernard Williams, to discovering within psychoanalysis "a robust, nonmoralizing moral psychology" (43).

These essays are moderate, beautifully written and very thoughtful. They represent an admirable and important attempt to overcome the intellectual isolation in which psychoanalysis is traditionally done, and to knit psychoanalysis in with the longer and deeper traditions of Western thought.

Notes

1 A review essay on Jonathan Lear: *Wisdom Won from Illness* (2017, Cambridge, MA and London: Harvard U.P.).
2 The "allegory of the Cave" is an extended metaphor conveying Plato's teaching that the ordinary world of "appearance" conceals from us the profounder reality of the Forms, and ultimately the Form of "the Good." The myth of Er is a report by a resurrected hero, who has lived through an afterlife with rewards and punishments for his good and evil deeds, and has now reincarnated in circumstances he has himself chosen. This story enables Plato to affirm the supreme importance of ethical decision-making.

References

Freud, S. (1912). Recommendations to physicians practising psychoanalysis. *SE* 12: 111–20.
Freud, S. (1927). The future of an illusion. *SE* 21: 5–56.
Lear, J. (1990). *Love and Its Place in Nature*. New York, NY: Farrar, Straus and Giroux.
Lear, J. (2006). *Radical Hope: Ethics in the Face of Cultural Devastation*. Cambridge, MA and London: Harvard UP.
Lear, J. (2017). *Wisdom Won from Illness*. Cambridge, MA and London: Harvard UP.

Chapter 4

Who founded Buddhism?

Notes on the psychological action of religious objects

In this chapter, I shall attempt to understand better the psychological forces at work in the development of religious "objects" by looking at one thread in the history of Buddhism. The simplicity of the initial story of the Buddha's Enlightenment, and the philosophical carefulness of the Buddhist tradition, allow such developments to be seen with particular clarity in Buddhism.

Introduction

Those who look, even superficially, at an outline of Buddhist history are often astonished that what appears to have sprung from a rather modest root, the "enlightenment" of Gautama Siddhartha as he meditated under a peepul tree, grew as it spread across Asia into a vast religious structure, with priestly hierarchies and ceremonies, many schools of philosophy and meditational practice, and mythologies speaking of countless Buddhas and bodhisattvas in this and many other realms and worlds, hells and Paradises, epochs and galaxies.

In this essay, I shall look at one of these later Buddhas in particular, Amitābha (Amida in Japanese), the Buddha of boundless light. His cult derives from Sanskrit texts originating in Northern India but is explicitly first heard of in second century China where it became one of many cults of Buddhas "without form" (i.e. non-historical). It reached Japan in the seventh century, where it had varying degrees of importance but didn't become a school in its own right until the twelfth century, when a priest named Hōnen brought it centre-stage. Hōnen's disciple Shinran founded the Jōdo Shinshū, a Buddhist denomination centred on the cult of Amida which is now the largest denomination in Japan.

The key-notion of Amidist Buddhism is love. Meditation is set to one side, the acquisition of wisdom ("Enlightenment") is downplayed and the goal of the Amidist Buddhist is to achieve rebirth in Amitābha's Pure Land, a sort of Paradise from which the attainment of nirvana is now certain. The language of goals is not really appropriate: all the emphasis is on Amitābha's love. It is the recognition of that love, with appropriate joy and gratitude, that causes the believer to be reborn in the Pure Land; it has nothing to do with the believer's own power or merit.

DOI: 10.4324/9781003451679-4

The extraordinary simplicity of this "salvation," achieved by being intensely moved by the love of an invisible figure (with no back-story that Amitābha ever "existed") is a little breath-taking. Early Western scholars, discovering Buddhism and impressed by its psychological and philosophical profundity, tended to be dismissive of a development that reminded them of a rather simplified evangelical Christianity. The historian of Buddhist thought, E.J. Thomas, writing in the 1930s, despatched Amidism in a couple of pages: "mere devotion," he remarked, "... cannot achieve salvation" (1933, 258). This is clearly not the view of the Amidist. The questions I want to consider are: what relation does the cult of Amitābha have to mainstream Buddhism (superficially so different), and how, psychologically, can it be understood, given traditional Buddhist teaching? The answer to these questions throws light, I think, on the functioning of religious objects more generally. But we need to start at the beginning.

The Buddha's Enlightenment

Virtually, all we know of the historical Buddha, Gautama Siddhartha, is legend. Some scholars have questioned whether he existed at all. Recent scholarship, however, tends to support the common-sense view that a coherent, radically new teaching is plausibly the creation of a single individual, even if, in an oral culture, it was then modified, misremembered, etc., in ways we can no longer track. The Buddhist scholar Richard Gombrich (2009, 194), noting the coherence of Buddhist ideas, has commented that to doubt the existence of a single mind behind them is like believing a team of blindfolded monkeys might accidentally type out the complete works of Shakespeare. He suggests that the Buddha, as a thinker, deserves a place alongside Plato or Aristotle.

I shall assume, therefore, that Buddhist teaching originated with a real person, Gautama Siddhartha. The details of his life, however, may be almost entirely mythical. For example, Gautama is said to be the son of the King of the Śākyas; but the Śākyas didn't have a king (Williams 2012, 18). His birth, by standing up from the lotus position in his mother's womb, and stepping out of her right side, is plainly a folktale. But myths have their own interest, psychologically speaking, so we don't need to dismiss them. The psychoanalytic thinker Mark Epstein, for example, has recently (2013) reflected fruitfully on the legend that the Buddha's mother died when he was seven days old. In what follows, I too will use elements from the traditional story.

The events leading up to the night of Enlightenment can be summarised briefly. Depressed by encountering four "presaging signs," an old man, a sick man and a corpse being carried to cremation – all emblematic of transience and suffering – and finally an ascetic in monk's robes, emblematic of the solution – Gautama abandoned his wife and new-born son and went off into the forest. For six years he practised extreme asceticism, under two famous teachers. But, despite his gift for concentration and enduring austerities, he remained dissatisfied: he felt no nearer a solution to the suffering caused by loss and transience. He therefore abandoned his ascetic practices and accepted some milk-rice from a young woman named Sujātā, the daughter of the local village headman. Strengthened by the food, he sat down under a peepul tree, vowing not to stand up until he had solved his problem. Assailed by distractions (represented by the demon Māra and Māra's seductive daughters), he called on the Earth to witness that he was fit to attain Buddhahood. The Earth responded with a roar of approval.

The night that followed was one of intense intellectual activity. In the first watch, he became able to recall his former lives; in the second, he saw that karma is dependent on ethical behaviour (Gombrich sees this "ethicisation of the universe" as one of the transformative innovations of Buddhism, differentiating it sharply from contemporary Brahmanism, in which karma was to do with fulfilling requirements for ritual action); in the third, he saw what became the founding teachings of Buddhism: the Four Noble Truths of suffering and the Noble Eightfold Path leading to its elimination (*Mahāsaccaka-sutta*, see Thomas 1949). (In other versions, in the third watch, he perceived the truth of "dependent origination" [*pratītya-samutpāda*], the recognition that nothing has an independent self or essence because all apparent "things" are moments in a vast cascade of causally conditioned, transient processes. Somewhat differently from Western science, in Buddhism the emphasis is on the multitude of "conditions" that make up causality: it's more like an ever-changing four-dimensional lattice than the familiar Western example of one billiard-ball imparting motion to another. (The "no-self" teaching is one consequence of this insight.) As dawn broke, Gautama knew that his search was ended.

What had he understood in this Enlightenment? It was, first, that what is most crucial about human beings is their ethical intentions, and, secondly, that suffering is caused by cravings which in turn depend on the belief in an enduring self. In reality, there is no enduring self: the world is not a world of enduring things, mental or physical, but a cascade of causally conditioned processes where nothing has independent reality and there is no enduring "I" to be the subject of suffering. These teachings are traditionally summarised in formulas involving numbered lists (Four Noble Truths, Three Marks of Conditioned Existence etc), mnemonic devices helpful in an oral culture, and some of which may well go back to Gautama himself.

In more modern language, we might say that the Buddha was a phenomenologist. Heidegger's distinction between the "universe" (that science tells about) and the "world" (that we live in) is one the Buddha also recognised, and similarly Heidegger's understanding that we have no facts without interpretations. The intellectual conundrums to which the no-self teaching gave rise are comparable to many of the issues discussed in modern phenomenology (Lusthaus 2002). The attempt to think what phenomena add up to the delusory experience of a "self" caused Buddhism to generate an extremely complex psychology, and the great Sri Lankan and Indian Buddhist thinkers, Buddhaghosa, Nāgārjuna and Asaṅga, deserve a high place in any global history of philosophy.

Following his Enlightenment, Gautama realised he had solved his problem: he had seen the path to the ending of the suffering caused by "birth and death," by the transience of everything. At first, he doubted what more he could usefully do.

"This *dhamma* (doctrine)," he thought, "is not easily understood, it goes against the stream … those who are slaves to passion will not see it …. My mind was inclined toward indifference and toward not teaching the *dhamma*" (*Ariyapariyesana sutta*, Holder 2006, 10). Briefly, it looked as if the story of Buddhism might end there, with a tranquil sage under a peepul tree. But then something remarkable happened. The god Brahmā appeared to the Buddha and urged him to teach his insights to others: you are now released from suffering, said Brahmā, but

"… look down at the people
afflicted with sorrow, oppressed with birth and old age."

The Buddha was persuaded by Brahmā. "Feeling compassion for beings," he set off from Bodh-Gaya to "turn the wheel of the Dharma." He preached his first sermon to his former fellow-ascetics in the deer-park at Isipatana, near present-day Varanasi.

The irony of this is apparent. The Buddha had freed himself from suffering by recognising that there were no selves, and that the gods themselves were only transient beings, bound on the wheel of rebirth, with no authority comparable to that of an "awakened one," an enlightened Buddha who has understood its mechanism. And yet here was one of the great brahmanical gods playing a key-role in advising him to teach, an activity meaningless unless there are "others." What was happening?

Gombrich (2006, 31) has suggested that the irony is deliberate. Like Thich Nhat Hanh (Hanh & Berrigan 2009, 117), he sees the teaching of the Buddha as a response to the teachings of the Upanishads, and the no-self doctrine as a deliberate reference to and contradiction of the central Upanishadic teaching that *ātman* is *brahman*, that the self is identical with divinity. For the god Brahmā (who is, so to speak, the personal version of impersonal *brahman*[1]) to beseech the Buddha to teach a flat contradiction of brahmanical doctrine is surely a joke at the expense of the brahmins. And it's easy to imagine that, when the story was told, that was one way in which it was heard.

Psychologically, however, we may notice something else. The Buddha's Enlightenment gave him a coherent intellectual picture of reality, an "ontology" in the light of which suffering had no place. But this teaching supplied no motive for action. Motives require subjects who are moved by them; to eliminate the self is to eliminate any place for motivation to occur. In psychoanalytic language, we might say Gautama's insight had left him in an intellectual space, removed or split off from any motive for action. What is split off often reappears first in projection, and for Gautama motivation reappeared in the figure of Brahmā. Brahmā here is not a "religious object" in the sense that he need be prayed to, worshipped, etc.: he plays a third-person part in an allegorical narrative.

There are many conundrums in this account: if there is no self, how can there be others? who has achieved Enlightenment? and so on. Out of these conundrums, the whole vast history of Buddhist thought will develop. But for the moment, the god Brahmā gives a useful starting point.

If we go back into the Buddha legend, we see that Brahmā was not without psychological precursors. Gautama had, apparently callously, abandoned his wife and new-born baby; he had practised extreme austerities, seemingly with no kindness to himself. But kindness came on the scene rather silently, in his recognition that his austerities were not helping him, and then appeared explicitly in the figure of Sujātā, who gave food to Gautama believing he was the god of her local banyan tree, to whom she had prayed for a baby and now wished to thank for answering her prayer. Her story seems designed to emphasise that, just before his Enlightenment, Gautama received milk from a young mother, recalling both the mother he had lost seven days after his birth and the mother-and-baby he had recently abandoned. Kindness appeared again in the generous response of the Earth when he called on it to confirm his excellence. Mark Epstein, reflecting on Gautama's early trauma, the loss of his mother, sees Buddhist meditation as providing a maternal holding function for the mind (Epstein 2013). In parallel fashion, we may see Sujātā, and the Earth, as representing a projected maternal kindness which Gautama remained unable to own in his own right. His Enlightenment takes the form of an ontological vision; compassion or love is not explicitly part of it.

Let us look more directly at this conundrum, which I suggest was the fuel or irritant powering the whole subsequent intellectual development of Buddhism. It's that the central "wisdom" of Buddhism, the content of Gautama's Enlightenment, had no place in it for kindness, love, or compassion. This was not a mere contingent fact that it just happened not to mention these things. It was intrinsic to the "wisdom" that, by systematically excluding selves, it abolished precisely what compassion demands, a self to be the subject of compassion, and the selves that could be its object. Compassion, if we accept the "wisdom," is delusory and finds no purchase.

Nevertheless, Buddhism has never been without compassion, certainly not since Brahmā appeared immediately after the Enlightenment. How are we to explain this? Gautama might, in principle, have become the teacher of a desolate truth, like some bleak pre-Socratic or some Nietzschean *Übermensch*, proclaiming that "what the world really is" is a meaningless cascade of causal processes. In fact, he founded one of the most compassionate traditions humanity has known. How can this have happened?

Buddhism was of course (as Buddhists always insist) never simply a philosophy – it has always been a "way of life" in which conceptual formulations were merely "fingers pointing at the moon" (its formulations were always eminently translatable, unlike the Semitic religions, where the words, being the Word of God, were sacred and had an un-displaceable authority). Nevertheless, the evolution of Buddhism and its expansion into new cultural contexts has always been powered by reflection on its formulations, and its thinkers have always struggled to express more adequately what seemed to them its central insights. So it is legitimate to highlight the questions raised by the way the Buddha's Enlightenment is described.

In saying something is "split-off" psychologically I am not invoking the strong (Kleinian) use of the term "splitting" to name a psychotic defence. I mean a psychic content that is not yet integrated into the I, the everyday person who is the subject of consciousness. A familiar example is the place of sexuality in adolescence, when sexuality appears in moods, stray thoughts, sudden hilarity – and may sometimes be acted out – but is not yet integrated into the personality, owned by the self and enacted in conscious relation to ideals and social norms. The Buddha's intellectual "Enlightenment" followed the abandonment of his family and a long period of austerity, in which bodily desires and ordinary domains of feeling had been subordinated to the felt need to make sense of psychological suffering.

What is split off from the awareness of the I is not, however, necessarily invisible to others. The emotions of the adolescent are often obvious, even though invisible to herself. It is convincing to suppose that the kindness that was no part of the Buddha's conscious thinking during his Enlightenment, and which was then encountered in projection in Brahmā, was perfectly apparent to others. We also know from clinical experience that if someone feels their unhappiness is being taken seriously and is being put into words, they may feel they are being "loved" – a fact which may require careful handling in the transference. For both these reasons, both because of Gautama's personal qualities, and because of his direct naming of life's painfulness in the first Noble Truth, his hearers may have felt "loved" and accurately recognised, and therefore drawn to follow him. (The Zen teacher D.T. Suzuki makes a similar point about the importance of the Buddha's personal qualities in addition to his teachings [1949, 79].)

The process by which unintegrated parts of the self gradually become integrated is one that involves interaction with others, evoking the full range of emotions, including painful ones like envy, exclusion and rivalry. Such interaction enables us to perceive our impact on others and the profound importance of ethics, and it promotes development because unacknowledged aspects of the self are first recognised in the other. Brahmā in the Buddha story may be conceived as embodying a projected element in this sense – destined for integration, but not yet recognised as part of the brightly-lit central "I", the newly enlightened Gautama. An incompletely integrated person sometimes acts from one of the split-off parts, and we are taken by surprise: she "isn't who we thought she was."

We may summarize all this by saying that when Buddhism began, its teachings had the form of a sophisticated phenomenological ontology, but they were accompanied by attitudes of kindness and compassion of which there was no mention in the theory. Or we might reverse the emphasis, as in the optical illusion called duck-rabbit, in which duck and rabbit are inseparable but cannot both be perceived simultaneously. We would then say that Buddhism started with an impulse of kindness towards the self, which allowed Gautama to step down from austerity and accept the kindness of Sujātā, and then found as its instrument an intellectual picture by which suffering could be overcome. Having achieved its goal with respect to Gautama, the motive of compassion could then enlarge its field of operation and teach that picture to others.

As is often the case, therefore, when someone is unintegrated, it isn't quite clear which part of her has initiated the action: was the Buddha's teaching primarily the product of his Enlightenment, or of the split-off compassion represented by

Brahmā; was Buddhism founded by Gautama or by Brahmā? Later this ambiguity appeared more explicitly in another teaching: Gautama declared there were four dwelling-places of Brahmā, the *Brahma-vihāras* (sometimes called the "Four Immeasurables"), which were direct paths to nirvana. These were: kindness, compassion, sympathetic joy (*muditā*, joy in the happiness of others) and equanimity. The fifth century Pali commentator Buddhaghosa (1964, 347) pointed out that these may be conceived as four sorts of maternal love. They are, he says, the different sorts of love of a mother with four sons: a baby, a sick child, a young man proud of his prowess and a mature man competently engaged with his life. Gombrich again suggests that the title, *Brahma-vihāras*, points to the style of a witty polemical teacher, explaining to the brahmins where Brahmā or *brahman* is *really* to be found (Gombrich 2009, 78–88). But in the light of Brahmā's role after the Enlightenment, we may wonder whether, in the mind of the Buddha's early followers, the figure of Brahmā had already acquired allegorical status, had come to represent compassionate states of mind – states increasingly recognised as important but with no place in the explicit teaching.

The Mahāyāna

The need to affirm selves, if "compassion" is real, and the need to deny selves, if Buddhist "wisdom" is correct, soon generated a variety of views. The historian of Indian Buddhism, Paul Williams, lists five recognisable schools in early Buddhism, all divided by different teachings on the nature of reality and how to understand the continuities that stubbornly persisted in demanding recognition despite universal transience. There was even one school, the *Pudgalavādins* (pudgala = person), which claimed there was a "person" who experiences the continuities required by karma and reincarnation. It was criticised, unsurprisingly, as reinstating the self under a different name. The *Sarvāstivādins* (sarva = all, asti = exist) claimed that there were "primary existents" that were real, into which "conceptual existents," like selves, could be analysed. The *Theravādins*, the only one of these schools that has survived into the present, believed in a basic unconscious level of the mind, called *bhavaṅga* (becoming), which links together experiences through a lifetime and across rebirths (Williams 2012, 83–97).

But the paradox went deeper than such theories could reach. For if there was no self, there was no one to reach Enlightenment, and what could it mean to say someone had become enlightened (and someone else, presumably, had not)? The rise of the Mahāyāna (Great Vehicle) was an attempt to relocate the subject of Buddhism altogether, from the individual to the totality of "all beings" – for apart from that totality there could be (according to Buddhist "wisdom") no singularity at all. The ideal shifted from the idea of the individual meditator who attains Enlightenment to that of the bodhisattva who works for the Enlightenment of all beings, a goal of incomprehensible vastness (for "all beings" included every mosquito and earthworm, proceeding through infinite numbers of rebirths) and requiring unimaginable tracts of time.

Even so, however, the fundamental paradox wasn't resolved. Infinitely compassionate though the bodhisattvas might be, in reality neither they nor the "all beings" had a self, and wisdom was to recognise the ultimate reality of "emptiness" (*śūnyatā*). Nāgārjuna in the second century CE made this teaching the centre of his philosophy and claimed that all things were "akin to illusions" (Williams 2012, 105). This took Buddhism back towards the Hindu teaching of *māyā*. As time went on, worshippers of Vishnu returned the compliment; they brought Buddhism back into the embrace of Hinduism by declaring Gautama to be one of Vishnu's several incarnations. Over the centuries, Buddhism disappeared from India.

The Mahāyāna was the version of Buddhism that spread to China and thence to Tibet, Korea, Japan, Vietnam etc, dividing as it did into many schools of thought and practice. Despite the Buddha's emphasis that truth can never be adequately expressed in concepts – that his teachings, in a famous image, were only a raft to get you across a river, to be discarded when no longer useful – theory continued to proliferate. The *Yogācāra* (Mind-only) school, founded by the half-brothers Asaṅga and Vasubandhu in the fifth century CE, examined the implications of Buddhist phenomenology with a psychological subtlety that perhaps went beyond anything Western philosophy has yet achieved (Lusthaus 2002). And Buddhism was strongly accretive: rather than conflict with local religious traditions, Buddhists preferred to interpret them buddhistically and then incorporate them. The difference in style between, say, Tibetan and Japanese Buddhism reflects the difference between pre-Buddhist Tibetan shamanism and a distinctive Japanese culture that already when Buddhism arrived on the scene combined careful intellectuality with passionate loyalties and acute aesthetic sensitivity.

The no-self teaching raised many questions for common sense. Who was the Buddha if there was no self? One of the precursors of the Mahāyāna, the *Mahāsāṃghika* school, questioned the nature of Gautama's apparently ordinary human life: was it only an "appearance" by a transcendent spiritual Buddha, who in reality never left the Tuṣita heaven? Or did Gautama, though really present, perhaps only *seem* to have ordinary needs, to suffer, grow old and finally die? Was he always *really*, perhaps, in a state of suffering-free meditation? The Mahāyāna was like someone who responds: all of the above. The Buddha was said to be discoverable in three bodies, the *nirmānakāya* (his ordinary historical body), the *sambhogakāya* (his "body" as met with in teachings, visions etc) and the *dharmakāya* which was ultimate reality.

Mantras and visualisations were also adopted extensively in some Mahāyāna developments, particularly the magical and sometimes deliberately antinomian tantric schools. Such techniques created a sense of a world of inner mental "powers," different from the world of sensory objects. But from a psychological point of view, perhaps the most interesting development was the sort of reverse construction made possible by the idea of a world whose ultimate reality was "mental experience" or "emptiness." For in such a world, the mind was sovereign. What one could imagine was as real as the physical world; what one encountered or created in mental space had the same sort of reality as everything else, was ultimately "empty" or ultimately a set of mental experiences (and nothing more) – just as everything else was.

Such thinking licensed the unlimited production of new spiritual entities: new Buddhas, "celestial bodhisattvas," ferocious guardians of the Dharma and so forth. Early Buddhism had been free of gods and demons (or rather, had retained them as part of a subsidiary mythology), but they had become secondary to the human story of suffering and release from suffering – with the single exception of Brahmā's intervention following the Enlightenment. In the Mahāyāna, spiritual beings returned in force, but they differed from the gods or demons of other religions in being clearly labelled as "mental constructs"; they could be invoked, worshipped, prayed to – but they didn't have to be "believed in" and there is no equivalent in buddhology to the agonised question, so familiar in Western religion, of whether God actually "exists." (A parallel in psychoanalysis, to which I shall return in a moment, is in Winnicott's account of transitional space and phenomena – a realm which, like that of Mahāyāna "mental constructions," is both imaginary and yet efficacious.)

To return to the main argument: the paradox of early Buddhism, the maintenance of compassion together with a "wisdom" that explicitly abolished both the subject and the objects that compassion requires, tended in the Mahāyāna to be increasingly tilted towards compassion: the bodhisattva's career was motivated by compassion, and the attainment of Enlightenment, though never omitted, had become secondary. Williams (2012, 104) emphasises that to say that bodhisattvas "postpone entry into nirvana," as many Western writers do, is inaccurate: in the Mahāyāna, the duality of nirvana and samsara was transcended, as was the idea of individual nirvana as a desirable goal.

The Mahāyāna became in all but name more like a mystical theism than early Buddhism (Wallace 2007) – perhaps at first glance a polytheism, but all distinctions among Buddhas and bodhisattvas were purely provisional. In the Tibetan meditation practice known as Dzogchen, the "mirror-like primordial consciousness" to which the meditator attains was given a Buddha's name – Samantabhadra – an immanent Buddha, so to speak, discovered at the heart of the meditator's awareness (Wallace 2007, 2009, 194). And externally, there were the so-called Dhyāni Buddhas at the centre and in the four cardinal directions, Vairocana, Ratnasambhava, Amitābha, Akṣobhya, Amoghasiddhi (Govinda 1960) and also Maitreya, the future Buddha – who might all be described as transcendent Buddhas. The celestial bodhisattvas represented qualities rather than locations – Avalokiteśvara compassion, Mañjuśrī wisdom etc. All these figures were the objects of local cults and rivalries, and their status wasn't stable – Mañjuśrī, for example, though usually a bodhisattva, was sometimes a Buddha (Williams 2012, 140). All these, and many others, were embodiments of the ultimate Dharmakāya (Dharma = teaching, kāya = body), the ultimate reality that all Buddhas "bodied forth" in their different ways.

The Buddha Amitābha

It's easy to see the Mahāyāna development as a sort of gigantic spray, flung up in all directions as the waves of devotion struck the hard rock of the founding paradox, which I have stated as the question: who founded Buddhism, the Buddha or

Brahmā? The question is of course unreal, if Brahmā is understood as a projection of the Buddha's own motivation, but if we think the reason why the Buddha's teaching was initially attractive was because of his personal kindness, and not only because of the intellectual conviction carried by his description of a world of universal transience, then the question captures an important issue. The proliferation of imaginary helpful figures in the Mahāyāna may be seen as a sort of multiplication of Brahmās, the creation of a very different sort of world, one in which love was abundantly available, and questions of ontology, though never settled and continuing to preoccupy specialists, could be bracketed and set aside by ordinary believers.

Paul Williams (2012, 220n) argues that as Buddhism became established, and large monastic communities were supported by settled populations of lay people, the need arose for a second sort of Buddhist career, that of the lay Buddhist. He suggests that monks who had left behind ordinary society might be content in parallel fashion to remember a departed Buddha, but ordinary householders wanted a Buddha they could contact directly in the present. We might rephrase this to suggest that there was psychological pressure to imagine ways in which, despite his death, one could still encounter the Buddha "in person," so to speak – and in the second person. One popular meditation practice in Northern India in the early centuries of the Christian era was "recollection of the Buddha," in which the Buddha was constructed in imagination in vivid detail. Practices of this sort may have contributed both to a belief that the Buddha was still present in some sense, and to further imagining of the "Pure Lands" in which Buddhas have their being. Early evidence of this is a text translated into Chinese in the second century CE, which describes the Pure Land of Akṣobhya: an ideal world of flowers, gentle breezes and music, where "all is clean, and all are interested in practising the Doctrine" (136).

The cult of Amitābha seems to have followed a similar path, and one of its foundational texts, the *Sukhāvatīvyūha-sutra*, was also translated into Chinese in the second century CE. This text became influential in China and in the seventh century it was brought to Japan. The different major schools of Buddhism in Japan all practised meditation on Amida but at first only as one among many Buddhas. It was only with Hōnen (1133–1212) that the cult of Amida gave rise to a school in its own right.

The *Sukhāvatīvyūha-sutra* tells the story of a monk named Dharmākara, who made 46 vows (48 in the Chinese translation) before attaining buddhahood. Of these, the 18th is the most famous. It stated that unless, when he attained buddhahood, all beings who aspired to be born in his Pure Land, and who pronounced his name ten times, would at once be reborn in the Pure Land, then "may I not attain the Supreme Enlightenment" (quoted Sato 2010, 28). In other vows, he made clear that anyone reborn in his Pure Land could be certain of attaining nirvana (Eliot 1935, 366–7). Dharmākara then attained Enlightenment and was reborn as Amitābha. His vows, therefore, had become effective.

Psychologically, these vows are of great interest. Why would Dharmākara make them? They seem to show, consonant with the central paradox I am discussing here, that there was a fear that Enlightenment could interfere with compassion, that something the "unenlightened" Dharmākara knew was precious could become lost if he went forward too enthusiastically into buddhahood. This is surely psychologically accurate. Those who commit themselves to particular beliefs are indeed at risk of narrowing the breadth of their sympathy. Amitābha's vows compelled him not to lose touch with it. At a purely psychological level, as well, there seems to be an understandable determination not to triumph over his fellow-aspirants, his "siblings".

It was to the *Sukhāvatīvyūha-sutra*, along with two similar sutras, that Hōnen turned. Hōnen's father had been murdered when Hōnen was eight years old. Legend says that the dying father told Hōnen not to seek revenge but to acquire Buddhist compassion. The boy went to study at the temple complex on Mt Hiei in Kyoto and was quickly recognised as outstandingly gifted. At a violent time in Japan's history, when there were two civil wars, Hōnen was noted for his gentleness and his concern to make his points in non-provocative ways. He became an admired teacher, and a "reclusive priest," a technical term for those who retreated, not only from the world but also from the religious orders of the time, which they felt had become overly concerned with wealth and ambition.

But in his late 30s, Hōnen became depressed. He felt that meditation was getting him no nearer to Enlightenment, and he is said to have read through the entire vast corpus of Buddhist scriptures, the Tripiṭaka, five times in an attempt to find the solution. Finally, aged 43, he came across a statement by the Chinese scholar Shandao (613–681 CE) that there were two right ways to practise: one was the familiar path of meditation, but there was also a second practice:

> Only repeat the name of Amida with all your heart – whether walking or standing still, whether sitting or lying never cease the practice for even a moment. This is the practice which brings salvation without fail, for it is in accordance with the original vow of the Buddha.
>
> (quoted Eliot 1935, 262)

This passage moved Hōnen deeply. He became convinced that "in this turbulent and degenerate age mental and moral discipline is of small avail and that peace can only be discovered in self-surrender and in reliance on a higher power – in Tariki or the strength of another, that is Amida, not in Jiriki or one's own strength ... he abandoned all other religious practices and devoted himself to the recitation of the Nembutsu only" (Eliot 1935, 262). The *nembutsu* is the formula *Namu Amida butsu* (meaning "Homage to the Buddha Amitābha"). which is repeated frequently in Jōdo Shinshū practices. (Hōnen himself was said to repeat it 60,000 times a day.)

We may note some parallels between Hōnen's story and the Buddha legend. Hōnen's father died when Hōnen was a boy, so like Gautama Hōnen too had the loss of a parent to deal with; he too had renounced the world, and he too reached a point where he recognised that the spiritual techniques taught by respected teachers were getting him nowhere. And he too turned in the direction of compassion. But this time it was explicit: "salvation" (it is hard to find religious terms in English that are free of Christian associations) was achieved, explicitly, through love and the recognition of love. Buddhist Enlightenment was no longer foregrounded but it was now "assured" as the sequel to rebirth in Amitābha's Pure Land.

Kemmyo Taira Sato, a Buddhist scholar who is also a Jōdo Shinshū priest, emphasises that the importance of the *nembutsu* is not in the number of repetitions, but in the sincerity of the spontaneous joy and gratitude they express for Amitābha 's love. He also emphasises that, contrary to some Western assumptions, the recognition of the necessity of *tariki* (the power of another) is an *advance* on the belief in *jiriki* (one's own power). This is a teaching reminiscent of Augustine's doctrine that we have no power of our own to do good but do so only by God's grace. Sato quotes Hōnen's disciple Shinran:

> … there is a distinct turning-point from the Path of the Sages to the Path of the Pure-Land Buddhist …. However much love and pity you may feel for others in this life, it is hard indeed to save them in the way you would wish; hence such love can never be perfect. Only the pronouncing of the *nembutsu* can manifest the mind of great unconditional love.
>
> (quoted Sato 2010, 46)

The change instituted by Hōnen was radical. In traditional Buddhism, practitioners used their "own power" (*jiriki*) to embark on a difficult Path, with active practices such as meditation that helped in perceiving the realities of impermanence and the delusory nature of selves. In the Mahāyāna, emphasis was placed on the "sky-like" spaciousness and stability of the consciousness one then discovered, to which the practitioners of Dzogchen gave the name of the Buddha Samantabhadra. Honen's experience, however, seems to have been that he was unable to give himself to the liberation offered by such teaching. Aided by a psychoanalytic picture in which psychic structure is built up vertically in response to experience, we might say that Honen lacked a foundational experience that could allow him to feel safe in letting go of self-preoccupation. He needed the assurance of being loved with a patient, non-narcissistic love before he could move on. For him, the cult of Amitābha allowed the affect to move into the foreground of the picture: what mattered now was not primarily meditative effort and intellectual insight but a relational event, the experience of recognising love and responding with spontaneous gratitude and joy. Such emotions had never been absent from Buddhism, and their importance was hinted at very early on, for example, by Sujātā's generosity to Gautama, or in the four Brahma-vihāras. But it was not until Hōnen arrived at a reformulation of the effective components of Buddhism (from *jiriki* to *tariki*) that the conundrum of the founding paradox could be deferred to a secondary position and the foundational quality of relational affect be recognised.

The effectiveness of religious objects

The Japanese psychoanalyst Takeo Doi, following Michael Balint, noted that European languages don't readily distinguish between active and passive object-love. In Japanese, the important verb *amaeru* clearly points to this distinction. It means "to depend and presume upon another's love or bask in another's indulgence" (and also: to long for that state) (Doi 1989, 349). It is used both for the baby's first recognition of its feelings toward the mother and also of adult situations of safe depending, highly and explicitly prized in Japanese culture. It describes very precisely, better than any single word in English, the emotion of the Amidist towards Amitābha.

To put things in this way is not to psychologise Buddhism. On the contrary, it is to recognize that Buddhism, like other major religions, has over the centuries moved towards finding ways to affirm the foundational importance of the conscious experience of being safely loved, out of which is born the "new life" and high ethical standards that developed religions claim to make possible. D.T. Suzuki, recognising the extraordinary nature of the Pure Land development, claimed that Hōnen's insight was profoundly original (1949). He was seeing that, differently from previous religious teachers, Hōnen had opened a path to discover, without having to believe mythology, the crucial experience of being the object of love.

This phrase, "without having to believe a mythology," marks the true originality of Buddhism among the world's religions, and its significance in the modern world in which educated people are increasingly unable to "believe in" mythological entities and have not yet found any other way to understand their significance. If the literal truths of science are the only model for truth, then religious entities become indistinguishable from novelistic fictions; if we take them seriously, we can only be deluded.

The Western religious insistence on belief, therefore, sets up a dialogue of the deaf: the fundamentalist who passionately believes versus the rational person who doesn't. We get nowhere by taking sides in this debate.

Buddhism, however, by making no demand for belief, and indeed by explicitly denying that its "great" Buddhas and bodhisattvas have any existence in the "world of form," bypasses the argument. In Amidism, a claim is made for the transformative potential of something very specific, the nature of which is indicated by Amitābha's Vow, and "Amitābha" has a central place in the functioning of the religion. Amitābha is not presented as merely an adjunct or heuristic aid along the path to Enlightenment; it or he is the crucial factor, the transformative object, in psychoanalytic language, that enables "salvation" – the experience of joy, gratitude and liberation. What sort of object are we dealing with?

Freud famously spoke of religion as illusion (1927), and Donald Winnicott, in a striking paradox, spoke of "the substance of illusion" – "that which is allowed to the infant," he said, "and which in adult life is inherent in art and religion" (1951, 230). Winnicott's use of the word illusion has been immensely fruitful and widely followed, including by psychoanalysts so sympathetic and perceptive about religion as Rizzutto (1979) and Meissner (1984). But in relation to religion, the word illusion is not adequate to fulfil the role required of it. Winnicott himself commented that psychoanalysis uses ordinary words "with a splash of paint" (1935, 129); that may be harmless within the profession, but if we wish to speak to a wider culture, our splash of paint will cause confusion. (Freud remembered the paint-free usage when he said emphatically: "our science is no illusion" [1927, 56].) The word illusion is an ordinary word implying that something is deceptive and awaits more correct description. Winnicott's discussion of transitionality also speaks of the need to avoid challenging enquiry into the real nature of the phenomenon ("the question is not to be formulated" [1951, 240]). This may be insightful when discussing a child's relation to a teddy bear, but it isn't clear how it applies to a religion like Buddhism, which has pressed its enquiries with a seriousness fully comparable to that of science.[2]

For Buddhism, the whole of the presented world is the product of our complex interaction with it – not exactly illusory, but "empty," not substantially existent as it appears. It is ethics that gives access to something significantly real. At least four steps on the Noble Eightfold Path are to do with ethics; ethical intention, as Gombrich emphasised, is the ground of karma in Buddhist understanding; and the moral teachings, the Vinaya, are the first of the Piṭakas, the big groupings of Buddhist scriptures. According to the Buddha's insight in the second phase of his Enlightenment, our ethical intentions are our most consequential reality; they determine our karma. The vigour of Dharmākara, in making his vows, expresses his determination not to lose touch with ethical concern. Conformably to the belief in the importance of *tariki* (other-power), however, for the Amidist the power of Amitābha's vow is so great that it overcomes karma, the entailments of one's own ethical history (Sato 2010, 29–31).

To use psychoanalytic language: what sort of "object" is Amitābha? The question is perhaps initially best approached using the language of Franz Brentano (1838–1917). He was the philosophy professor at the University of Vienna who taught Freud (who was briefly very impressed by him [Gay 1988, 29]) and also Husserl, Meinong and many others. Brentano had been a Catholic priest but left the Church when he was unable to accept the doctrine of Papal infallibility. He remained fascinated, however, by the nature of God's existence. He attempted to create a rigorous philosophical base for psychology, in which "mental phenomena" were distinguished from physical phenomena by three main criteria, one of which was that, when they appeared, they were always "about something," always directed towards an "in-existent object" (Brentano 2015, 92–5). This characteristic, known as "intentionality," became influential in many schools of thought, particularly Husserl's phenomenology (which influenced Heidegger) and Meinong's theory of objects (which influenced Russell). Brentano is viewed as the last major linking figure before the paths of analytic philosophy and continental philosophy diverged (Critchley 2001; Huemer 2015).

Brentano's concept of an intentional object implies a third sort of "existence." An intentional object is not externally existent, like the objects of natural science but nor need it be illusory; it may be reliably present to the mind and capable of being present to more than one mind. The category includes numbers and mathematical and logical relations.

For Brentano, this gave a way to speak seriously about certain objects, such as God, without having to make claims about the empirical world as science knows it. We may say the same about Amitābha. But the question arises: how can such an object have importance? With a figure from fiction, like Mme Bovary, we may compare our understanding of female psychology with Flaubert's, or we may compare nineteenth century attitudes to sexuality with our own – and this may have value – but if we said Emma Bovary was "important" to us, it would seem an affectation, at most a way of saying that we are moved and caused to reflect by reading Flaubert's novel.

A religious object is an intentional object in Brentano's sense, but it must be different from a fictional object – perhaps in some ways more like a mathematical object, which is also "intentional" but has a stable presence and can be used reliably in repeated mental operations and also by others. And this is confusing, because, for the non-religious person, the stories of religion read like fictions. How are they different for the religionist?

The difference, I think, lies in the third-person nature of fictional objects, and the potentiality of religious objects to be encountered in the second person. It may be helpful at this point to distinguish mythology from religion: the objects of mythology, like Brahmā in the initial Buddha legend, are encountered in the third person; as such they are more like fictional objects; they may become, but are not yet, religious objects. And religious objects are always at risk of falling back into being mythological objects. It is intense emotion, experienced as second-personal "response" to a "subject" that distinguishes the religious object and allows it to be efficacious in the individual's life. Sato quotes the founder of Jōdo Shinshū: "Shinran Shōnin does not state that salvation is realised 'when you utter the *nembutsu*', but 'at the very moment when the thought that moves you to say the *nembutsu* is awakened within you'"(2010, 30). This "thought" is the affect, the emotion of delight, love and gratitude that arises in response to Amitābha's Vow, and this is the experience described as rebirth in Amitābha's Pure Land.

When Shinran said: "Only the pronouncing of the nembutsu can manifest the mind of great unconditional love" (Sato 2010, 46), he was recognising that the capacity that enables the subject to relate with full emotion to Amitābha's Vow creates at the same moment the capacity for Amitābha's motive to awaken in the subject: the person who responds with joy to Amitābha's unconditional patient kindness simultaneously discovers the capacity for such kindness in himself. But he also discovers that it is not in his own control. If it seems to be, it becomes a source of vanity and limitation; it must not be *jiriki* (own-power) and must be *tariki* (other-power). Putting it psychoanalytically, we would say the good object must remain an object; if it is identified with, it becomes a source of inflation and mania.

The "good object" in this sense is an idea we owe to Melanie Klein, though it has its parallels in other psychoanalytic schools. She spoke of it initially as a way to understand the variable quality of resilience in young children. "When the infant reaches the crucial stage of about three to six months and is faced with the conflicts, guilt and sorrow inherent in the depressive position, his capacity for dealing with his anxiety is to some degree determined ... by the extent to which during the first three or four months of life he has been able to take in and establish his good object which forms the core of his ego. If this process has been successful – and this implies that persecutory anxiety and splitting processes are not excessive and that a measure of integration has come about – persecutory anxiety and schizoid mechanisms gradually lose in strength, the ego is able to introject and establish the complete object and to go through the depressive position" (Klein 1952, 76).

Klein makes clear that the establishment of a "good object" in this sense owes a great deal to the mother's handling and capacity for relationship, and to the confidence the child develops in the mother's reliable presence and support for his achievements, his understanding of the world and his capacity to make reparation when his aggressive impulses interfere with good contact (73). Klein uses the language of "objects," but it's clear that these formative events are intensely subjective "second-personal" experiences of "I" and "you," not in the third person. Doi's concept of *amaeru* (1989) – of the joyful dependence on another's love – beautifully captures one element in the child's experience with an actual good mother.

To describe the good object as the "core" of the ego cannot be quite right, as it overrides the necessary primacy of the baby's own being, but it recognises the inextricable complexity of the earliest identifications (Lear 1990, 161–6) and is on the right level (that of Erikson's "basic trust"). As development proceeds, the good object is fundamental to the ego's good feeling, both about itself (self-esteem) and about others (whom it approaches in a spirit of cooperation and curiosity [the emotional equivalent of Bion's K – see Fisher 2011]). Part of the hope of psychoanalysis is that it may help to establish or strengthen a reliable "good object" in its patients.

Some analysts nowadays might question Klein's confidently developmental picture, but, without debating that point, it's clear that her account can readily be converted into a structural picture: for psychic health, for an engaged and reasonably hopeful attitude to the world, it is necessary to the ego to have a sense of an object (a subject) that affirms it. "… (W)hat it is for the world to be lovable," as Jonathan Lear said in an important argument about the functioning of love, "is for it to be loving" (1990, 154). Neville Symington's idea of "the life-giver," the alternative choice, as he put it, to the narcissistic object, which determines the capacity of a person to be "emotionally alive" (1993, 35) and which "comes into being through being chosen" (40), misses, I think, the necessary priority of the passive experience, but captures the sequel to it, the active choices that flow from conscious or preconscious contact with a loving object.

A non-technical way to put this would be to say that the importance of the experience of "having a good object," of "feeling loved," of being able to "amaeru" (all necessarily second-person experiences), is so great that it would not be surprising if humans created, as Freud said, a wish-fulfilling fantasy of an external loving God to supply it (1927). Such a fantasy is no doubt very common, and (put in that mythological form) is indeed illusion; what is remarkable about Amidism is that it finds a way to provide/affirm the experience, not by resorting to illusory wish-fulfilment, but by supplying a story that is effective. It's effective, presumably, by creating not experience as such but a recognition of experience – perhaps, rather like the transference in psychoanalysis, by linking to the person's preconscious memories of having had the experience, even if historically their encounters with it were not necessarily in the form or to the extent that they would have wished or

were able at the time to appreciate. Thus, the Amidist arrives at the delighted recognition that Amitābha's motive (very much resembling non-ambivalent maternal
love) does exist in the world he or she occupies.

Allegorical objects

I have described religious objects elsewhere as "resources for consciousness,"
because when meditated upon, worshipped etc, they represent potentials for the
expansion of the subject's capacities and sympathy (Black 2004, 2011). We might
more precisely call them "allegorical" objects because, like the objects of allegory,
their function is to embody, pure-culture, some crucial motive and allow it to be
recognised, related to and gradually assimilated (or, in the case of motives seen as
negative, repudiated). Prior to the development of scientific psychology, allegory
gave a way of thinking – sometimes, in the hands of a master like Dante, very
subtle thinking – about the conflicting or cooperative relationships among human
motives, by "(representing) what is immaterial in picturable terms" (Lewis 1936,
44). (I discuss this further in Chapter 6.)

The importance of second-person relationship has been discussed by Western
philosophers in the twentieth century, particularly by Martin Buber and Emmanuel
Levinas. It was Buber's important insight (1970) that we perceive the world in two
very different relational registrations, the third-person objective vision of natural
science, which he called I/It, and the second-person vision of encounter, which he
called I/Thou. In Buber's poetic prose, this insight can seem, though perhaps mis-
leadingly, somewhat "romantic"; it was taken up by Levinas with less emphasis on
the affect, but with very far-reaching consequences, to become the foundation of
his understanding of ethics.

Levinas was one of the first philosophers to introduce Heidegger's thought into
France. Ethical issues were of passionate concern to him; he sought above all to
understand the basis of "responsibility." (I discuss different aspects of his thought
in the last three chapters of this book.) He saw the recognition of responsibility as
arriving inexplicably, like "an order that (slips) into my consciousness like a thief"
(1998, 13) when I perceive "the face of the Other." This is a technical term in
Levinas' philosophy, a development of Buber's Thou, and it means, not the literal
face, but something more like the reality of the other as a vulnerable human subject (Levinas 1958). Levinas's account was not ostensibly of religious experience,
but his recognition of the importance of this encounter caused him to speak of it
as a moment of "epiphany," a recognition of the subjective reality of both "I" and
other, in which the commanding values of the I are clearly seen. So powerfully did
he conceive this experience that he described ethics in a way reminiscent of Buddhism, as having priority over ontology and as the source of truly human being.
In the less vivid language of psychology, we might summarize Levinas' insight
by saying that we don't feel responsibility is required of us when we conceive
another as an "object"; responsibility arises when we become aware of the other
as a "subject."

Levinas's "face of the Other" is, like Amitābha, an "allegorical object." The characteristic of allegorical objects is that, unlike actual human beings, they embody a single psychological quality, compassion in Amitābha's case and the potential for suffering in the case of Levinas' concept. An allegorical object therefore acts as a vector: it exerts a directional pull on the subject who encounters it, and it tends to cause psychic change. The encounter with the allegorical object, therefore, is potentially consequential: it kindles awareness of value and it awakens the individual to the desirability, perhaps the necessity, of change.

Allegorical objects are not correctly described as "illusion." It would of course be an illusion to believe in the existence of Amitābha in space and time, but Amitābha's "motive" is perfectly real, it exists in the universe and has been encountered, in imperfect but real forms, in the individual's experience; it is truly an emotional potential for the self, however much the religious "object" as such may be imaginary or a "mental construct." Differently from how it is with the allegorical object, in any actual person the motive will always be one of many; the ideal simplicity of the allegorical object may be aspired to, but it can never be attained. Nevertheless, to a greater or less extent, the epiphanic moment, the second-person encounter with the allegorical object, has an effect in reality. William James observed that the emotions of religious conversion often revert over time to something only slightly altered – but altered nonetheless – from the pre-conversion personality. And in some cases, as in Hōnen, they result in lasting psychological transformation.

Conclusion

Looking back at Buddhist history in the light of the emergence, many centuries later, of the cult of Amitābha, we see a move from the perception of compassion in the third person, in Brahmā, to a perception of it in the second person in the figure of Amitābha to whom the devotee relates directly. (The *nembutsu* isn't grammatically in the second person, but the crucial emotion of gratitude goes direct to Amitābha.) It's plausible to think that the need for second-person relating drove a great deal of Mahāyāna theorising about the Buddha's existence, the Buddha's three bodies and so on – which was probably in origin not only theoretical, but an attempt to make sense of emotional experiences of relatedness occurring in meditation, dreams and "epiphanic moments" (see Chapter 9). By contrast, damage resulting from the idealization of all-too-human Buddhist teachers, documented in recent American contexts by Jeffrey Rubin (1998), is a consequence of having no internal "allegorical object" in relation to which such emotion would be harmless.

"An allegorical object, a sub-species of intentional objects, that can be encountered in the second person" is a clumsy formulation to describe a religious object. But what it attempts to do is to affirm the importance of the world of experience, and to eliminate the need to discover (illusory) religious objects in the world known to physics. It gives a way of thinking further about the objects of other religious traditions, which are not always as careful as Buddhism in making reality-claims. It also echoes certain thinkers from other traditions, notably Martin Buber, who once in a lecture said that he believed in God when he was spoken of in the second person, but "when I speak of him in the third person … my tongue cleaves to the roof of my mouth" (quoted Horvitz 1988, 105).

In psychoanalysis, this formula relates to the recognition of the importance of conscious appreciation of the "good object," derived from reflection on the crucial impact on the baby or small child of aspects of maternal functioning. And it relates as well to the Winnicottian account of the transitional object, which allows something that is empirically unreal to be efficacious and indeed transformative in the world of experience. But Winnicott's choice of language – "illusion," "fantasy" – carries an implicit subordination of the transitional object to the sort of realities known to physics and natural science. This has no equivalent in Buddhism, which, like Emmanuel Levinas, gives first place to experience.

Notes

1 See Gombrich (2009, 41).
2 Reviewing a book by Marion Milner, Winnicott himself acknowledged the limitations of the word *illusion*. "For what is illusion when seen from outside is not best described as illusion when seen from inside; for the fusion which occurs when the object is felt to be one with the dream, as in falling in love with someone or something, is, when seen from inside, a psychic reality for which the word illusion is inappropriate. For this is the process by which the inner becomes actualized in external form and as such becomes the basis, not only of internal perception, but also of all true perception of environment" (1989, 391–2). (I am grateful to Sarah Richmond for drawing my attention to this passage.) Winnicott was wrestling with the limitations of the language available to him. As we saw in Chapter 2, his thought was pregnant with the insights of phenomenology, but he was unable to quite give birth to them.

References

Black, D.M. (2004). Sympathy reconfigured: Some reflections on sympathy, empathy and the discovery of values. *Int. J Psychoanal.* 85: 579–96.
Black, D.M. (2011). *Why Things Matter: The Place of Values in Science, Psychoanalysis and Religion*. London and New York, NY: Routledge.
Brentano, F. (2015). *Psychology from an Empirical Standpoint* (first publ. in German 1874). Trs. L.L. McAlister and others. London and New York, NY: Routledge Classics.
Buber, M. (1970). *I and Thou*. Trs. W. Kaufmann. Edinburgh: T. and T. Clark.
Buddhaghosa (1964). *The Path of Purification (Visuddhimagga)*. Trs. Nyānamoli. Colombo: A. Semage.
Critchley, S. (2001). *Continental Philosophy: A Very Short Introduction*. Oxford: Oxford University Press.
Doi, T. (1989). The concept of *Amae* and its psychoanalytic implications. *Int. Rev. Psycho-Anal.* 16, 349–54.
Eliot, C. (1935). *Japanese Buddhism* (reprinted 1969) London: Routledge and Kegan Paul.
Epstein, M. (2013). *The Trauma of Everyday Life*. New York, NY: Penguin Press.
Fisher, J. (2011). The Emotional Experience of K. In C. Mawson (ed) *Bion Today*. London and New York, NY: Routledge New Library of Psychoanalysis.

Gay, P. (1988). *Freud: A Life for Our Time*. London: J.M. Dent.

Gombrich, R. (2006). *How Buddhism Began* (2nd ed.). Oxford and New York, NY: Routledge.

Gombrich, R. (2009). *What the Buddha Thought*. Sheffield: Equinox.

Govinda, L.A. (1960). *Foundations of Tibetan Mysticism*. London: Rider & Co.

Hanh, T.N. & Berrigan, D. (2009). *The Raft Is Not the Shore*. Mumbai: Jaico Publishing House.

Holder, J.J. (2006). (trs.) Ariyapariyesana sutta. In *Early Buddhist Discourses* 1–18. Indianapolis: Hackett Publishing Co.

Horvitz, R. (1988). *Buber's Way to "I and Thou": The Development of Martin Buber's Thought and His "Religion as Presence" Lectures*. Philadelphia, PA: Jewish Publication Society.

Huemer, W. (2015). http://plato.stanford.edu/archives/fall2015/entries/brentano/.

Klein, M. (1952). Some Theoretical Conclusions Regarding the Emotional Life of the Infant. In *Envy and Gratitude* (1975), 61–93. London: Hogarth Press.

Lear, J. (1990). *Love and Its Place in Nature*. New York, NY: Farrar, Straus and Giroux.

Levinas, E. (1958). Martin Buber and the Theory of Knowledge. Trs. P.A. Schilpp & M. Friedman. In S. Hand (ed) *The Levinas Reader* (1989). Oxford: Blackwell.

Levinas, E. (1998). *Otherwise than Being, or Beyond Essence*. Trs. A. Lingis. Pittsburgh, PA: Duquesne University Press.

Lewis, C.S. (1936). *The Allegory of Love*. Oxford and New York, NY: Oxford University Press.

Lusthaus, D. (2002). *Buddhist Phenomenology: A Philosophical Investigation of Yogācāra Buddhism and the Ch'eng Wei-Shih Lun*. Oxford and New York, NY: Routledge.

Meissner, W.W. (1984). *Psychoanalysis and Religious Experience*. New Haven: Yale University Press.

Rizzutto, A.-M. (1979). *The Birth of the Living God*. Chicago, IL: University of Chicago Press.

Rubin, J.B. (1998). The Emperor of Enlightenment May Have No Clothes. In Molino, A. (ed) *The Couch and the Tree* 200–13. London: Open Gate Press.

Sato, K.T. (2010). *Great Living in the Pure Encounter between Master and Disciple: Essays on the Tannisho*. New York, NY: American Buddhist Study Center Press.

Suzuki, D.T. (1949). The Shin Sect of Buddhism. In J.C. Dobbins (ed) *Selected Works of D.T. Suzuki Vol II: Pure Land* (2015) 75–114. Oakland: University of California Press.

Symington, N. (1993). *Narcissism: A New Theory*. London: Karnac.

Thomas, E.J. (1933). *The History of Buddhist Thought*. London: Routledge and Kegan Paul.

Thomas, E.J. (1949). *The Life of Buddha as Legend and History* (3rd ed.). London: Routledge and Kegan Paul.

Wallace, A. (2007). *Contemplative Science: Where Buddhism and Neuroscience Converge*. New York, NY: Columbia University Press.

Wallace, A. (2009). *Mind in the Balance: Meditation in Science, Buddhism and Christianity*. New York, NY: Columbia University Press.

Williams, P. (2012). (with Tribe, A. and Wynne, A.) *Buddhist Thought: A Complete Introduction to the Indian Tradition* (2nd ed.). New York, NY and Oxford: Routledge.

Winnicott, D.W. (1935). The Manic Defence. In *Through Paediatrics to Psychoanalysis* (1958), 129–144. London: Hogarth Press.

Winnicott, D.W. (1951). Transitional Objects and Transitional Phenomena. In *Through Paediatrics to Psychoanalysis* (1958), 229–242. London: Hogarth Press.

Winnicott, D.W. (1989). *Psychoanalytic Explorations*. London: Karnac.

Chapter 5

Dante's two suns

The psychological sources of the *Divine Comedy*

Introduction

Dante's *Divine Comedy*, one of the most remarkable poems ever written, is of great psychological interest. Overtly, it is a vivid account of a journey to the three realms of the afterlife, Hell, Purgatory and Paradise; in passing, it contains numerous reflections on politics, history and personal morality; but it is above all a psychological drama, leading the protagonist, also called Dante, from an initial moment of existential crisis, alone and astray from the right path, to the sublime vision of the love that moves the universe with which it concludes. The story is told with such simplicity and grace that almost anyone can read it with pleasure, but the fact of its continuing appeal, even to readers who give no credence to Dante's theological reference points, is very surprising. It depends on an underlying acute psychological truthfulness, which causes us to feel in safe hands even when we don't fully understand what is being spoken of.

I want in this chapter to consider what Dante's initial personal crisis was about, and the nature of the huge intellectual struggle he undertook to render his complex feelings coherent – in terms, necessarily, of the stock of ideas available at the start of the fourteenth century. Working in conflict situations in the modern world, Vamik Volkan (2009) has emphasised the extraordinary difficulty for individuals in wars and other conflicts of preserving their human and individual judgement over against the irrational force of "large-group identities," largely imaginary self-perceptions tenaciously held in place by cultural symbols (flags, languages, religious labels etc.) having compelling power. Especially at risk is the individual's continuing commitment to personal ethical responsibility. This too was part of Dante's predicament. His personal crisis confronted him in a context of civil war and constant political confusion, and he had to deal with both.

I begin in the middle of things with a curious episode that occurs as Dante, the protagonist of the poem, with Virgil his guide, is climbing to the higher terraces on the Mountain of Purgatory.

The meeting with Statius

As they leave the Fifth Terrace, that of the Avaricious, Dante and Virgil are overtaken by the shade of the Roman poet Statius. He has completed his many centuries of purgation for his sins and is now free to enter Paradise. The following two cantos

DOI: 10.4324/9781003451679-5

(21 and 22) consist largely of conversation with Statius; in Canto 25, he again takes a central role when he describes the nature of the soul for Dante's benefit; otherwise he becomes a silent presence, but he accompanies them to the top of Purgatory and even stays with Dante for some time after Virgil, unable as a non-Christian to go further towards Paradise, leaves and returns to Limbo.

What is especially remarkable about Statius is that Dante tells a carefully crafted fiction about him. With most of the "shades" Dante and Virgil encounter, Dante's account is truthful to his own knowledge and judgement about them, though sometimes the account is slanted by the external requirements of the poet's life. Almost all of the time Dante was composing the Comedy he was living the life of an exile, under sentence of death by his native Florence, in the chaos of chronic civil conflict among the city-states and feudal lords of central Italy: from time to time, he needed to flatter the family of his latest patron, or to blacken the reputation of his patron's enemies. Such diplomatic considerations aside, Dante's descriptions of individuals in general may be taken as representing his honest view. With Statius, however, he is quite clearly making up a story.

I'll tell the story first as Dante tells it and then discuss which bits of it are fiction, and some possible implications of Dante's creation of them.

At the end of Canto 20, an earthquake gives Dante an enormous shock and causes him to fear death. (He is alone in this, of course, as everyone around him is already dead.) Canto 21 begins with a flurry of strongly Christian imagery, including references to the "living water" of God's grace that Jesus offered to the Samaritan woman (the only true cure for the fear of death), and then to the account in Luke's gospel of Christ's appearance after his resurrection to the two disciples on the road to Emmaus. Thus powerfully heralded, the shade of Statius now appears to Dante and Virgil, coming from behind and giving the traditional Christian greeting: "may God give you peace." Virgil responds courteously, but in a way that draws attention to the fact that he, Virgil, being pagan, is excluded from Paradise. Statius is surprised: if so, how can they have come so high on the Mountain? Virgil explains that he is only there as Dante's guide. But, asks Virgil, what was the cause of the earthquake?

Statius (still unnamed) explains that the Mountain shakes whenever a soul has completed its purgation and is released to go forward into Paradise; this earthquake was because of his own new freedom. He now introduces himself: he is Statius, a Roman poet who was inspired by Virgil. He speaks in such glowing terms of Virgil (who died before Statius was born), not realising whom he is speaking to, that Dante gets the giggles. Statius is offended, and Dante explains that the shade Statius is addressing is, precisely, the Virgil he's speaking of. Statius, overwhelmed with emotion, falls at Virgil's feet, but Virgil reminds him they are both merely "shades": veneration should be reserved for God who alone deserves it.

Canto 22 jumps smartly forward to the Sixth Terrace (that of the Gluttonous). Virgil is now intrigued by Statius. He has met him on the Terrace of the Avaricious, and he asks him now how someone so thoughtful could have been guilty of avarice? It is now Statius's turn to be amused: he explains that his sin was the opposite of avarice, it was prodigality, and he learned it was sinful from Virgil himself. He quotes the relevant passage from the Aeneid in Italian translation (*Per che non reggi tu, o sacra fame....?* 22, 40–1) and explains that Virgil's words allowed him to recognise that "sins" are departures from a mean: avarice and prodigality, being opposites, are therefore related and are repented on the same Terrace.

Virgil next asks Statius how he, a classical Latin poet, became a Christian (a fact that is evident because Statius is about to enter Paradise). Statius replies that this too he owes to Virgil. He again quotes the relevant passage in Italian translation (*Secol se rinova;/torno giustizia...*, 22, 70–1) – from Virgil's Fourth Eclogue, where the Cumaean Sybil prophesies the return of the Golden Age. These words, says Statius, so chimed with what Christian teachers were preaching that he became convinced of the truth of Christianity. However, it was too dangerous to be known publicly as Christian and so he kept his faith a secret. He then asks Virgil about the fate of the other great classical poets; Virgil replies that they are all in Limbo like himself. (Limbo is a sort of antechamber of Hell, reserved for the souls of the unbaptised.)

That, in very brief summary, is the surface story told in Cantos 21 and 22. The fact that it is fiction is well-known to Danteans. Auerbach (2001, 136) simply refers to it as "Dante's fiction" without further comment. Sinclair (1939, 280) remarks: "it is of no great consequence for a reader of Dante if scholars do not support... Statius's account of his conversion." However, it's rare that any detail of the *Divine Comedy* is of no consequence, and it's worth enquiring further.

The first and most obvious fiction is that Statius became a Christian. This is untrue and there's no likelihood that Dante would have believed it. So the first question we should ask is: why would Dante have imported a Latin poet to play this role, of the saved soul newly freed from Purgatory, when there were any number of indisputably Christian souls who could have played it? And second, if he wanted to present a Christian Statius, why would he describe him as converted by the mani- festly non-Christian Virgil?

Moreover, once alerted to the fact that something strange is going on here, we start noticing further details. Statius twice directly quotes Virgil and both times completely misunderstands him. In the first example, he takes lines from *Aeneid Book III* out of context and gives a reading of them that the context clearly con- tradicts. Virgil was telling the story of Polydorus, a boy to whom when Troy was defeated King Priam entrusted his gold. The King of Thrace undertook to protect Polydorus but then transferred his allegiance to the Greeks, murdered Polydorus and stole the gold. Virgil exclaims: *Quid non mortalia pectora cogis,/auri sacra fames?* (lit. "To what will you not drive mortal hearts,/accursed hunger for gold?") Jackson Knight translates, loosely but correctly: "no wickedness is beyond a man whom that accursed gold-lust drives" (1956, 76).

It is this passage that Statius powerfully mistranslates: *Per che non reggi tu, o sacra fame/dell'oro, l'appetito de' mortali?* (lit. "Why don't *you* rule, O sacred appetite/for gold, the lusts of vulnerable mortals?") – an impossible reading, given the context, though just possible if the passage is isolated and the ambiguous word *sacra* (accursed) apparently inverted from its obvious meaning. But this (mis)read- ing makes room for another part of Dante's fiction about Statius, that he owed not only his poetry, and his Christian faith, to Virgil, but also his recognition of sin, which allowed him to repent and arrive in Purgatory (with prospect of salvation) and not in Hell (with no such prospect).

In the second misreading, it's clear in the Eclogue that the Sybil is presenting an astrological, cyclical picture, the return of the constellations and of the Golden Age, very different from the Christian linear history of Adam's sin and Christ's redemption. What links the two pictures is their emotional tonality of joy and relief, not their content.

All this of course has been much debated by scholars, most interestingly I think by William Franke (1996), who weaves it into his brilliant Heideggerian reading of Dante as a whole. But to keep focused on the central question, I think in the fiction it is crucial, first, that Statius owes *everything* that is precious about him to Virgil, and second, that Dante has invented a story that bridges across from the classical world, with its balanced and rational vision of nobility and virtue, to the Christian world with its vision of God's love, judgement and condemnation/forgiveness. There is abundant evidence that Dante himself found this gap difficult to cross, and found particularly difficult the fact that Christian teaching appeared to exclude from Paradise all the great classical poets and philosophers (including Virgil) who meant so much to him.

The philosopher Steven Berg (2012) describes Statius as "a great misinterpreter of things generally speaking" (45), and even as "a figure of fun" (52). He lists almost every intervention by Statius as based on misunderstanding. This is certainly interesting (though I'm not sure he is right about Statius's Aristotelian account of prodigality, which I think Dante would have agreed with). But Dante isn't slow to condemn those of whom he is critical, and Statius is after all a soul bound for salvation (explicitly linked with Christ after the resurrection), and treated with affection by both Virgil and Dante – so I think we have to view him as finally a positive figure in Dante's eyes.

Franke, from his Heideggerian viewpoint, suggests that what Dante is drawing attention to, in presenting Statius's elementary misreadings of the poet he admires so passionately, is the fact that all our readings of the world are "interpretations," and what matters to us in our *Dasein* is not what is "really" there but what we perceive to be there. In consequence, though Statius has plainly by any ordinary judgement misunderstood the texts before him, what matters is that his misreadings have been effective: they have become the basis of huge changes in his life by which he will, finally, arrive in Paradise.

There is, however, one point at which Statius's eager but ambiguous utterances throw us into profound uncertainty. As he introduces himself, saying enthusiastically that the *Aeneid* was both "mother" and "nurse" to him – two roles we will consider shortly – he goes on:

And could I but have lived on Earth when Virgil
also was living I'd have gladly paid
a year more than I owed to Purgatory!
                    (21, 100–102 [Black 2021])

The Dante scholar Marco Andreacchio (2012, 61) has noticed that this is a very extraordinary statement. If Statius (45–96 CE) had lived when Virgil (70–19 BCE) lived, he would have had no chance at all of being in Purgatory: he would have been in Limbo with the other classical poets. "Would Statius," asks Andreacchio, "have preferred knowing Virgil to knowing Christ?"

With regard to Statius, we can take that challenging question no further. But if we think of another poet with a huge love and admiration for Virgil, we may find it fertile. Dante has two outstanding and consistent passions, which persist through the whole of the *Divine Comedy*: his gratitude and admiration for Virgil, and his similar though even more intense feelings for Beatrice. He finds it painful, and feels it to be unjust, that even the best of pagans, such as Virgil, are apparently barred forever from Paradise, whereas even very second-rate Christians have only to re-pent on their death-beds to be assured of it. In Paradiso Canto 4, Beatrice reassures him that such doubts are not heretical – are in fact evidence of faith – presumably because they derive from "love" and not from a Satanic wish to dispute God's ordering of the universe; also, Dante (the poet) is friendly to doubt and sees it as a necessary part of intelligent questioning. He makes his point, without departing too far from orthodoxy, by making Virgil the guide of Dante (the protagonist) right up to the top of Purgatory, a mountain ordinarily reserved for Christians. What is implied is that the pagan virtues of rational thought, nobility and moderation, which Virgil exemplifies, can take one very far indeed into the world the Christian knows by revelation.

When Statius speaks impulsively, in a way implying, if we took him literally, that he would rather have known Virgil than Christ, this is perhaps not so much a "mis-interpretation" as what psychoanalysts call a parapraxis, a slip of the tongue saying more than the speaker intends – more perhaps than he knows. In the poem, Virgil is silent in response, but Dante, overcome by laughter, creates a diversion, and the topic is never returned to. Could it be that this very uncharacteristic laughter in Dante (the protagonist) was a response by Dante (the poet) to a danger-signal, which caused him to take the story smartly off in another direction?

The attraction of classicism to Dante

Much earlier, in the *Vita Nuova*, Dante has told us that, grief-stricken after the death of Beatrice in 1290, when he was 25, he was suddenly attracted to a "young and ex-ceedingly beautiful" woman whom he saw watching him from a window. He began to "delight too much" in seeing this woman (Musa 1962, 76), and later he refers to his feeling for her as an "evil desire and empty temptation" (80); he reinstates Beatrice as the supreme object of his love. In a later prose-work, the *Convivio*, he tells us that this tempting woman was "the Lady Philosophy."

Psychoanalysts are familiar with the idea that one is forever revising one's au-tobiography in the light of the changing present, and of no one is this more true than Dante. So whether we should understand this distractingly beautiful woman as always having the same solely allegorical character is not a question it will be profitable to explore. We do know, however, that in the early 1290s, following Beatrice's death, Dante devoted himself to studying philosophy, and when, in 1304 or 1305, after the political *coup* in Florence that led to his banishment from the city, he came to write the *Convivio*, he brought to it the intimate knowledge of Aristotle and Aquinas that later influenced much of his thinking in the *Divine Comedy* (written almost entirely between 1306 and his death in 1321). And, however, we understand the beautiful woman, his attraction to her is presented in the *Vita Nuova* as an infidelity to Beatrice.

The same event is spoken of when, at the very top of the Mountain of Purgatory, Dante at last meets Beatrice (and Virgil vanishes: Beatrice now takes on Virgil's role as guide). Dante is overwhelmed by "the great power of former love" (*d'antico amor senti la gran potenza*, 30, 39), but Beatrice is restrained if not severe. She tells Dante's familiar story from her viewpoint: in youth, she had led him in the right direction (*in dritta parte volto*, 123) by her beauty, but when she died and rose from flesh to spirit he turned his steps to an untrue path (*e volse i passi suoi per via non vera*, 130), following "false images of the good that keep no promise fully." She ends (remarkably in this Christian text but in a way that we begin to recognise) by expressing her gratitude to Virgil, with tears (*li preghi miei, piangendo*, 141) for bringing Dante safely through Hell and Purgatory – perhaps one of the clearest implications that, for Dante, the *Divine Comedy* is no mere report of sight-seeing, but an account of his own journey and recovery from sin through penitence to salvation.

We glimpse the same theme in the extraordinarily moving Canto 4 of Paradiso, in which Dante uncharacteristically loses his voice; he is unable to speak after he has heard Piccarda Donati's account of her history and her broken vows. Not until the very end of the canto does he recover his voice; he is at last able to ask Beatrice the question that troubles him. It is: if someone has broken their vow to Beatrice, can she ever take them with full seriousness again? To which she responds with a look "so full/of sparks of love, and so divine" that he is overwhelmed.

All these many references point to a period following Beatrice's death when Dante feels that he went astray, and in a way that he fears may be unforgivable. And of course the *Comedy* itself, nominally set in 1300 when Dante was 35, begins with Dante (the protagonist) "finding himself" (*mi ritrovai*) "in a dark wood/where the straight way was lost" – *mi ritrovai per una selva oscura/che la diritta via era smarrita*, Inferno 1, 2–3.

The final Terrace of Purgatory, which Dante passes through before he can encounter Beatrice, and while Virgil is still with him, is the Terrace of the Lustful. To negotiate this, he has to go through a wall of flame, hotter than boiling glass; only when Virgil tells him that Beatrice is on the far side – using her name, which is rarely spoken – does Dante find the courage to enter it. The vividness and painfulness of this image would certainly give support to the idea that sexual desire for an actual other woman might have caused Dante to feel he was being unfaithful to the memory of Beatrice. On the other hand, the physicality of Dante's imagery for mental torments, in Inferno particularly, may equally allow us to imagine he was describing a solely mental "infidelity", such as turning to the pagan philosophers.

Dante's personal qualities

It is hard for the modern imagination to conceive the social world in which this ardent love-poetry was written. Dante put his admired precursors, the love-poets Arnaut Daniel and Guido Guinizelli, on the Terrace of the Lustful, perhaps implying that "spiritual" love can only be fully reached by those who have truthfully confronted the experience of sexual desire. But we should remember that in everyday life Dante was married from age 18 to Gemma Donati, and Beatrice from age 15 to Simone dei Bardi. Both Gemma and Simone were from well-known families in Florence; the Bardi were one of the great Florentine banking families (they employed Giotto to decorate their private chapel) (Santagata 2016, 39). Dante's feelings for Beatrice, however, and her imagined feelings for him, seem to take place in a world in which such facts can be ignored. (Such evidence as there is suggests that Dante's marriage was a reasonably happy one. He and Gemma had three children, all of whom, and perhaps Gemma too, joined him in exile. After his death, both his sons wrote admiringly of their father and his work, and his daughter, becoming a nun, took the name Suor Beatrice.)

Dante's biographer, Marco Santagata, seems inclined to accept the portrait of Dante's character given by Giovanni Villani, a Florentine who knew Dante (though perhaps not well) and whose account of him as scornful, impatient and contemptuous, "taking delight" in "grumbling and complaining" (Santagata 2016, 5) has given rise to the conventional picture we have of him. Santagata repeatedly emphasises Dante's enormous self-importance ("we needn't worry," he writes, "about overestimating Dante's egocentric nature" [294]) and he accuses Dante of an "astonishing lack of gratitude" (308) towards the Malaspina family, who helped him greatly during his exile, but who receive no mention in the Paradiso cantos in which Dante's ancestor Cacciaguida foretells Dante's experience of exile. But it's easy, reading the Comedy, to underestimate the reality of the daily political pressures under which its author was living. When he wrote the Cacciaguida cantos, the city of Florence had recently renewed his sentence of exile, and moreover declared Dante to be fair game: anyone could assault him with impunity. He was staying in Verona, at the court of Cangrande della Scala, an aristocrat whose father Dante had unfortunately condemned in an earlier and already published part of the poem. Not an easy situation! Cangrande didn't greatly like him, and paying off earlier debts of gratitude could not have been Dante's most pressing need at that moment: Cacciaguida praises to the skies the della Scala family. Need this be seen as "astonishing ingratitude" to the Malaspinas?

In the *Divine Comedy*, Dante is depicted in two very different sorts of relationship. One is with the many people he encounters along the way, in Hell, Purgatory and Paradise. Most often those he speaks to tell him why they are in their particular location. Sometimes he is very moved by their plight, for example by Farinata degli

Uberti in the Circle of the Heretics (Inferno 10), or Brunetto Latini in the Circle of the Sodomites (15); sometimes, as with Pope Nicholas III among the Simonists (14), Dante joins in the condemnation. In Inferno, all these people are, so to speak, exemplary: they speak vividly as their individual selves, but they are also allegorical, embodying some single quality, a "ruling passion" which has resulted in their being in their hellish state. Dante's poem is in this sense profoundly psychological, even psychoanalytic. He is thinking what the sin, unrepented for, leads to by its own nature; in what way, as we might put it, a particular motive, unrecognised and therefore "unmourned," can become destructive of a person's happiness. He is not, as is often supposed, merely imagining arbitrary torments for those whom he, or God, happens to disapprove of. (So hideous do some of these torments become that the Dante scholar Robert Pogue Harrison has recently suggested that Dante went "mad" in devising them [2016]. Given his unceasing formal control, I think this unlikely, but it points to the huge breadth of Dante's emotional imagination.) In Purgatorio, there are similar sins, and indeed often similar torments, but the shades now have seen the larger truth of divine love; though not yet free of their sin, they are becoming able, with varying degrees of success and over immense tracts of time, to hate the harm it does and to wish truly to inhabit a more loving world. (Working through takes time, as psychoanalysts are accustomed to saying: insight alone is not enough.)

The other sort of relationship is with the two guides, Virgil and Beatrice. Dante meets Virgil right at the start of the Comedy. Dante is lost in the wood, comes out onto a desert mountain-side at dawn and encounters three beasts, leopard, lion and she-wolf. The leopard he thinks he can escape, the lion terrifies him, but the wolf, so emaciated it seems driven by every hunger (*di tutte brame.... carca,* Inf. 1, 49), causes him to despair. He flees down the mountain and sees a figure – and we are at once in the ambiguous territory we will inhabit for the next 14000 lines: is it man or shade (*omo* or *ombra*)? And Dante's first words are surprising: not a cry for help with the wolf but something with religious overtones: *Miserere di me,* "have pity on me." It's as if the wolf, the embodiment of the extremity of need, has had the function of a dream-image: it has allowed Dante to feel his own need for pity and recognition.

The figure turns out to be Virgil, and learning this Dante responds (not unlike Statius many cantos later): "You are my master and my author" (*lo mio maestro e'l mio autore,* 1, 85), "you alone are he from whom I took/the beautiful style that has brought me honour." In the following canto he learns that Virgil wasn't there by chance. The Virgin Mary had observed Dante's plight; she gave instructions to Saint Lucy, who passed them on to Beatrice – all these women being in Paradise – who descended to Limbo to tell Virgil that "my friend" (Beatrice's friend) has turned back on his journey out of fear. *Amor mi mosse, che mi fa parlare,* she explained (2, 72) – "love moved me and makes me speak." Virgil obeyed at once.

The psychoanalyst at this point is likely to think of Dante's mother, of whom we know nothing except that she died when he was a child (perhaps when he was very young, and certainly before he met Beatrice at the age of 8) – it is as if, at this darkest moment of despair in front of the famished she-wolf, something in him has also been enabled to remember a loving and protecting female presence. Consciously, the woman he loves is Beatrice, but the hierarchy behind her suggests an intuitive awareness that her huge importance for him is supported more deeply by another female presence. This being medieval allegory, it is also an account of Dante's own understanding of the hierarchy of forces requiring him to write his poem: the supreme Christian motive of transcendent love represented by Mary, which requires clarity of understanding and insight (Saint Lucy, the patron saint of eyesight – her name derives from *lux*, light), which in turn requires direct personal knowledge and concern (Beatrice) – which in turn spurs to practical action, in Dante's case to write at the summit of his poetic powers (Virgil).

So although Dante in the poem has two guides, one is essentially the emissary of the other: Beatrice is present behind Virgil, and Dante's attitude to both is very similar, one of profound respect, gratitude and love. It is this emotion that gives its unique music and atmosphere to the Comedy and endows it with its remarkable quality of beauty and delicacy, despite the strangeness, monstrosity or distressingness of much that it describes.

At the same time, there is a radical intellectual discrepancy between these two guides that Dante is consistently aware of. The scrupulously Christian hierarchy of women who have come to Dante's rescue has very remarkably chosen as their emissary not, say, Saint Paul, or Augustine, or Aquinas – virtuous Christians – but a pagan poet who lived before Christ and whose chief objects of praise were the Emperor Augustus and the Roman Empire. Dante's love for Virgil is continually hurt by the recollection that Virgil, at the end of the day, will return to Limbo and has no place in Paradise.

Moreover, how are we to understand the fact that Virgil can have so much virtue that he can guide Dante right up to the threshold of Paradise – though there are several points in Purgatory when Virgil doesn't know his way around and has to ask the shades or trust his intuition (Purg. 13, 10–21, for example). It is here, I think, that we begin to glimpse the reasons for Dante's creation of the fictional Statius.

The divide between the pagan world with its highly developed philosophy (including the "master of those that know," Aristotle – also in Limbo, of course) and its understanding of courage and nobility (Virgil), and the Christian world with its recognition of the transcendent importance of divine love, represented by Jesus and the Virgin Mary – a love which, in psychoanalytic terms, so closely resembles a non-ambivalent maternal love – is not one that can easily be knitted together. In fact, it was traditionally represented as a contrast: Christian teaching was, said Saint Paul, "to the Greeks foolishness." And yet Christian teaching had been, as Dante knew, greatly enriched by Augustine's learning from Plato and Aquinas's from Aristotle. And Dante himself, if we take seriously his saying in the *Convivio* that the "lady" by whom his fidelity was threatened after Beatrice's death was "the Lady Philosophy," seems to tell us of a time when he felt his devotion to philosophy had jeopardised his faith.

Erich Auerbach, discussing Dante's self-accusation for "grave errors" when he meets Beatrice at the top of Purgatory, makes the same point. "Purely carnal transgressions," he writes, would not have justified Beatrice's reproaches or Dante's self-accusation, and he goes on: "It seems very likely that for a time Dante doubted the Christian verities and inclined towards a radical Averroism or a free-thinking sensualism" – but we don't know enough to say this with certainty (2001, 70–1). If so, however, this would make sense of Dante's painful doubts in Paradiso IV.

The larger project

On a yet larger scale, it would also make sense of the whole project Dante was engaged on in writing the *Divine Comedy*, which begins with Dante's terrifying experience of being lost in the *selva selvaggia* and his encounter with the wild beasts. This clearly describes an episode of existential terror, of "lostness" in the sense of no longer knowing what one's values are and being at the mercy of any impulse, including ones we might label psychotic. In the previous chapter, I discussed a similar sort of crisis in the legend of the Buddha, which caused him to abandon his wife and child, and it's in response to such profound existential crises that religious visions have often emerged. David Aberbach, studying the relation between trauma and creativity (1989, 83) quotes T.S. Eliot: "A man does not join himself with the universe as long as he has anything else to join himself with."

Christianity teaches that no man can serve two masters, and if Dante was not to be torn apart between his two allegiances, neither of which he could bring himself to surrender, he would have to work very hard to build a larger structure to contain them both. That structure, I think, was the *Divine Comedy*. With this in mind, we can begin to understand better the role Statius plays as the moment approaches when Virgil will give way to Beatrice as Dante's guide.

Statius allows Dante to represent in more complex detail the links between the classical world and the Christian, or in political terms between Empire and Papacy. In personal terms, Dante had spent his twenties largely as a private person, acquiring some celebrity as one of the high-minded love-poets of the "sweet new style," the *dolce stil nuovo*; increasingly after Beatrice's death, he moved into public life, and in 1300, he became a "prior" of Florence, one of the nine members of the government, the Signoria. Such responsibility necessarily called for profound thinking about the relation between practical politics and high-minded values. The fictional Statius, outwardly classical but secretly Christian, yet guided to Christianity by a pagan poet, was comparably complex to Dante himself, undoubtedly Christian but unable to forget the excellence of the classical world, both in its admirable poetry and in its rational facing of political reality – both of which excellences were exemplified in Virgil. With the defeat of the White Guelfs, and Dante's own death-sentence and banishment, these issues could only become even more acute.

If we recall that, in his daily life, these were the dilemmas that Dante was continually confronting, the *Comedy* appears in a clearer light. In Inferno 2, he attempted a traditional solution: he said that Rome and its Empire came into existence, in the divine plan, in order to provide a seat for the Papacy. But perhaps so early in the Comedy (the first seven cantos of Inferno were probably written as a group in about 1301, before his exile), his thought was still developing. By the time of *De Monarchia* (1312), he goes much further: he says Pope and Emperor are two suns; each derives its authority direct from God; it was not the case, as was often said, that they are like sun and moon and that only the Pope has divine authority from which the Emperor's power derives. When Christ chose to incarnate in the reign of Augustus, he was affirming the excellence of Roman imperial government; anyone criticising it, therefore, was committing a grave sin (Santagata 2016, 268).

This strong affirmation of a duality of spiritual and secular powers was matched, theologically, by Dante's introduction, probably original to him, of the Earthly Paradise at the top of Purgatory, prior to the move to the spiritual Paradiso. This carries the implication that even now, subsequent to Adam's Fall, a sinless humanity could once again "inhabit Eden," that a good life is possible on earth and not only in heaven. This was emphatically not the view of orthodox Christianity, nor of Aquinas whom in many ways Dante followed closely. According to orthodox thought, the Fall had "permanently cut out of the programme" the earthly beatitude God had intended for man (Wicksteed 1913, 219), and which Adam and Eve had enjoyed for about six hours. Dante-the-poet, therefore, is redrawing the map of conventional Christianity when Dante-the-protagonist is restored to primal innocence: after Virgil "crowns and mitres" him – the double coronation of a Holy Roman Emperor – and declares that he can now trust his own judgement: "Your will is straight now, vigorous, and free:/it would be sin to act against its wisdom" (*libero, dritto e sano e tuo arbitrio,/e fallo fora non fare a suo senno*, Purg. 27, 140–1).

This "imperial coronation" corresponds to one of the "two suns." Dante uses the image in *De Monarchia* when he says that man pursues two beatitudes and therefore is given two guides, Pope and Emperor. (He uses it again later in Purgatorio 16.) Virgil represents the imperial sun, and what is original to Dante is that he gives it so high a place that for a moment it may seem to the reader as if the whole task of Purgatory has been completed. But Dante is about to discover that, though he is now sinless, and may enter the Earthly Paradise, he will require a second guide if he is to get through it unscathed. Virgil can no longer help. The second guide is Beatrice, who represents the second sun, the Christian revelation.

This bold theological move, of declaring that there are two Paradises, earthly and heavenly, to both of which we may aspire, sheds light on the many dualities we encounter in Dante. It clarifies the role of Virgil and Beatrice and reminds us of the importance of esteeming both. But (as Dante also says) Pope and Emperor should not be in conflict. In the Comedy, Virgil and Beatrice are very clearly in harmony: they repeatedly praise one another, and as we have seen, it is at Beatrice's request that Virgil came to Dante's assistance in the first place.

If (fictional) Statius is in some ways a proxy for Dante himself, allowing Dante to acknowledge that his Christianity stands partly on a classical base – and showing a figure from the classical world who can cross over with Dante into the wholly Christian realm where Virgil's voice is silent – then for all his apparent misinterpretations, Statius is certainly not a "figure of fun." He allows Dante to express his immense gratitude to Virgil, to whom, like Dante, he owes his vision of poetry (all three wrote epics) and his central career. Statius is presented as indebted to Virgil for everything that matters most: his poetry, his Christianity and also his recognition of his own particular sort of sin, enabling him to repent and finally to enter Paradise – a larger debt is hard to imagine. It is the sort of debt one might owe to a loving parent, but instead it is the *Aeneid* that he describes as his "mother" and his "nurse" – a nurse provides the milk that becomes the stuff of the body, a mother provides the recognition that gives birth to the emotional self. (Five centuries later, W.B. Yeats echoed Dante when he wrote: "I owe my soul to Shakespeare... and to the English language" [Vendler 1989, 20].)

The psychoanalyst will be struck, encountering this imagery, by the absence of reference to sexuality, and it would be easy, and perhaps correct, to attribute this to Dante's personal psychopathology. I am inclined to think, however, that it is also more generally characteristic of medieval thought, that, though the powerful response to a woman's beauty clearly includes sexuality (Harrison 1988), when sexuality emerges as a component in its own right, apart from or predominating over love and praise, then it is viewed as the sin of lust (one of the three sins – the others are avarice and gluttony – in which what is good in its own nature "is loved in disproportion" (Purg. 27, 126); or of obsession, as in the case of Paolo and Francesca (Inferno 5). In such a view, there is a certain taken-for-granted character about physical sexual response which parallels the silence about the actual wives of the *dolce stil* poets. Perhaps, in the crowded intimacy of medieval social and family life, the danger of losing contact with sensual response to others was less great than in our own urban world of separate bathrooms, bedrooms and the internet. Perhaps masturbation and excited solitary fantasy, so supportive of psychological splitting in the modern world, were less accessible in thirteenth century Florence. When, in Purgatorio 25, Statius describes human sexual reproduction, his account is as factual and free of moralising as any modern biology text.

Discussion

The puzzling episode of Statius gives the best opportunity we have in the *Divine Comedy* to glimpse Dante's feeling about the role of Virgil – emblematic here of the entire tradition of classical philosophy and poetry – in relation to Beatrice, the revelation of Christian love. Apart from Dante himself, Statius is the only figure in the Comedy who bridges the gap between a full understanding of classicism and Christianity, and his adoring reaction when he learns he is speaking to Virgil shows that he has by no means renounced his first love. But for him the two traditions have become compatible, thanks to his (we might say: ingenious) misreadings of Virgil.

But to speak of them as "ingenious" is to miss the more important point of their spontaneity. In this sense, Franke is right to invoke Heidegger, who emphasised that we are "thrown" into an interpreted world – that we never encounter the world in uninterpreted form. The importance to psychoanalysis of this picture is enormous. (Hans Loewald's thought was pervasively influenced by Heidegger [see Mitchell 2000, 11–2] and Heidegger has been well discussed, for example, by Robert Stolorow [2011].) From a psychoanalytic point of view, given the inevitable ambivalence of all emotion, there can never be in reality a perfectly "non-ambivalent maternal love." Nevertheless, for the establishment of a secure good internal object, the baby needs to have the experience of such an "impossible" external object. It is in this paradoxical territory that Statius's life-changing and ecstatic "misinterpretations" are located, and it is also in the light of this that we can understand the importance of the religious creation of objects that are univocal, "all-good," "all-loving" etc.

Melanie Klein, no doubt inadvertently, provided a psychoanalytic back-story for such objects when she said (1946) that the baby splits both itself and its object in order to protect goodness from the destructive fury of the death drive. Less concretely, we may think that the baby tends to live in a present tense of very direct experience, simpler and less ambivalent than the world of older children and adults who have reached more secure object-permanence. But saying this need not imply that the use of a univocal allegorical object, such as Dante's Beatrice, is necessarily regressive. As Heidegger's student and later critic, Emmanuel Levinas, argued, the encounter with a univocal object is an essential step in the establishment of a reliable base for ethics.

Eyal Rozmarin (2007), in a detailed study of the relevance of Levinas's thought to psychoanalysis, criticised Levinas for the use of such an object (Levinas named it, famously, the "face of the Other") and for placing it as the foundation-stone in his account of the genesis of obligation and responsibility. Rozmarin argued that Levinas' position is too absolute and overlooks what psychoanalysis knows about the universality of ambivalence. In the light of the *Divine Comedy*, however, we may think that Levinas arrived not at a psychoanalytic but a "transcendent" truth, comparable to that represented by Beatrice in the *Comedy*, and like Dante he embodied it in an allegorical object, the "face of the Other." Like Dante too, Levinas recognised the necessity for such a non-ambivalent perception if a universal ethical attitude, based not solely on feeling, which is inevitably transient, but also on considered judgement and commitment, is to be securely held to. (I take such an attitude to be the meaning of the *diritta via*, the "straight way" from which Dante was astray at the start of his poem.)

But the psychological realities of ambivalence and complexity require in addition something very different from what is represented by Beatrice: they require the rationality, balance and thoughtful knowledge of the world that Dante found in the classical tradition. These were not a mere derivative (as moonlight from sunlight) from the love of Beatrice; they were "another sun" and had their own authority. It was Virgil's role to represent this other sun, and it was a delicate matter for Dante to reach this understanding, and to declare it, in the forceful world of medieval Christianity.

If it is not too paradoxical, we may say that Dante goes beyond Levinas, in that he sees the fundamental necessity, not only for the non-ambivalent allegorical object that gives rise to a true basis for ethics (Beatrice), but also for the boundaried rationality and practical good sense that mediates, without betraying, the lofty aspiration of ethics into the actual complexity and ambiguity of human affairs (Virgil). Psychoanalysis, with its favouring of "maturity," ambivalence etc. – understandable, since psychoanalysis exists primarily as a therapy – has tended to undervalue the first of these by its use of terms such as "illusion" and "regression". (See the previous chapter.) We may see Dante's achievement here as of finding a way to a balanced appreciation of two very different levels or modes of ethical value, without having either disparage or diminish the other.

If we think that Dante's infidelity to Beatrice, after her death, was that he turned to pagan philosophers, and perhaps for a time his deeper Christian faith was in question, that would make sense of the painful guilt and shame he fears and acknowledges when he re-encounters her. It makes sense too that his existential crisis, at the start of the Comedy, was the huge turmoil this had created. On the level of personal psychology, we may imagine that Beatrice's death, echoing the trauma of the death of his mother in childhood, stirred very deep anxieties about the possibility of love and goodness. We know from the *Vita Nuova* that, even when Beatrice was alive, encounters with her created great disturbance in him. In the opening episode, at age 18, when she greeted him in the street, he experienced the "summit of bliss" but then went home and had a disturbing vision in which Love (personified) compelled Beatrice to eat Dante's heart; in the following days, he was so obsessed by her that he became "frail and weak" and his friends expressed concern for him. In the *Convivio*, in the canzone *E' m'incresce di me si duramente* ("I feel such deep pity for myself"), he describes a childhood experience in which he lost consciousness. (He associates this episode, improbably, with the day Beatrice was born; it is tempting to wonder if it might be the day his mother died.) These physical reactions to emotion were so powerful that some commentators have suggested that he suffered from epilepsy (Santagata 2016, 30–5). More likely, however, Aberbach is right (1989, 45–7) that for Dante the prospect of love aroused intense ambivalence, awakening a terror of being abandoned again, and of the rage, hatred and desperation that might ensue. (In the vision, Beatrice is naked except for a loose crimson cloth, so thoughts of sex are also clearly close to consciousness [Harrison 1988].) Aberbach compares Dante's history with that of the French poet, Gérard de Nerval, whose mother abandoned him as a baby and died soon after. Profoundly committed to literature, de Nerval had poignant visions of divinely beautiful women, but wrote: "Seen at close quarters, the real woman revolted our ingenuous souls.... above all, she had to be unapproachable" (147). (De Nerval never married. He committed suicide at the age of 46.)

Following this line of thought, and remembering Klein's recognition that splitting can have a protective function, we can understand that Beatrice's beauty, adored but carefully and of necessity kept at a distance, allowed Dante to feel that goodness existed after his mother's death. (We don't know what age he was when she died. We do know that his father re-married and had at least one son by his new wife before his death when Dante was about ten.) Beatrice became, we might say, an external "good object" in the psychoanalytic sense, not unlike the Virgin Mary but physically present. (As Pogue Harrison has emphasised [1988], her physicality is never forgotten, even in Paradise.)

Beatrice's death, therefore, when Dante was 25, was – if we follow this train of thought – especially devastating because it was a repetition of the trauma of his mother's death and threatened him with a recurrence of the unbearable emotions of that first trauma. (These emotions are perhaps symbolised by the wild beasts that block his upward path and cause him to despair at the start of Inferno.) Such emotions would entail doubting the Christian teaching that love is the source of salvation, and the turn to pagan philosophy, and to urgent "thinking," would be understandable, along with a feeling of being lost and astray from the right path. The paradoxical *mi ritrovai* in the second line of the Comedy – "I refound myself" lost – is psychologically very accurate, and it's symbolised shortly afterwards in the remarkable hierarchy of women who send Virgil to find him – Beatrice's love has remained alive if remote from consciousness. It suggests that Dante, despite his loss, carried good, perhaps unconscious memories of his mother from childhood. (No such efficaciously caring figures appear in de Nerval's visions.) This is a recognisable moment in psychoanalysis, when someone in crisis becomes able to acknowledge their conflict and own the need for help from an external figure.

We see a development in Dante's thought in the course of writing the *Comedy*: at the beginning, he presents Virgil as simply following Beatrice's bidding, but later on, by the time of the Statius cantos, Virgil has become much more of an authority in his own right. In Purgatorio 16, Dante uses the imagery I have already quoted: he has Marco Lombardo speak of Pope and Emperor as "two suns", both deriving their authority directly from God; though they should be in harmony, they should not become entangled.

Dante was very directly involved with the civil warfare in Florence and more widely on the Italian peninsular, and the horrors of the Inferno may well reflect horrors he had actually witnessed. Conflict between Pope and (Holy Roman) Emperor was very much part of the political scene he had to inhabit. So this was an important political position, which he had thought hard to arrive at. And we may equally translate it in terms of individual psychology. The implication then would be that the individual has two goals that he or she needs to fulfil. They are "two suns" that each have irreplaceable importance. We may think of them as practical ambition and love: ambition has to do with life "on earth," the need to make a contribution to life in society; to this, classical philosophy is relevant; it calls for the Aristotelian virtues of courage, justice, temperance, prudence, the capacity for friendship and so forth (virtues entirely recognisable to Virgil), and for conditions, the *pax romana*, that an ideal Emperor would put into place. (Having lived through decades of civil strife, Dante wrote in *De Monarchia*: "universal peace is the greatest of the blessings ordained for human beatitude" [Santagata, 267].) Love is a different sort of thing; to speak in a way Dante would not have used, it is essential but it involves an element of luck: to be born at the right time, to encounter the right "revelation" – as psychoanalysts know, to have access to a "good internal object" depends partly on the fortune of life, on having the experience of being loved to a sufficient degree and on having the capacity to respond to it. I have suggested in the previous chapter that responsible religions are under psychological pressure to evolve until they are able to help their followers to the recognition of such experience.

The intensity of Dante's dependence on Beatrice, and his crisis at a time when he felt he had been unfaithful to her, reveals both the insecurity and the tenacity with which he held on to his experience of the good object. It reveals also the necessary primacy of that experience, its ultimate importance, beyond the sphere of ambition and "this world," which Dante symbolised by making Beatrice his guide, not to the complex psychological terrain of Hell and Purgatory, which call for careful thought and discrimination, but to Paradise, where the visor of ambivalence could at last be let go. Erich Auerbach provocatively subtitled his study of Dante: "Poet of the secular world". That aimed to correct an important imbalance, but it too is not quite right: Dante saw the importance of both the secular and the spiritual world, and he was determined to give each its fullest possible due.

In psychoanalytic language, we could say that the *Divine Comedy* shows how fundamental to human happiness is a stable connection to a loving internal object, and that that is essential too for a proper ethical orientation in the world (the *diritta via*); in an ideal world this might be a natural outcome of the experience of "good mothering," but in reality it's interfered with by a multitude of factors, sometimes catastrophically and sometimes, as in Dante's case, very nearly catastrophically; he had to work extremely hard and very consciously to maintain it. As Elliott Jaques put it, using a Kleinian language, for Dante his poem was a true working through of the depressive position: "not the reinforcing of manic defence and denial which characterizes mystical experience fused with magic omnipotence; but rather the giving up of manic defence, and consequent strengthening of character and resolve, under the dominion of love" (1965, 505–6). At the same time, while engaging with absolute seriousness in this inner work, Dante refused to accept any down-grading of the importance of living a mature, contributing adult life "in the world," the domain of classical philosophy and Virgil. These were his "two suns," and the colossal mental energy required to write the *Divine Comedy* in the midst of Italy's constant civil strife is a measure of his commitment to affirming both of them.

We may think he was assisted by three contingent factors. One, perhaps surprisingly, was the medieval custom of arranged marriage, so that regardless of personal pathology he was placed from age 18 in a family structure, and later (we don't know dates) in the role of a father; a second was the presence of the Christian mythology, including such elements as the Virgin Mary and the afterlife, so that what we would call his "psychopathology" could link up with a socially recognised structure of ethically meaningful allegorical internal objects (Rizzutto 1979); and a third, paradoxically, was the civil conflict itself, which compelled him to face the issues of destructiveness and take up a very conscious position in relation to them. To mention these historical contingencies is in no way to belittle the personal qualities of energy, originality and seriousness with which he addressed his situation.

References

Except where otherwise noted, translations from Dante are translated by the author. (Those from Purgatorio are from Black, D.M. 2021, below.)

Quotations from the Vita Nuova are from Musa, M. 1962, below.

Aberbach, D. (1989). *Surviving Trauma: Loss, Literature and Psychoanalysis*. New Haven, CT and London: Yale University Press.

Andreacchio, M. (2012). Dante's statius and Christianity: A reading of Purgatorio XXI and XXII in their poetic context. *Interpretation* 39: 1, 55–82.

Auerbach, E. (2001). *Dante: Poet of the Secular World*. New York, NY: NYRB Classics.

Berg, S. (2012). Dante's Statius: The comedy of conversion. *Interpretation* 39: 1, 37–53.

Black, D.M. (2021). (Trs). Dante: *Purgatorio*. New York, NY: New York Review Books.

Franke, W. (1996). *Dante's Interpretive Journey*. Chicago, IL: Chicago University Press.

Harrison, R.P. (1988). *The Body of Beatrice*. Baltimore and London: Johns Hopkins University Press.

Harrison, R.P. (2016). Dante: He went mad in his hell. *New York Review of Books* LXIII: 16, 30–2.

Jaques, E. (1965). Death and the mid-life crisis. *Int. J. Psychoanal.* 46, 502–14.

Klein, M. (1946). Notes on Some Schizoid Mechanisms. In *Envy and Gratitude and Other Works 1946–1963* 1–24. London: Hogarth Press and Institute of Psychoanalysis.

Knight, W.F.J. (1956) (Trs). *Virgil: The Aeneid*. Harmondsworth: Penguin Classics.

Mitchell, S.A. (2000). *Relationality: From Attachment to Intersubjectivity*. New York, NY and Hove: Routledge.

Musa, M. (1962) (Trs). Dante: *Vita Nuova*. Bloomington, IN: Indiana University Press.

Rizzutto, A.M. (1979). *The Birth of the Living God*. Chicago, IL: University of Chicago Press.

Rozmarin, E. (2007). An other in psychoanalysis: Emmanuel Levinas's critique of knowledge and analytic sense. *Contemp. Psychoanal.* 43: 327–60.

Santagata, M. (2016). *Dante: The Story of His Life*. Trs. R. Dixon. Cambridge, MA and London: Harvard University Press.

Sinclair, J.D. (1939) (Ed and trs). Dante: Divine Comedy vol 2: Purgatorio. Oxford and New York: Oxford University Press.

Stolorow, R.D. (2011). *World, Affectivity, Trauma: Heidegger and Post-Cartesian Psychoanalysis*. New York, NY and Hove: Routledge.

Vendler, H. (1989). Yeats as a European Poet: The Poetics of Cacophony. In A.N. Jeffares (ed) *Yeats the European*. Savage: Barnes and Noble.

Volkan, V.D. (2009). Large-group identity, international relations and psychoanalysis. *Int. Forum Psychoanal.* 18: 4, 206–13.

Wicksteed, P. (1913) *Dante and Aquinas*. London: J.M. Dent; New York, NY: E.P. Dutton.

Chapter 6

Dante, duality, and the function of allegory

Introduction

When I said to friends that I had decided to translate Dante's *Purgatorio*, several responded: Why? Is another translation necessary? To which the answer was undoubtedly no. There are already many excellent translations.

But I wanted to find a way to get close to the texture of Dante's thinking. Dante writes, usually though not always, with extreme concision, and it's easy to read him quickly, to be perhaps moved, intrigued, or bored by his allegorical inventions, but to miss the continual play of *thinking* that guides the movement of the story. Allegory tends to have a bad press nowadays, as if it were old-fashioned, rigidly moralizing, decidedly primitive compared with today's rational and scientific thought. But at its best, and certainly in Dante's hands, allegory is an extremely sophisticated instrument.

And from a psychological point of view, it has the advantage over the objective language of science that it speaks the subjective language of dream. That's to say, where science perceives a world of objects, to be understood by an abstract single subject, the thinking mind, giving what Thomas Nagel famously called the "view from nowhere" (1986), allegory presents a world of subjects, who each have their own point of view, comparable to "mine," but always other and always, in some way, to be learned from. In dreams, we see the spontaneous occurrence of such a language; Dante's allegory is a very conscious and deliberate use of it. And like dream, allegory does not require belief: it requires interpretation.

The structure of Purgatory

The curiosity that took me to *Purgatorio* had been triggered first by a well-known fact about the *Divine Comedy*, that in it Dante chooses two very different people to be his guides, the Roman poet Virgil and his Florentine neighbour Beatrice. The more I thought about it, the more surprising this pairing seemed: Virgil, the supreme epic poet of Augustan Rome, who lived in the century before Christ and devoted his work to praise of the Roman Empire; and Beatrice Portinari, an upper class girl whose family went to the same church as Dante's, and whom he fell in love with, as he tells the story, when they were both aged eight.

DOI: 10.4324/9781003451679-6

As he tells the story, he barely ever spoke to her, though he was a close friend of her brother. Both were put into arranged marriages to other people, Beatrice at 15, Dante at 18, and in 1290, aged 25, she died. Five years later, Dante published a little book entitled *La vita nuova* (The New Life), in which he told the story of his intense and idealizing love for her, illustrating it with sonnets and other poems he had written for her, many with a wonderful clarity of emotion and formal beauty. At the end of *La vita nuova* he broke off, saying he was not yet ready to write of Beatrice as she deserved, but he hoped in future to write of her "that which has never been written of any other lady" (Musa 1962, 86).

Rather astonishingly, a few years later, he kept that extravagant promise. He began to write the *Comedy*, perhaps in 1301 – the action is nominally set in 1300, when he was 35, "*nel mezzo del cammin di nostra vita*" (in the middle of our life's path). In 1302, he was banished from Florence for political reasons; thereafter he lived in exile, under sentence of death if he ever tried to return, in the frightening chaos of chronic civil war among the city-states and feudal lords of the Italian peninsula. He wrote almost the whole of the *Comedy* (he never called it "divine") in exile, completing the final cantos of *Paradiso* a few months before he died in Ravenna in 1321.

The story of the *Comedy* is well-known: it describes a journey through the three realms of the afterlife, Hell, Purgatory, and Paradise. Dante is initially lost in a dark wood ("even to think of it renews my terror"), and Beatrice puts in an early appearance when she descends from heaven to ask Virgil to go to Dante's assistance. Virgil does so, and he becomes Dante's guide through Hell and then right up to the top of the Mountain of Purgatory. There he disappears, and his role is taken over by Beatrice herself; she becomes his guide through the highest realm, the spiritual Paradise.

Dante is sometimes said to represent Christian orthodoxy. He was of course a child of the intensely Christian Middle Ages/early Renaissance, born a generation after Saint Francis and Saint Thomas Aquinas, and a contemporary of Giotto. His thought is saturated in that of Aquinas, Albertus Magnus and other theologians, and the intensely coherent and meaningful world he portrays is the world of medieval systematic theology. But the medieval world was also in close dialogue with classical (that is, non-Christian) philosophy. Aquinas himself was hugely influenced by Aristotle, whose work – it's a fascinating story – having been preserved in Arabic translation by Muslim scholars, had only recently been translated back out of Arabic into Latin and therefore become accessible to Christian thinkers.

The dialogue between Christianity and classical thought is central to the formation of Dante, as it was of Aquinas, and this dialogue is represented by the two guides, both of whom are treated by Dante with the utmost respect, and neither of whom is ever repudiated. And once one has this clue to a duality in Dante's value system, one discovers it repeatedly: classical thought and Christianity, Virgil and Beatrice, emperor and pope (whom Dante describes as the "two suns" that together guided Rome when it "made the good world" [*Purgatorio* 16, 106–14], but which are now damagingly entangled because of the temporal power of the papacy), and most strikingly of all, perhaps, in the structure of the Mountain of Purgatory itself, where the Earthly Paradise is reached by way of the penitential terraces.

This duality also informs Dante's central psychological insight. It enabled him to bring an extremely sophisticated understanding to the place of religion, which remains a puzzle to many people in our rational and scientific epoch. To the psychoanalyst, aware of not only the power but also the inadequacy of Freud's dismissal of religion as "illusion" – "the fairytales of religion," said Freud magisterially in his central text, *The Future of an Illusion* (1927) – this is where Dante's thought opens up territory that still awaits deeper exploration.

He demonstrates his position – shows but not tells – by having Virgil, representing the power of classical thought without benefit of Christian revelation, escort Dante right up to the top of the seven Terraces on the Mountain of Purgatory. Virgil explains their structure in Canto 17. All human motives, he says, are variants on love. There is no innate wickedness, and no equivalent of Freud's "death drive." Love is quite simply "natural":

> The natural is always without error,
> but the heart can err by choosing a wrong object,
> or by excessive or too little ardor.
> (Purg. 17, 94–96, Black 2021)

The most severe sins are repented on the lowest three Terraces; they are examples of love that chooses a "wrong object": pride, envy, wrath. The three upper Terraces are examples of love for something good in itself, but loved excessively: avarice, gluttony, lust. And, in between, the fourth is an anomaly: the Terrace of "too little ardor," usually though not very adequately translated "sloth." These seven sins are all within Virgil's understanding, and though psychologists no longer use the language of sin, they are still all entirely recognizable as sources of "problems for self or other." In Purgatory, they all give rise to penitence, that is to say, to conflict between the motive of the sin, on the one hand, and the recognition of divine love on the other, by which their deformity and obstructive power can be perceived. All the souls in Purgatory suffer their penance in graphic and distinctive ways, expressive of the nature of the sin they have to repent.

What is especially remarkable, however, and original to Dante is that this process of purgation is not the whole story. The conventional view of Purgatory is that it's the place where you repent, for however long, and then, like a prisoner who has done his time, you are free to go upward to heaven; and sometimes Dante speaks as if this is the case. More often he makes it clear that repentance involves psychological work, analogous to psychoanalytic "working through": the will is being trained by its purgation and is required to change radically. In Canto 21, Statius explains that the Mountain quakes in celebration whenever a soul completes this task and its "free-will becomes free" to ascend to Paradise. But Dante is about to show us there is a further step.

When the pilgrims emerge from the final Terrace, that of the lustful, Virgil tells Dante that this is as far as he can guide him:

> I have brought you here by thoughtfulness and skill:
> henceforth let your own pleasure be your guide[...]
> No longer look to me for word or signal!
> Your will is straight now, vigorous, and free—
> it would be sin to act against its wisdom.
> You over yourself I therefore crown and mitre.
>
> (Purg. 27, 130–131; 139–142)

I discuss this passage in Chapter 5. It seems at first glance to mark the climax of what has to be achieved in Purgatory: repentance is complete, sinlessness has been attained. And indeed, shortly afterwards, Dante walks ahead of Virgil into the Earthly Paradise, a restored Eden, where he meets the whole pageant of Christian history. And here he re-meets Beatrice at last.

But refinding Beatrice, in this new world, is not at first the ecstatic experience we might expect. Dante, as so often in the past (he told us so in *La vita nuova*), is profoundly disturbed by the sight of her. He is dismayed by "the power of former love." He turns to the faithful Virgil for support – but Virgil has vanished ("Virgil my sweetest father, Virgil/to whom I gave myself for my salvation" [30: 50–1]); Dante breaks down in tears. It is one of the most moving moments in Purgatorio. But Beatrice shows no sign of sympathy. She tells Dante not to weep yet; he's going to have something else to cry about.

A second world of values

This is the moment at which we begin to perceive that there is an altogether different world of values from that of Virgil. Beatrice is concerned with something else entirely. She asks two challenging questions:

> How did you deign to approach the Mountain?
> Did no one tell you that here man is happy?
>
> (30, 74–75)

These are very surprising questions. It's as if her picture of Dante is of someone too proud to surrender his unhappiness and sense of grievance. This is very different from the self-portrait Dante has so far shown us, of himself as frightened, longing to be comforted, eager to learn, and profoundly grateful to Virgil for his support. But to the psychoanalyst, it is very suggestive, because the changed picture is also a recognizable one: we know that those who have suffered trauma they have not been able to verbalize, perhaps in infancy, or perhaps, like some Holocaust survivors, too terrible to be remembered explicitly, are often unable to surrender their sense of sadness and grievance, even though they have no way, consciously, to know what it's about or to tell any adequate story to account for it.

Such people very often, consciously, pine for love but may then be unable to respond to love when they meet the opportunity. David Aberbach, in *Surviving Trauma* (1989), has shown how often people who are exceptionally creative have suffered trauma of this sort. He discusses Dante in particular, whose mother died when he was a child (we don't know at what age, but certainly when he was still very young, perhaps four or five). Aberbach suggests that Dante's "overwhelmed" reactions of disturbance at meeting Beatrice in person – becoming faint, becoming confused, having disturbing visions and on at least one occasion becoming unable to eat, so that his friends worried about his health – were the product of an unbearable conflict between his conscious feelings of love and delight, on the one hand, and on the other, an unconscious terror of repeating some terrible, unbearable grief process, including rage, bewilderment and desperate fear at abandonment. If this grief reaction, a chaotic response to traumatic and incomprehensible loss, is not available in explicit (episodic) memory, it can't be processed and worked through but can only be enacted repeatedly in the form of recurrent un-understandable symptomatic behaviour. (Freud would have spoken of "repetition compulsion"; the story of an unconscious memory of trauma, perhaps now built into the brain's neuronal structure, makes the repetition understandable.)

However, the poem is being written, not by Beatrice, but by Dante. Her questions therefore represent a moment of at least partial insight on his part – not into the part played (perhaps) by his mother's death, but at least into the character of his own reactions. And his response to Beatrice's questions is now not guilt, the response to sin throughout the Terraces of Purgatory, but *shame*:

Ashamed, I dropped my gaze to the clear water,
but seeing myself reflected there removed it
to the grass, so painfully my shame weighed on me.
(30, 76–78)

It's a wonderfully convincing description of shame and conveys a sense of Dante's absolute acceptance of the truth of Beatrice's reproach. But what is Beatrice reproaching him for?

This is the beginning of a sustained passage, continuing directly across two cantos, in which Beatrice retells Dante's history from her point of view, that is to say, from the viewpoint of non-punitive but truthful and clear-sighted love. Where Virgil represented the love for *doing,* Beatrice represents the love for *being*. It is often a latent question for a child: Am I loved for what I *do* (when I'm good, when I get things right), or am I loved for who I *am* (am I loved simply for the person I am, even when I make mistakes, even when I'm naughty, and so on)? It corresponds to a profoundly important distinction, even if in human reality the two sorts of love may never be met with entirely separate from each other. The "trainings" of the Purgatorial Terraces have been trainings of Dante's will: he is now a "man of good character" in Aristotle's sense and can be trusted to act seriously and to make good choices. But Beatrice represents the second sort of love. This is what is also allegorized by Dante as "divine love."

She explains that while she was alive her beauty guided him on the true path, but when she died he became unfaithful to her:

> But then when I was on the threshold of
> my second age, and entered a new life,
> all at once he abandoned me and chose another.
> And when I rose from flesh to spirit,
> and beauty and virtue both increased in me,
> I was to him less dear and less delighted-in.
>   (30, 124–129)

We know from another of Dante's writings, the *Convivio*, that after Beatrice's death, he turned to study, both classical philosophy and Christian theology – and he spoke of this as turning to the "Lady Philosophy" – so perhaps this is the infidelity she is talking about. Or perhaps he really turned to another woman, as *La vita nuova* seemed to suggest. At all events (since Dante is writing the poem), he has come in middle age to see this event, whatever it was, as a betrayal of his deepest love, to Beatrice, and therefore as something that put his ultimate salvation at risk.

And in the following canto, he meets "the point of her sword." She asks him directly: Does he agree with what she has just said? Dante breaks down in painful tears. He confesses she is right: following her death, he succumbed to the lure of "things present/and their false pleasures" (31: 34–5).

This confession is the pivotal moment in the long and subtle account of self-insight that this conversation with Beatrice represents. She responds by congratulating him on his truthfulness: this honest admission, she says, is what allows the whetstone's wheel to start turning the other way, to blunt and not to sharpen the sword of reproach. And shortly afterwards he says that "the nettle of repentance" so stung him that "whatever else once drew/me into love now seemed repulsive to me" (31: 85–7).

Thinking of this psychoanalytically, what is happening has ceased to be primarily guilt, or even shame, and has become grief, the mourning for what had not been possible because of the damage done to his capacity to love and to receive love straightforwardly and with gratitude. This is what the self-insight represented by Beatrice's questions leads on to: a recognition not only of trauma but also of loss, the irretrievable loss of life time and life experience, and of the development that life experience makes possible; with this comes a recognition, too, that the other things that "drew him into love," whatever their merits in themselves were substitutes for her and therefore not for him the equal of what he had not been able to live directly. This is why the sword of reproach now becomes blunter: the reproaches and self-criticism of guilt have now changed into the less noisy but no less painful emotion of grief.

Soon afterwards, something altogether new happens: the angels surrounding Beatrice start to sing, not of Dante's infidelity to Beatrice, but of his fidelity to her in spite of everything:

"Turn, Beatrice, turn your holy eyes," they sang,
"to this man who has been so faithful to you,
who has taken so many steps to come to see you."
(31, 133–135)

Dante is becoming able to forgive himself. The angels now represent a new way to think about his history, and also a new and more ordinary way to think about Beatrice, not so much as the representative of an overpowering beauty, goodness and perfection, but as friendly to him and appreciative of his love. The journey has much further to go, but from this point on Dante and Beatrice can have (in general!) a mutually trusting relationship.

In terms of the topic of this chapter, the working of allegory and of the dual value systems in Dante's thought, the crucial point has now been made: what Beatrice represents is the more profound (is "necessary for salvation"), but what Virgil represents (practical good sense, courage, justice, wisdom, friendship – the sum of the virtues required for Aristotelian *eudaimonia* or flourishing) can take you a very long way indeed and is essential for coping in a world that contains, and in which you contain, the sinful motives on display in Hell and Purgatory. Virgil and Beatrice are "two suns" – two independent sources of illumination – but each should be in harmony with the other, symbolized by the fact that at the outset it is Beatrice who asks Virgil to assist Dante (and Virgil responds without hesitation), and at all points, though he never addresses her again, Virgil speaks of Beatrice with the greatest respect.

Allegory and the logic of incarnation

Dante has made his point: living necessitates a duality of ethical value systems, the one practical, to deal with the unpredictable realities of a complex world, the other transcendent, to provide the ultimate compass bearing that guides the whole project. Now, to show the radical nature of this truth, he needs to make the same point in theological terms. He does so again by the use of his allegorical method.

When he meets Beatrice in the Earthly Paradise, she is part of an extended pageant. This is allegory of the sort that often seems artificial and rather alienating to the modern reader. A gryphon, representing Christ, draws a chariot (the Church), with three ladies dancing at the right wheel (the theological virtues: faith, hope and love) and four ladies dancing at the left wheel (the classical virtues: prudence, justice, temperance, courage) – and so it goes on; other figures represent the four evangelists, the different books of the Bible, and so forth. But Dante makes something remarkable of this highly artificial and conventional construction.

A gryphon is a composite mythological beast, with the head and breast of an eagle and the body of a lion; it can therefore represent the dual nature of Christ, both god and man. At first, Dante can't see Beatrice clearly, but when he does, she is looking not at him but at the gryphon. As he looks into her eyes, he sees the gryphon reflected:

> And there within them, like the sun reflected
> in a mirror, shone that double animal,
> revealing now the one, now the other nature.
> Imagine, reader, how I marveled, seeing
> that thing that in itself remained unchanging,
> yet, where it was reflected, changed continually!
>
> (31, 121–126)

What Dante is describing is the central mystery of Christianity, the Incarnation: Christ is both god and man, and yet one person. This is a double truth that the human mind cannot fully conceive as it reflects: it can only oscillate between its perceptions of the "two natures."

A moment later, in response to the angels, Beatrice turns her eyes to Dante; then she also removes the veil that conceals her mouth. (The eyes represent her truthfulness; her mouth, her smile, represents her loving kindness.) Dante, no longer overwhelmed and now articulate, exclaims:

> O splendor of eternal, living light!
> Who has grown so pallid in Parnassus' shadow,
> or drunk so deeply its abounding springs,
> as not to seem to have a clumsy mind
> if he attempts to tell how you appeared
> when, shadowed only by the loving sky,
> you let yourself be seen in open air?
>
> (31, 139–145)

By saying "you" to mean both the eternal light and Beatrice, Dante is declaring that he too now sees a double nature. Beatrice at this moment comes close to being, or perhaps actually becomes, a gryphon in her own right, a Christ-like revelation of the twofold nature of reality.

It is tempting to say that what Dante is suggesting here is that the doctrine of the Incarnation, understood in its fullness, implies that to the eyes of love, every human being may give access to the divine, may be both god and man, and yet one person. But it's possible that he is saying that Beatrice is so special that she uniquely displays this Christ-like attribute. On either interpretation, Dante's fidelity to his own perception is again taking him beyond conventional Christian teaching. Without resolving the ambiguity, we can see that in Dante's hands, the ultimate nature of what we call religious language is allegorical: it's an attempt to say certain things that can't be said simply, in our univocal ordinary language, and can only be pointed to by using the equivocal or double-natured language of allegory. "God us keep," said William Blake, "from single vision and Newton's sleep." Blake meant – and Dante would have agreed – that a "single vision," the univocal language that describes material reality so successfully, creates a limitation in our capacity for understanding if we want to go deeper into the nature of being and consciousness.

Mainstream Christianity has caused a great deal of confusion by its insistence on "belief," and by presenting a creed in which historical and allegorical statements stand side by side ("suffered under Pontius Pilate" alongside "sitting at the right hand of God the Father"), as if they were the same sort of thing and should be believed in the same way. Other religions, Buddhism for example, as discussed in Chapter 4, or mysticisms such as the thought of Meister Eckhart or Jacob Boehme, recognize quite explicitly that their religious objects are "mental constructions," necessary way stations for the imagination, which cannot be regarded as "ultimately" true but which open up deeper perspectives of meaning and, because of the limitations of the human mind, can never be gone beyond entirely, or not for long.

It is this conceptually difficult territory that Dante was illuminating with his enormous and subtle poem. In the process, with his notion of a dual system of values (represented by Virgil and Beatrice), he also made a contribution to ethical thinking that philosophy has yet to take fully on board. (In modern times, Emmanuel Levinas has perhaps come closest to it.) Dante affirms both an ideal ethic of love and a practical ethic of justice, kindness and the recognition of social reality – and the necessity for both these ethical levels if we are to achieve our two goals of living responsibly in the world and also of attaining "salvation." Salvation perhaps means being able to die feeling we have lived without betraying what we have loved most.

Conclusion: wider implications

In some ways, Dante's thinking marked a culmination; Christian theology then went off on another road into "nominalism," a sort of theology in which God and nature were opposed, very different from Aquinas's integrated picture in which "grace does not contradict nature but perfects it." Nominalism in turn led to Protestantism, and then to the rise of science in the seventeenth century, in which God and nature had ever less to do with each other (Milne 2018). Dante's poem became a monument, but his thinking did not become a foundation. Allegory came to be thought of as a mere literary device, and not as a mode of thinking in its own right (one which, recognized as such, enables religion and science not to be in conflict). Today's scientific thinkers typically have little useful to say about religion except, like Freud and Richard Dawkins, that it is illusory. (The concern with illusion is understandable, of course, as a response to the insistence on belief.)

I'd like to end this chapter by suggesting that Dante, thinking through the implications of his emotional response to Beatrice in such detail with a vocabulary derived from Christian theology, shows us the way to a psychological understanding of religion that is less concerned with whether it is or isn't illusory but instead helps us to understand the strength and importance developed religions can have as ethical instruments to think with. And, despite the clamour of institutional orthodoxy, we should not imagine that a developed religion is a static and collective thing. Anyone, like Dante, who attempts to live its truth through his or her own experience, necessarily modifies and extends it. The role of Beatrice in Dante's poem, as he foresaw in *La vita nuova*, goes beyond that of any precursor, although it echoes that of the Virgin Mary in a hymn such as the "Salve Regina." And Beatrice, because in addition to being an allegorical figure she was also an ordinary Florentine girl, whom Dante saw across the aisle when he went to church with his family, also becomes an instrument to think with about the nature of incarnation.

The theologian Raimon Panikkar, one of the greatest twentieth century believers in interreligious dialogue, used to say that different religions are like different languages: you can tell the truth in every language, he said, but the truths you can tell in any one language are always slightly different from those you can tell in the others. (Every translator knows the truth of the last part of that sentence!) Many people, including the Dalai Lama and the Catholic theologian Hans Küng, have pointed out how similar the ethical and human values are that the different developed religions support. In Chapter 4, I described the emergence of Pure Land Buddhism in Japan, in which the figure of the Buddha Amitābha came to embody a value strikingly similar to the divine love of Christ or Mary. A similar value is undoubtedly present in Ramakrishna's Vedantic Hinduism, in Islamic Sufism, and in Martin Buber's and Emmanuel Levinas's Judaism. Buber, with his emphasis on the importance of relationship to a "Thou," the unique, second person singular (1970), and Levinas, with his claim that ethics has priority over ontology (Levinas 1984), are especially helpful in coming to grips with the sort of psychology and ethical system that Dante's allegory discusses.

This variety in developed religions, all achieving a similar ethical outcome despite wholly different "allegorical" stories, is impossible to understand if the model for belief is that of the sciences, in which what is believed is the hypothesis best supported by empirical evidence. It becomes comprehensible, however, if the emphasis on belief is dropped in favour of a recognition that the language of religion is the language of allegory. That's to say, that religious objects tell a story that conveys or reflects on an ethical attitude. Levinas, a Jew who survived the Second World War in a German POW camp, knew that ultimately it is ethical response that is supremely important. To see "the face of the other," in his phrase, is of "transcendent" importance, because it makes one aware of a dimension that is altogether new, namely that of obligation and responsibility, notions that can have no commanding power in a purely "ontological" account of the world such as that of science.

I think that intuitively many people have some awareness of this, although often nowadays, particularly if they are highly educated, they have no vocabulary in which to affirm it or account for it. What allegory offers is such a vocabulary; it allows us to live in a world of subjects, not objects, with the possibility of discussing values from many different perspectives. What Dante emphasized in addition is duality, the recognition that the transcendent value represented by the religion is an ideal, in no way to be sidelined for that reason, but needing to be mediated realistically into the world of human events and history – forever at a new and unique moment for cultural and political (and, we may now add, ecological) reasons – in accordance with practical knowledge and principles that can only be learned by experience. This need for a second deck of practical ethical values is what Dante symbolized by the figure of Virgil. When Dante spoke of Pope and Emperor, or Christianity and the classical world, as "two suns," emphasizing that both transcendent ethical vision and practical wisdom are independent sources of illumination, he also made clear that they should closely support one another. Together they make up yet another version of the gryphon: two natures, with one ultimate purpose.

Dante described Aristotle as the "master of those that know," the supreme philosopher. Virgil, as an allegorical figure, represents rational and realistic thinking, of which Aristotle's *Ethics* remains an impressive example. Dante certainly had Aristotle's thought in mind as part of the illumination provided by the classical sun. In a recent extension of Aristotle's thinking, the philosopher Jonathan Lear, who is also a psychoanalyst, has suggested that, if we are to have adequate access to the conscious values and decision-making capacity that Aristotle in his account of human flourishing took for granted – and which we now know to be the outcome of a long process of social and psychological development – it will be necessary to include an account of psychoanalysis, the distinctive modern technique to help us discover and reflect on our fundamental motives. Aristotle said that the rational and non-rational parts of the soul needed to "speak with the same voice." Lear agrees, but, he says, in the absence of psychoanalysis, Aristotle could give no account of how this desirable outcome was to be achieved. In his collection of essays, *Wisdom Won from Illness* (Lear 2017 – discussed here in Chapter 3), Lear considers how psychoanalysis can contribute to establishing the basic psychological conditions without which Aristotelian *eudaimonia* cannot be pursued.

Some such large picture of the relation between religion, philosophy and psychoanalysis is necessary if we are to find a steady place to stand in the swirling tangles of theory that make up the modern and postmodern intellectual scene. Dante, like us, lived at a time of great danger and political confusion. It is not a coincidence that in such a context, he felt compelled to work out in careful detail his extended but very clear vision of the deep structure of ethics and the two levels of value.

References

Quotations from the Divine Comedy are the author's translation. (Those from Purgatorio are from Black, D.M. 2021, below.)

Quotations from the Vita Nuova are from Musa, M. 1962, below.

Aberbach, D. (1989). *Surviving Trauma: Loss, Literature and Psychoanalysis*. New Haven, CT and London: Yale UP.

Black, D.M. (2021). Dante: *Purgatorio*. New York, NY: NYRB.

Buber, M. (1970). *I and Thou*. Trs. W. Kaufmann. Edinburgh: T and T Clark.

Freud, S. (1927). *The Future of an Illusion*. Trs. J. Strachey. Standard Edition vol 21. London: Hogarth.

Lear, J. (2017). *Wisdom Won from Illness*. Cambridge, MA and London: Harvard UP.

Levinas, E. (1984). "Ethics as First Philosophy." Trs. S. Hand and M. Temple. In S. Hand (ed) *The Levinas Reader* (1989). Oxford: Blackwell.

Milne, J. (2018). *The Lost Vision of Nature*. London: Temenos Academy.

Musa, M. (1962) (Ed and trs) *Dante: La Vita Nuova*. Bloomington, IN: Indiana University Press.

Nagel, T. (1986). *The View from Nowhere*. Oxford: Oxford UP.

Chapter 7

Freud and idealisation[1]

Introduction

There is a recognised moment in the history of successful institutions, when the generation of the "founders" comes to an end, and the "followers" have to take over. "Founders" need qualities, including "charisma," that are not needed, and may even be serious obstacles, in the running of a continuing organisation. The temptation for the successors to avoid the pain of loss by idealisation, by avoidance of criticism and by seeking to perpetuate the founders' characteristics has to be overcome.

In the history of psychoanalysis, idealisation is a theme with deep roots. Freud himself famously identified with heroes: Moses, Oedipus, Hannibal, Oliver Cromwell, Goethe; in 1900, he described himself to his friend Wilhelm Fliess as at heart a "conquistador" (Jones 1964, 297). When he spoke of himself arriving at his key ideas, he claimed to have worked for ten years in heroic isolation. "Like Robinson Crusoe," he said, "I settled down as comfortably as possible on my desert island" (1914a, 22). He told Ernest Jones that when he published his foundational work, *The Interpretation of Dreams* (1900), for 18 months there was no serious review of it in the scientific press, and for some years no sale at all.

No doubt that was how he remembered it. But recollection is an uncertain guide and tends to be re-shaped by fantasy. The reality is that Freud's book was reviewed, at length and respectfully, in at least 11 journals within, on average, one year of publication (Sulloway 1979, 449–50).

Similarly, Jones tells us that Freud's emphasis on sex was received with outrage. He wrote dramatically in his biography: "Freud and his followers were regarded not only as sexual perverts but as…. psychopaths. No less than civilisation itself was at stake" (Jones 1964, 381). The historian of Austrian thought, William Johnston, paints a different picture: "In a city where Sacher-Masoch, Krafft-Ebing, and Weininger were read with nonchalance, Freud's pansexualism hardly shocked anyone" (quoted Sulloway 1979, 452).

We needn't accuse Freud or Jones of telling deliberate lies. But an atmosphere of hyperbole has gathered around Freud's life, and it's hard to escape from. Even a sober biographer like Peter Gay falls into the language of legend: Freud worked in the laboratory of "the great Brücke" (Gay 1988, 32); he studied psychiatry under "the

DOI: 10.4324/9781003451679-7

great Meynert" (42); he visited Paris to attend lectures by the "genius," Jean-Martin Charcot (49). These rhetorical touches act like a sort of theatrical make-up: they create a world of oddly heightened excitement. The factual historian of psychiatry, Henri Ellenberger, wrote a trifle wearily: "The difficulty in writing about Freud stems... from the fact that a legend had grown around him, which makes the task of an objective biographer exceedingly laborious and unrewarding" (1970, 427).

This legendary quality attaching to Freud's life has made it difficult to see psychoanalysis itself in a sober light. Freud's need to be exceptional caused him to develop psychoanalytic training in local Societies, "apostolic successions" apart from the medical schools or philosophy departments that might have integrated his thinking into a wider texture of ideas. More recently, when his theory *has* appeared in academic contexts, it has done so cut off from the clinical experience that keeps it grounded. And the rhetorical vocabulary of idealisation has infected individual psychoanalytic societies, many of which derive from charismatic local practitioners who have themselves become idealised. The institution of "training analysts," with the dual function of deciding responsibly who may enter the profession and also of entering into the intensely intimate relationship of psychoanalysis with prospective candidates, has further complicated the picture. There is probably no other profession in which such a combination of intimacy with responsibility for assessment would not be viewed as potentially abusive.

In recent years, especially in America, there has been a serious attempt to address the negative consequences of such arrangements – see, for example, a group of papers in a recent issue of the *Journal of the American Psychoanalytic Association* (Fritsch and Winer 2020, Richardson et al. 2020, Cherry et al. 2020). But it has continued to create considerable problems elsewhere. Otto Kernberg proposed the abolition of the training analyst system altogether. In his words, it "fosters idealization, submissiveness, a paranoid atmosphere that fosters splitting mechanisms, rebelliousness, and above all an atmosphere of infantilization of candidates." He saw it as leading to a "combination of dogmatism and fearfulness regarding scientific questioning of accepted principles" (Kernberg 2014, 154).

It's into this landscape, of both legend and the conscious rejection of legend, that Joel Whitebook has published his "intellectual biography" of Freud (Whitebook 2017). "Intellectual" is not, I think, quite the right term: it is essentially a "psychoanalysing" biography, looking deeply into aspects of Freud's life that the "legend" skates past – above all, his complex relationship with his difficult and demanding mother Amalie, his avoidance of issues to do with the enormous importance of the mother to the pre-oedipal infant, his somewhat facile assumption that, for men, the rejection of passivity is "bedrock," and his "tin ear" in relation to both music and religion. It devotes no less than four chapters to Freud's "homosexual" love affairs (Whitebook doesn't avoid such language) with Fliess and Jung and comments on the psychological significance of Freud's "phallologocentrism" – his commitment to "science" seen as a masculinist posture.

As a biography, it suffers from certain limitations because of this focus. It doesn't centrally describe important parts of Freud's life, for example the cocaine episode, which led to the distressing death of Ernst von Fleischl-Marxow, or the quarrels with important dissidents such as Stekel, Adler or Otto Rank. Nor does it enquire into Freud's analysis of famous patients such as Anna O, Dora, the Ratman, the Wolfman or his own daughter Anna. It doesn't, therefore, replace the competent biographies we already have, such as those by Ronald Clark (1980) or Peter Gay (1988). It has a very definite and somewhat limiting focus, but one that is extremely important.

The originality of Whitebook's biography

At one point, Whitebook says of Freud: "To combat the pain, he mobilised the hypomania of extreme theoretical exertion and struggled to create meaning" (376). Whitebook was speaking specifically of the writing of *Beyond the Pleasure Principle* in 1920, in the months following the death of his "favourite daughter," Sophie. But it's tempting to extend the idea to the whole of Freud's prodigious writing output all through his life – not only the 24 volumes of his collected psychoanalytic writings, but also the more than 200 neurological books and papers, and the 15000 surviving letters, many of them lengthy and detailed. As Whitebook points out, Freud's passionate love affairs, with his future wife Martha Bernays and then with his "Messiah," Wilhelm Fliess, were above all conducted in writing. During his four-year engagement to Martha, Freud wrote her over 900 letters, pouring out his feelings, thoughts and hopes for the future. After they married, when Freud was 30, there was no more need for letters. He and Martha rapidly became a good work-team, Freud absorbed in his career, Martha in running the home and bearing and looking after the six children. By the time, he was 37, according to Peter Gay, it had become a "*mariage blanc*," a marriage without sex. In 1897, aged 41, Freud wrote to Fliess: "Sexual excitement is of no use to someone like me" (Whitebook, 133–4).

Since Fliess lived in Berlin, that relationship too, perhaps the most intense of all of Freud's many passionate and ambivalent friendships with men, was conducted largely in writing. Whitebook describes the relationship as "homosexual" and even speculates that it may have been acted out physically, but perhaps a more fruitful line of reflection arises from his phrase, "the hypomania of extreme theoretical exertion." Most creative thinkers are necessarily caught up in such "extreme exertion" for some part of their career, but Freud is extraordinary in that in his case it seems to have almost never let up throughout his long adult life. His passion for Fliess was no doubt intense, but it also gave him the opportunity to plunge into his world of imaginative ideas without risk to his career. Major emotions always precipitated Freud into writing. This was true even in his last 16 years, after 1923, when he was in constant physical distress from his cancer of the jaw and the 30(!) gruelling and painful operations it necessitated. Even in such appalling conditions, he continued to advance psychoanalysis and to write some of his most important and original papers.

The originality of Whitebook's biography, and what differentiates it from the generally admiring and often worshipful tone of much psychoanalytic writing about Freud, is that he looks carefully at the costs of, and the reasons for, this astounding productivity. To use the word *hypomania* is of course to hint that something is missing at the root of this creativity. To be manic is to be avoiding something. Whitebook puts this very clearly towards the end of his biography: "It has been a persistent thesis of this work that a lacuna in Freud's own psychological development colored and limited his theoretical work. Simply put, his difficulties with the figure of the early mother proved to be the source of a range of wrong-footed theoretical formulations" (407).

I would like to look at this briefly under three headings: Freud's relations with women; with science; and with his Jewishness and understanding of religion.

Freud and women

Freud was born in 1856, in the predominantly Catholic town of Freiberg in Moravia. In the legend, he was the adored son of a beautiful young mother. He often wrote as if such a relationship is the best thing life can offer, at any rate for the mother. "A mother is only brought unlimited satisfaction by her relation to a son – this is the most perfect, the most free from ambivalence of all human relationships," he wrote in 1933 (1933b, 133). In his paper on Leonardo, he writes that a mother's love for her baby son is "in the nature of a completely satisfying love relation, which not only fulfils every mental wish but also every physical need" (1910, 197). Such a formulation is manifestly hyperbolic. How could it satisfy every physical need? But it's plausible that Freud did imagine that his own first months with his mother were blissful, and that this good experience was the source of much of his impressive resilience in later life. But within a year she became pregnant with a brother, Julius, who was born when Sigmund was 19 months old (Whitebook says on page 37: "when Sigmund was eleven months old"! No doubt it felt like that). For a short time, he was looked after by a local Czech woman, a Catholic, whom he remembered with affection.

Julius developed tuberculosis and died at the age of seven months. Four months later when Sigmund was 2 ½, Amalie gave birth to a daughter, Anna; at the same time, the nanny was abruptly sacked, allegedly for theft. This must have been a very traumatic time for Amalie and for the whole family. Anna was the first of a succession of five girls, who were born in rapid succession over the next seven years. The only other surviving boy, Alexander, was born when Sigmund was 11. Whatever else was true of Amalie, she certainly had a lot on her mind in addition to Sigmund. No wonder, too, confronting this relentless procession of sisters, that it felt pretty special to be the one with a penis!

It's likely that Sigmund was very much favoured, not to say spoiled. There is a famous story of his sister Anna being forbidden to play the piano, so that "the scholar Sigmund" could have the quiet he needed. Though both Anna and Amalie loved music, the piano was removed from the house. It's hard not to think that he was allowed to grow up something of a domestic tyrant. The story of the expulsion of the piano would find a parallel later when he married Martha Bernays.

Martha was from a pious Jewish family. On the first Friday after the wedding, Freud forbade her to light the Sabbath candles – "one of the most upsetting experiences of my life," she later told a cousin. We glimpse something important about the Freud marriage when Whitebook tells us that, 50 years later, on Freud's death, Martha "immediately" resumed the familiar Sabbath ritual (124–5).

Many people have noticed that Freud's family of origin had little in common with the family Freud imagined in the Oedipal triangle. Whitebook tells us that Amalie, though indeed beautiful, was described by those who met her – she lived to the age of 95 – as a difficult, self-centred, infantile and aggravating woman. Freud's father, Jacob, is described as amiable and rather ineffectual. (Ruth Abraham [1982] suggested that Freud's picture of the Oedipal father was in fact derived from his mother.) It's something of a mystery that the family, which was extremely poor when Freud was born, became moderately prosperous after their move to Vienna. Whitebook speculates that they were supported by Jacob's sons from his first marriage, who had emigrated to Manchester. Much remains mysterious about these early years. Gay tells us that Jacob's brother, Josef, had been convicted in 1856 for trading in counterfeit roubles, and that perhaps Jacob and Jacob's two older sons were also involved. At all events, all three left Freiberg, the sons Emanuel and Philipp going to Manchester; Jacob left in 1859, when Sigmund was three. After a year in Leipzig, the family moved to Vienna.

With five younger sisters, it's perhaps surprising that "woman" should remain such a "dark continent" for Freud; the "repudiation of the feminine" is more understandable. Intensely hard-working, always top of his class, he grew up extremely shy; prior to meeting Martha when he was 26, there is only one story of his being attracted to a girl, the 13-year-old Gisela Fluss when he was 16. He was too shy to speak to her but wrote rapturously about her to his friend Eduard Silberstein. When Gisela married, three years later, Freud wrote jeeringly about her to Silberstein but privately recorded feelings of jealousy so painful that they made him think of suicide.

Such an adolescent boy is rather recognisable. He is likely to go in one of two directions: he may throw himself into work and achievement, probably at the cost of a somewhat narrow or impoverished personal life; or he may throw himself into personal life, probably get severely hurt, and his work and career will suffer, perhaps irretrievably (the phenomenon of the "brilliant student" who suffers a breakdown). Freud, very remarkably, did both, but in different departments of himself, so to speak: he gave a huge, overwhelming priority to his scientific career and his "fame" – and subordinated his personal life to that end – but, at the same time, he made his emotions, his sexuality and his inner life the subject of his work. His career took off, finally, when he could derive its subject-matter from his "self-analysis," and his theory, as Whitebook shows very clearly, reflects in crucial ways the strengths and the limitations of his own personality.

His relationship with Martha is understandable in these terms. In its four-year epistolary phase, Freud the writer-about-emotion is powerfully in evidence, loving, domineering, passionately jealous (he seems always to have suffered from severe doubts about his personal attractiveness); then, when they marry and there is no need to write letters, the relationship quickly fell into a conventional division of roles. Both were extremely hard-working, and as far as we know there were no infidelities on either side. After the rapid birth of six children, the marriage apparently ceased to be sexual, and Martha showed no interest in her husband's work which she referred to on one occasion as pornography (Whitebook, 132). Both were devoted parents, though Freud's heavy workload, both of patients and of writing, meant that he was rarely available. Later, Freud's analysis of his daughter Anna – an astounding violation of parental responsibility, as he must have known very well – established an extreme closeness to her. Anna was the only person he would permit to nurse him physically during his last 16 years, when he underwent the 30 operations on his jaw; she was the only one permitted to see him in states of extreme vulnerability. (He referred to her as his Antigone, the daughter who tended the blinded Oedipus, and who, like Anna, never married.)

Apart from Martha and his patients, women played little part in Freud's adult life until after the two crucially important "homosexual" relationships with Wilhelm Fliess and Carl Jung. Female patients were of course discussed with male colleagues, usually in the clearly inferior role of "hysterics." Whitebook tells in harrowing detail the story of Emma Eckstein, the original "Irma" of Freud's famous "specimen dream" in *The Interpretation of Dreams*. Fliess, a Berlin ear nose and throat specialist, had fanciful theories about the special kinship of the nose with the female genitals: both are subject to bleeding, and there are, said Fliess, morphological resemblances between the female genitals and the turbinate bones in the nose. Eckstein was Freud's patient, who had come to him because of her premenstrual depression. Infatuated with Fliess, Freud ignored his doubts about Fliess' competence and sent her to Berlin to see him, first for diagnosis and then for surgery. Fliess, an inexperienced surgeon, operated to remove one of Emma's turbinate bones. The operation went disastrously wrong, Fliess left a length of gauze in the wound, she had recurrent haemorrhages, nearly died, and was left with a lifelong facial disfigurement.

Whitebook tells this painful story at length and vividly. Freud, obviously feeling horribly guilty, became very depressed. But in an act of what Gay called "willed blindness," he refused to be critical of Fliess: "such a distressing affair for you," he wrote to Fliess. Whitebook suggests that this bonding with another male at the expense of a female was a recurrent triangularity in Freud's history – first in his childhood uniting with his nephew John, back in Freiberg (John was nine months older than Freud), against John's sister Pauline (who was seven months younger); later in his bonding with Eduard Silberstein to cope with his painful feelings about Gisela Fluss; and then, beyond Eckstein, in his later correspondence with Jung about Sabina Spielrein. (We might add that a similar pattern is present in what Freud regarded as the successful outcome of the Oedipal triangle.) We should of course make allowance for the generally "patriarchal" nature of European society, and the medical profession in particular, at that time. Nevertheless, we are bound to think that Emma Eckstein paid a high price for male bonding and male insecurity.

It was not until after the breakdown of his relationship with Jung that Freud, by then in his late 50s, became able to have more equal friendships with women, including his sister-in-law Minna and Lou Andreas-Salomé. Whitebook credits Jung with the beginning of important changes in Freud's theory. For the first time, in his papers on Leonardo (1910) and on Narcissism (1914b), Freud began to recognise the significance of mothers, although he would never be fully able to acknowledge straightforwardly the primary place of the mother in a child's life. Whitebook borrows from Hans Loewald the idea of an "official" and an "unofficial" Freud. The official Freud continued to assert that only the father can give a child the protection it needs, and that "castration anxiety," the "repudiation of femininity," is "psychic bedrock." The unofficial Freud began increasingly to make room for the important role of mothers and the pre-oedipal phases of development. Alongside this development, he increasingly recognised the importance of specific relationships, not merely drive-satisfactions, and the crucial role of mourning. It was the unofficial Freud, too, who was made acutely uneasy when he heard from his admired friend Romain Rolland about religious feeling (although the official Freud quickly stepped in to put Rolland straight. I shall discuss this further in a moment). The gradual replacement of "libido" by "Eros," too, heralded a greater change than Freud was ever quite able to take on board. Not until Hans Loewald came on the scene was the major implication of this change recognised (see, for example, Lear [2017a, 2017b]).

I shall comment briefly on the "homosexuality." It seems surprising nowadays that Freud would use that word so freely, about his love for both Fliess and Jung. But, especially in his earlier writings, Freud is very respectful of the "innately bisexual" nature of the human psyche, and in his *Three Essays on the Theory of Sexuality*, he speaks of "inverts" "whose efficiency is unimpaired" and who are distinguished "by especially high intellectual development and ethical culture" (1905, 139). So he didn't need to feel threatened by recognising that he too could have homosexual feelings. And of course his theory required that he claim all loving feelings unflinchingly as expressions of "libido." It's probably simplest to see his delight in a male best friend as rediscovering his boyish pleasure in playing with his nephew John (the child of Philip, Jacob's son by his first marriage) – an inseparable and intense best friendship that was abruptly terminated when Freud was taken from Freiberg at the age of three. That too, of course, Freud would have described as "homosexual."

Freud and science

Whitebook is at pains to deny that Freud was a "positivist." The charge, he says, "has become monotonous. It is too facile" (398). A positivist is someone who believes that science, together with what can logically be deduced from its findings, gives us our only path to truth. In 1847, Freud's teacher, Ernst Brücke, along with Hermann Helmholtz and Emil du Bois-Reymond, had espoused a "biophysics programme," committed to finding no explanations of life that couldn't be reduced to physics and chemistry (Sulloway 1979, 66–7). That was an extreme of positivism, and by the time Freud came on the scene in the 1880s, none of these men still asserted it. Nevertheless, post-Darwinian science in general continued to speak as if "reality" could only, ultimately, be "material reality," and logical positivism continued to be an important philosophical school right up until the 1940s.

Freud, as so often, is hard to pin down. From the time of the abandonment of the seduction theory in 1897, much of his theory is one of psychological causes: "phantasies" could govern human action, affects could give rise to physical effects, including apparent medical conditions ("conversion symptoms"), dreams were caused by "wishes". Yet in the background, he never let go of the vision he described in his (unpublished) *Project for a Scientific Psychology* (Freud 1895), in which all psychological events could be traced back to an ultimate reality in brain events.

In his 70s, formulating the world-view (*Weltanschauung*) of psychoanalysis, he declared straightforwardly that "psychoanalysis is part of science and can adhere to the scientific *Weltanschauung*" (1933c, 181). This asserts that "there are no sources of knowledge of the universe other than the intellectual working-over of carefully scrutinised observations" (159). Psychoanalysis had extended this research to include "the mental field," but it remained a science, and in his paper Freud devoted most of his effort to rejecting the rival claims of religions, philosophy, Marxism etc., which might offer alternative world-views.

Here we meet Freud on his best behaviour as a thinker. He writes very carefully and doesn't forget to say that science is a forever unfinished project; he gives no hostages to fortune like the 1847 biophysicists – he doesn't pretend to know in advance that the answers will all be "reducible to physics and chemistry" or even to "neurology." And as long as he remembers to be so careful, he is not, I think, a positivist. Although he reaffirms his repudiation of religion, claiming that it "prohibits thought" (a claim that any Buddhist, and most Jews, would view with astonishment) he does note the important matter of ethical values. He says they need to be obeyed and declares them "indispensable to human society" (168). But he doesn't take time to discuss the matter, or to consider what sense a purely scientific *Weltanschauung* could make of a "requirement to obey" the commands of ethics.

I think to describe Freud as a positivist is not a charge (an accusation), as White-book says. It is a description, and what is confusing is that it often fits but sometimes doesn't. When Freud is dismissing things, the "fairytales of religion," for example, he often forgets his own best guideline, the need for careful scrutiny, and becomes someone who "knows the answers." Unlike religion, "our science is no illusion," as he said emphatically (1927). But he can also write in quite different modes. In some papers – *On Transience* (1916) for example, or *A Disturbance of Memory on the Acropolis* (1936) – he writes with great charm but more as a literary essayist, and in others (*Beyond the Pleasure Principle* [1920] is a dramatic example), he allows himself the freedom to "speculate" to a quite startling degree.

Freud's scientific *Weltanschauung* therefore, like positivism, allows for truths that can be logically deduced from scientific findings; his arguments for a death drive in *Beyond the Pleasure Principle* go far beyond such careful limits

(Black 2001). Similarly, at the end of his life, in *An Outline of Psychoanalysis*, he likens the two great drives, by then called Eros and the destructive drive, to "the forces of attraction and repulsion which rule in the inorganic world" (1940, 149). Elsewhere (1937) he compares them to the cosmic forces described by the pre-Socratic philosopher Empedocles. It's hard to know how to categorise such speculations. The adoption of Greek names for the drives seems to imbue them with a sort of animistic force (and Freud spoke of them at one point as "our mythology" [1933a, 95]). Whitebook argues that in Freud's personal life, his astonishing courage and resolution in confronting his cancer, and his other losses as he grew older, stemmed in part from his fantasy of himself as battling against the goddess Anangke, Necessity herself. Here again, as with the claim to be a *conquistador*, we seem to meet a boyish level of Freud's imagination – or perhaps a mythological one – but certainly not one constrained by a scientific *Weltanschauung*.

He was other things too: the boy who tyrannised over his sister's piano-playing, and was indulged in doing so by his adoring and perhaps intimidated parents, became a tyrant over his wife's religious feelings, and a jealous leader of the psychoanalytic movement he created. In the earlier part of his psychoanalytic career, he made good use of his imaginative energy. Part of the appeal of Wilhelm Fliess – whose theories of the male menstrual cycle, and the morphological resemblance of nose and female genitals, fell notably short of the criterion of "carefully scrutinised observations" – was that in company with Fliess, Freud too could risk far-reaching imaginative hypotheses about the internal world: libido, unconscious, psychic defences, transference, Oedipus complex and so forth. He was always over-ready to believe his own hypotheses – his early colleague and friend Josef Breuer, who knew Freud very well, described him as "a man given to absolute and exclusive formulations" (Whitebook, 142) – but as history was to show, many of these early ideas proved highly adaptable, and they illuminated as time went on a great deal of experience. It is hard now, even outside the world of technical psychoanalysis, to think of subjective reality without using the Freudian notions of defence and transference.

Jewishness and religion

Freud always asserted his Jewishness very definitely, despite his clear rejection of the religion and his dislike of Zionism. Whitebook describes Freud's "weekly game of Tarock while schmoozing with his brethren at [the Jewish service organisation] the B'nai B'rith" (320), and in his address to the B'nai B'rith in 1926, Freud spoke of his attraction to "Jewry and Jews" as "irresistible" (1926, 274). It depended, he said, on "*die Heimlichkeit der inneren Konstruktion*," the comforting familiarity of Jewish "inner construction" – an important phrase well discussed by Erikson (1968, 21). This *Heimlichkeit* reflected both his family of origin, which was Yiddish-speaking – Amalie is said to have never perfectly learned German (Whitebook, 66) – and later, as an adult in Vienna, Freud's close circle of family, friends and colleagues, and most of his early patients, who were almost without exception Jews.

At the same time, his literary influences were above all the traditional European classics, including the ancient Greeks and Shakespeare. He claimed to model himself, both as a stylist and as a personality, on Goethe. (This is yet another of Freud's identifications with a "hero," and perhaps a surprising one. Goethe's personality, his delighted sensuality, and his generous and spacious temperament, were very far from Freud's jealous intensity; the man who wrote of being guided upward by *das Ewig-Weibliche*, the Eternal-Womanly, would have been surprised to learn that "repudiation of the feminine" was "psychic bedrock." Freud's literary style, however, often echoed Goethe's urbanity, and both men believed passionately in the importance of truthful observation. Freud too attributed his choice of a scientific career to hearing an essay, *On Nature*, which he believed to be by Goethe.)

Freud's discussions of religion are curious in several ways. One is that, until he came late in life to write *Moses and Monotheism* (1938), what he means by religion seems less like Judaism than a conventional sort of Catholicism. In his central text, *The Future of an Illusion* (1927), he puts great weight on Tertullian's "I believe because it is absurd," which is hardly a central tenet of most Christian theology and, as a formula, is clearly maximally vulnerable to rational attack. (It is generally agreed by modern scholars to be a misunderstanding of Tertullian's text.) In general, Freud ignores major religious thinkers, like Aquinas or Maimonides, and prefers to point out the "illusion" in naive literal belief – that God "the Father" will protect the believer from danger, or that someone dead might literally return to life.

It has been suggested that the Catholic flavour of the religion Freud discusses derived from his Czech nanny, who took him with her to churches in Freiberg. As the nanny was sacked when Freud was aged two and a half, this seems precocious even by Freud's standards. His father Jacob was intensely religious, but in a non-institutional way: he didn't attend synagogue or observe the religious festivals, but he spent a great deal of time studying the holy texts and the Bible. He also loved Jewish jokes, and the picture we get of this amiable man – so unlike the father of Oedipus – is of someone lovable, kind and perhaps exasperating in his refusal to "be a man" in the conventional, conquistadorian sense that became so important to his son. Perhaps Freud chose Catholicism for his model of religion because in fact he knew rather little about institutional Judaism – the world of the synagogue and the rabbinate. Catholicism was what he saw around him, in Vienna and on his trips to Rome. It also enabled him to speak of religion from his favoured position as an outsider.

I mentioned above that in his *Weltanschauung* paper, Freud makes reference to the importance of ethical values. He approaches them by way of his familiar dismissal of religion: "Its consolations deserve no trust. Experience teaches us that the world is no nursery. The ethical demands on which religion seeks to lay stress need, rather, to be given another basis; for they are indispensable to human society, and it is dangerous to link obedience to them with religious faith" (1933c, 168).

He doesn't, however, link them with anything else and doesn't stop to reflect that the scientific *Weltanschauung* that he's recommending offers no possible base for them to stand on; if they do indeed demand "obedience," that should give him pause. Instead, he moves quickly on. However, he could never quite let go of the topic of religion, and a few years later, he came back to it in *Moses and Monotheism*.

And here for the first time Freud seemed to become aware that more is at stake in the matter of religion than the wish of believers to remain in the nursery. Romain Rolland, a follower of the Hindu teacher Sri Ramakrishna, had responded to *The Future of an Illusion* by agreeing with many of Freud's criticisms of institutional religion, but commented that Freud had ignored "the true source of religious sentiments," namely, "the sensation of 'eternity'," which Rolland also described as "the oceanic feeling." Freud took 19 months to respond to Rolland, and when he did, he said Rolland's phrase had "left me no peace": "To me," he said, "mysticism is just as closed a book as music" (Whitebook, 409–10).

In *Moses and Monotheism*, the discussion of religion is made bizarre because of Freud's interpolation of his own mythology into the biblical story: Freud claimed that Moses was not a Jew at all, but an Egyptian, and he was killed off finally by the Israelites like the leader of the primal horde in *Totem and Taboo*. Both these assertions are Freud's invention, and there is no good reason to believe them. It's a little like saying that Oedipus wasn't really the son of Jocasta. Assertions of historical truth or falsity can only be distractions when one is dealing with what, writing about Dante, I have called "allegorical" statements (see Chapter 2). But Freud also arrives in this text at a truly important question about religion: the nature of the psychological impact of religion on the believer.

He was writing in part in response to the devastating anti-Semitism that was developing in Germany and Austria with the rise of Nazism. For Freud, it came very close to home. His books were publicly burned, his training institutes were disbanded (Whitebook, 435), and for one terrifying day in 1938, Anna was summoned for questioning to Gestapo headquarters, from which few detainees returned: most were sent on to concentration camps. Jones tells heroic stories of Freud's witty response to the Gestapo; perhaps these are true, but if so, they were surely extremely unwise. At any rate, less than three months after Anna's experience, Freud, along with his daughter, allowed himself to be brought out of Vienna, partly thanks to the good offices of Ernest Jones. In London, old and ill, perhaps dying, his thoughts turned again to the phenomenon of anti-Semitism and what on earth it was that evoked it.

His suggestion now was that the Jewish religion, with its prohibition of any image of God, had compelled the Jews to develop a capacity for abstraction: "'an advance in *Geistigkeit*' into world history," as Whitebook says (439). Whitebook discusses in detail the meaning of this important word, *Geistigkeit*, not quite captured either by *spirituality* (the choice of Katherine Jones, the first translator into English of *Moses and Monotheism*), or by Strachey's translation, *intellectuality*, in the Standard Edition. Its achievement has something in common, Whitebook suggests, with what Freud believed he had accomplished by critiquing religion as illusion – a "destruction of the idols." This Jewish triumph of *Geistigkeit* over *Sinnlichkeit* (sensuality) evoked the hostility of those still sunk in *Sinnlichkeit* and, thus, explained not only anti-Semitism but also the hostility encountered by psychoanalysis, that other, more recent advance into *Geistigkeit*. This reading enabled Freud to identify with yet another heroic figure, Moses, now ingeniously extracted from his religious role and redefined. As Philip Rieff pointed out, Moses on this reading becomes a precursor of the Enlightenment.

The "early breast-mother…. is the apotheosis of *Sinnlichkeit*" (442), so this advance in *Geistigkeit* was also a step forward into the realm of the father. There were suddenly all sorts of parallels between the invention of Judaism and the invention of psychoanalysis. The Israelites in the Exodus had left behind the "flesh-pots of Egypt," and Moses, in leaving Egypt, had left behind his Egyptian mother (his actual mother in Freud's version, his adoptive mother according to the Bible). This step had been hard to take: the Israelites in the wilderness, unable to endure the unalloyed *Geistigkeit* demanded of them by Moses, danced naked around the golden calf and yearned to return to the flesh-pots. (So much so that finally, in Freud's telling, they rose up and murdered him.) Whitebook sees this interpretation as yet again "Freud's devaluation of the pre-Oedipal realm," and "a debasement of the maternal dimension." It is also, yet again, Freud's identification with a heroic leader.

Freud was thus able to discover a parallel between psychoanalysis and what he declared to be the true nature of Judaism, and to make "the most impertinent claim that no more essential Jew than he had ever walked the earth" (444). (Whitebook also calls this claim "impudent" and "outrageous.") Freud claimed, "in short, that psychoanalysis constitutes the culmination of the Mosaic tradition…. The Standard Edition became the new Torah" (444). It is possible to be indignant about the "impertinence" of this claim, but perhaps Edward Said captures the tone of it better when he spoke of the aged Freud writing his *Spätwerk* (late work) with "a sort of irascible transgressiveness" (Said 2003, 29) – the elderly conquistador no longer concealing the excesses and departures from decorum of his unstoppable claim to greatness.

We might of course criticise the claim by saying, using Freud's own argument, that it fails because it lacks *Geistigkeit*: it remains an idolatry. Instead of relating to the ethical perspective of Judaism, Freud competes with Moses. What he momentarily glimpsed in his *Weltanschauung* paper, the necessity for a foundation for ethical values, is surely at the heart of what is compelling in Mosaic religion – the voice that spoke from within the burning bush. The notion that this is the special contribution of the Jewish tradition to human thought was taken further in Freud's lifetime by Martin Buber and Franz Rosenzweig, who would later influence Emmanuel Levinas. It remains unaddressed, however, in *Moses and Monotheism* except by implication. Freud's fantasy of the murdered patriarch and his descendents, kept in line by their "phylogenetic inheritance" of guilt and anxiety, followed the template he had already constructed in *Totem and Taboo* (1913), when he sought the origin of morality in the story of the "primal horde."

To have Moses finally murdered by the enraged Israelites allowed him, therefore, to construct Jewish history on a long-familiar model. Freud acknowledges this straightforwardly. "I acquired that conviction," he said, "a quarter of a century ago when in 1912 I wrote my book on *Totem and Taboo*, and it has only grown firmer since" (1939, 58). Freud seems close here to recognising what Breuer had early pointed to, his vulnerability to believing his own speculations[2].

If we look at Freud's life as a whole, there is something about this picture that is both familiar and touching. Once again, in the extremity of old age, illness and exile, Freud dealt with passivity by escaping into "greatness" – as he did when he suppressed his sister's piano-playing, as he did when he suppressed his wife's pious ritual, as he did after the humiliation of the cocaine episode and the disaster of Emma Eckstein's surgery, as he did after the death of his daughter Sophie, and as he did after the death of his grandson and the almost simultaneous shock of his diagnosis with cancer and the hideously painful first operations. What is remarkable, of course, is that, ever since the cocaine episode, he had something to be great about, so to speak. Where Fliess' ideas were pretentious and absurd, Freud's ideas were opening an important path into the future.

Nevertheless, the implications of Whitebook's word, *hypomania*, don't go away. The repudiation of vulnerability and passivity (we don't need to call them feminine) was indeed "bedrock" for Freud. When it came time for him to die, he was fortunate his old friend, the doctor Max Schur, was still at hand. Freud could take charge of his own death. "Don't fail me now," he said to Schur. And Schur didn't. He gave Freud "adequate sedation" (Jones 1964, 657).

Conclusion

With the help of Whitebook's biography, I think we become able at last to see Freud with reasonable clarity. The legend drops away: we see instead a man of outstanding talent and imaginative energy, always threatened perhaps by a fear of insignificance (it's plausible to associate it with his mother's distraction and grief at the illness and death of his brother Julius, when Freud was two years old), which he overcame by extremely hard work and the strenuous use of his extraordinary intelligence and gift for writing. His parents seem to have been not only strongly motivated to support his giftedness but also perhaps so dazzled by it that they failed to realise it needed to be kept in balance with the needs of others; his resulting need to be "great," a *conquistador*, has something about it that, from a distance, can seem touching and rather "boyish." But in reality, as so often, that need imposed huge costs in adult life, both on those close to him, and on Freud himself. It stands behind the wearisome rhetoric of greatness and heroism in the history of early psychoanalysis, the shedding of "dissidents" from the psychoanalytic movement, and also the curious atmosphere of excitement and isolation in which psychoanalysis developed. In the long run, it led to what I describe at the start of this essay, the tone of idealisation in both the theory and the practice of psychoanalysis, and also in much discussion of Freud himself and of certain "great" clinicians and theoreticians. As Ellenberger said, these idealisations and allegiances make the history of psychoanalysis difficult to see clearly, and "laborious" if one wishes to examine it honestly.

We are now, I think, at the end of that era. Psychoanalysis, if it's to survive, needs to take its place as one discipline among others. It finds itself in an intellectual landscape that includes other knowledge and other approaches to psychology and psychotherapy, and that allows it to be in dialogue on equal terms with philosophy, with sociology, with literature and with neurobiology. The Freud who identified with Moses might have found this development a bit diminishing, but I like to think a different Freud, Loewald's "unofficial Freud," would recognise it as necessary and an important advance.

Notes

1 Review essay on Joel Whitebook: *Freud: An Intellectual Biography* (2020, Columbia UP).
2 In early drafts back in Vienna Freud subtitled *Moses and Monotheism* "a historical novel" (see Yerushalmi [1989] for a detailed discussion of Freud's oscillations over this description). But he dropped the phrase, finally, and he had no intention that the final text should be read as fiction.

References

Abraham, R. (1982). Freud's mother conflict and the formulation of the Oedipal father. *Psychoanal. Rev.* 69: 4, 441–53.
Black, D.M. (2001). Mapping a detour: Why did Freud speak of a death drive? *Br. J. Psychother.* 18: 2, 185–98.
Cherry, S. et al. (2020). Professional and personal development after psychoanalytic training: Interviews with early career analysts. *J. Am. Psychoanal. Assoc.* 68: 2, 217–39.
Clark, R.W. (1980). *Freud: The Man and the Cause.* London: Jonathan Cape.
Ellenberger, H. (1970). *The Discovery of the Unconscious: the History and Evolution of Dynamic Psychiatry.* London: Allen Lane, The Penguin Press.
Erikson, E. (1968). *Identity: Youth and Crisis.* London: Faber and Faber.
Freud, S. (1895) *Project for a Scientific Psychology.* SE I.
Freud, S. (1905) Three essays on the theory of sexuality. SE VII.
Freud, S. (1910) Leonardo and a memory of his childhood. SE XI.
Freud, S. (1913) *Totem and Taboo.* SE XIII.
Freud, S. (1914a) On the history of the psychoanalytic movement. SE XIV.
Freud, S. (1914b) On narcissism. SE XIV.
Freud, S. (1916) On transience. SE XIV.
Freud, S. (1920) *Beyond the Pleasure Principle.* SE XVIII.
Freud, S. (1926) Address to the Society of B'nai B'rith. SE XX.
Freud, S. (1927) *The Future of an Illusion.* SE XXI.
Freud, S. (1933a) Anxiety and instinctual life. In *New Introductory Lectures.* SE XXII.
Freud, S. (1933b) Femininity. In *New Introductory Lectures.* SE XXII.
Freud, S. (1933c) The question of a *Weltanschauung.* In *New Introductory Lectures.* SE XXII.
Freud, S. (1936) A disturbance of memory on the Acropolis. SE XXII.
Freud, S. (1937) Psychoanalysis terminable and interminable. SE XXIII.
Freud, S. (1939) *Moses and Monotheism.* SE XXIII.

Freud, S. (1940). *An Outline of Psychoanalysis*. SE XXIII.

Fritsh, R.C. & Winer, R. (2020). Combined training of candidates, scholars, and psychotherapists: A model of psychoanalytic education for the twenty-first century. *J. Am. Psychoanal. Assoc.* 68: 2, 175–200.

Gay, P. (1988). *Freud: A Life for Our Time*. London: JM Dent.

Jones, E. (1964). *The Life and Work of Sigmund Freud*. Harmondsworth: Pelican Books.

Kernberg, O. (2014) The twilight of the training analyst system. *Psychoanal. Rev.* 101, 151–174.

Lear, J. (2017a). Eros and Development. In *Wisdom Won from Illness* 175–90. Cambridge, MA: Harvard UP.

Lear, J. (2017b). Mourning and Moral Philosophy. In *Wisdom Won from Illness* 191–205. Cambridge, MA: Harvard UP.

Richardson, J. et al. (2020). Beyond progression: Devising a new training model for candidate assessment, advancement, and advising at Columbia. *J. Am. Psychoanal. Assoc.* 68: 2, 201–16.

Said, E.W. (2003). *Freud and the Non-European*. London: Verso and Freud Museum.

Sulloway, F. (1979). *Freud: Biologist of the Mind*. London: Fontana.

Whitebook, J. (2017). *Freud: An Intellectual Biography*. Cambridge: Cambridge University Press.

Yerushalmi, Y.H. (1989). Freud on the 'historical novel': From the manuscript draft (1934) of Moses and Monotheism. *Int. J. Psychoanal.* 70, 375–94.

Chapter 8

The transcendent in everyday life

Introduction

To write about psychological reality, as TS Eliot and many others have pointed out, one can only use words that are best adapted to describing a world of external, enduring "things." The neuroscientist Iain McGilchrist has written about this perceptively in *The Matter with Things* (2021). In the world of psychoanalysis, to deal with this difficulty, as far back as in the 1970s Roy Schafer suggested that psychoanalysis would be better done in an "action language", a language of verbs (Schafer 1976). Unfortunately this was not practicable, but he was recognising a crucial issue (see Chapter 2).

I wrote the present chapter after working on a Commentary to Dante's *Purgatorio*. Dante was one of the most skilful users of words in recorded history. To tell the truth about his experience, which he intensely wanted to do, he took the falsification imposed by language for granted: he made no attempt to state "the facts" and instead wrote in allegory, a sort of fiction ("falsification" if you like) in which the pattern is continually adjusted to point more deeply to the truths of lived ethical experience.

This is not to imply that there are no facts in the ordinary sense of the word. But it is to imply that such facts, about the world seen as material and measurable, may "falsify" as well as convey truth. This is why a text such as Freud's "The question of a *Weltanschauung*" (1933) is misleading for all its carefulness. Freud said of science (which he thought provided a sufficient *Weltanschauung*, world-view, for psychoanalysis) that all it has done is develop certain features of ordinary thinking: "it takes an interest in things even if they have no immediate, tangible use; it is conceived carefully to avoid individual factors and affective influences; it examines more carefully the trustworthiness of the sense-perceptions on which it bases its conclusions; it provides itself with new perceptions which cannot be obtained by everyday means and it isolates the determinants of these new experiences in experiments which are deliberately varied. Its endeavour is to arrive at correspondence with reality – that is to say with what exists outside us and independently of us and, as experience has taught us, is decisive for the fulfilment or disappointment of our wishes. This correspondence with the real external world we call 'truth'. It remains the aim of scientific work even if we leave the practical value of the work out of account" (Freud 1933, 170).

DOI: 10.4324/9781003451679-8

That is an excellent description of science conducted with Cartesian presuppositions: there is an external world which is "real" and an objective language in which it can be correctly described. The mind appears to have no task except to arrive at this description (though the puzzling word "value" appears in the final sentence).

This essentially nineteenth century view of science was already out of date by 1933. The revolution in physics associated with the names of Einstein, Nils Bohr, Heisenberg and others had already shown that applying the language of classical physics – wave, particle, "thing," location – to the world of quantum physics resulted in impossible paradox; and in philosophy, Heidegger had enlarged a recognition that could already be found in Kant, that we always live in an already interpreted world – that the "world" of our experience is never the "universe" known to physics. Ironically, psychoanalysis itself had also made Freud's understanding of science inadequate, showing as it did that perception and projection can never be wholly unscrambled.

I want here to pick out one ingredient from this tangle of far-reaching topics, and it's the one he dropped in apparently casually in my long quotation above, the word "value." "Value" is clearly a notion that makes a bridge between subject and object; it requires us to say that some objective state of affairs gives rise in a subject to a feeling-toned response. To a committed Cartesian, values of every sort can only be a puzzle. Freud, whose natural-science perspective was inherited from Darwin, Helmholtz, and his own mentor, Brücke, saw no problem with the sort of values that are associated with bodily needs or pleasures: food is good because the organism needs it to survive; sex is good because the species has evolved on the basis of individual organisms engaging in an activity that enables it, the species, to continue. But in his perception, the "unit" of biological science can only be the individual organism; philosophically, this derived indirectly from Descartes, but more directly from the "materialism" that was an unquestioned metaphysical assumption in Freud's scientific milieu. In this picture, an individual organism is ultimately nothing but its body and all its acts derive from its body's "drives."

When it came to ethical values, things became more difficult. In 1930, Freud wrote: "Ethics is thus to be regarded... as an endeavour to achieve, by means of a command of the superego, something which so far has not been achieved" by any other means (1930, 142). Ethics, he said, derives essentially from a re-direction of the death drive: so much does man long "to satisfy his aggressiveness on the other, to exploit his capacity to work without compensation, to use him sexually without his consent, to seize his possessions, to humiliate him" (111) – Freud even cites the old adage, *homo homini lupus*, man is a wolf to man, as a rhetorical clincher to his argument – that the only way to manage these urges has been to internalise them. "Ethics" is the product of the death drive when it has been adopted by the superego and turned against the ego's unbounded selfishness.

Every psychoanalyst is likely to recognise some version of the sort of ferocious "superego" that Freud is describing here; it can result in symptoms such as feelings of worthlessness, depression, paralyzing perfectionism and the like. But to make this the source of ethics in general is to assimilate ethics to mental illness – to treat, so to speak, the pathology of a function as the function itself. Freud did something similar with religion, when he correctly identified many sorts of misuses of religion – wish-fulfilment, obsessional ritual, evasion of painful realities such as death and loss – and then treated them as the whole project (see Chapter 10). With both religion and ethics, the insufficiently examined metaphysical assumption of reductive "materialism," and its correlate "individualism," painted Freud into a corner.

What is at stake in this issue? It is both ethics and "meaning." As the philosopher Peter Singer writes: "our lives can be pleasurable or painful, but if we want them to have some meaning as well, we cannot create this meaning out of our subjective experiences alone. There can be no meaning to a life unless something is worth doing. To decide that something is worth doing involves making an ethical judgment" (Singer 1993, 250).

Freud was not alone in his inability to give any adequate account of ethical values. As Nietzsche foresaw, the replacement of religious belief by "science" as the ordinary educated person's *Weltanschauung* undermined from within the traditional vocabulary of ethics: the language of ethics continued to be used, but the words became increasingly empty shells. (A process well described by the philosopher Alasdair MacIntyre in his important study *After Virtue* [1981]. See too, for example, Marilynne Robinson [2010].) In recent years, the crucial importance of ethical issues has been increasingly recognised both in psychoanalysis and elsewhere. The accelerating dangers in the public domain, to do with climate-change, AI, and mendacious populism have made the devastating consequences of a failure to discover a compelling basis for ethics ever more apparent. The thinking of the philosopher Emmanuel Levinas (1906–1995) has been especially significant in making such a discovery possible.

The psychoanalyst Viviane Chetrit-Vatine has made use of Levinas' thought very directly. A French analyst who has worked in Israel for many years, she speaks of her concern for ethics as linked with her experience of working in Israel with Jewish patients and encountering "multiple aspects of the 'radioactive' effects" transmitted from the Holocaust, which bring up ethical issues at every turn (Chetrit-Vatine 2014, 167). She suggests that Freud, before he developed his full armoury of psychoanalytic ideas, indicated a less pathological path to thinking about ethics when he wrote in 1895: "The initial helplessness of human beings is the primal source for all moral motives" (Freud 1895, 318).

The fact that a baby cannot survive without the help of a responsible care-taker Freud initially connected with the need for ethics, but when, much later in his career, he returned to the topic, he was unable to return to the simplicity of his original thought. In a paper on the asymmetry of the analytic encounter, Chetrit-Vatine reverted to it, drawing on Levinas and the psychoanalyst Jean Laplanche to suggest that the early mother/baby relation gives a model for subsequent ethical situations, in particular for the relation between analyst and patient (Chetrit-Vatine 2004).

I have written about Levinas in several places, and specifically here in Chapters 9 and 10. In Chapter 10, I give a brief account of his moving and powerful life-story. He survived the Holocaust, very remarkably, as a prisoner of the German military.

After the war, he produced a succession of philosophical works in which he looked with great sensitivity at issues of ethics, which he declared to be "first philosophy," of prior importance and known with greater certainty than "ontologies" such as the natural sciences (Levinas 1984). He developed above all his notion of the "face of the Other" – meaning, not the literal face, but something more like the poignant human reality of the other – which, once "seen," is perceived to be the source of a "command," an obligation of responsibility in relation to the other. This command is "transcendent": it is infinite, it cannot be denied (though it can be ignored), and it cannot be accounted for (it is self-validating). Its call to respond singles out *me* as the unique person I am: " me who am me and no one else" (Levinas 1998, 14). "The unicity of the I consists in the fact that nobody can respond in its place" (Levinas 1962, 18). By obeying the call of responsibility for the other, one becomes "human." Humanity is an achievement in Levinas' conception, it is not given merely by belonging to a biological species.

Levinas always insisted on the "transcendence" of obligation. It was not an emotion: obligation is present, regardless of one's emotions. Nor was he doing psychology: Levinas doesn't speculate about the psychological background of ethical compellingness, as a psychoanalyst is bound to do. (Levinas was opposed to such speculation, which threatens to root "ethics" back in the earth of "ontology," to convert "the other" into "the same.") Chetrit-Vatine, however, like Freud in 1895, links the origin of ethics back to the initial helplessness of the infant. Freud had understood the adult wish to help the infant as based on an unconscious memory in the adult of having once been comparably helpless herself; this gives a basis to identify with the child's need, and therefore to wish to help him. Chetrit-Vatine comments that Freud's account of ethics is based "in an essentially narcissistic motivation" (2014, 72). With Levinas in mind, she proposes instead that what the child needs, and what, all being well, the mother provides, is a "matricial space."

Psychoanalysts differ in the degree to which they are comfortable using technical language. Its use can be very helpful in achieving greater precision. At the same time, language "imposes a pattern, and falsifies." My own preference, therefore, is to use language that is as ordinary as possible – which no doubt also imposes its pattern but is less intimidating and perhaps can be turned in more directions to catch the light. To spell out the notion of matricial space in my own words, which Chetrit-Vatine might not endorse: the word *matricial* is derived from the French *matrice*, a womb or matrix; the image is that the correct ethical stance of the mother creates in the psychological realm a "space" for the baby's developmental needs comparable to the space of the womb for the physical development of the foetus – a space characterised both by a standing-back (to influence a spontaneous process as little as possible) and by intense engagement (so the baby need have no anxiety that its development is not of the greatest possible interest to the mother). Writing this I am reminded of the Talmudic story: "Every blade of grass has its Angel that whispers over it: 'Grow! grow!'"

This is matricial space, which Chetrit-Vatine also says is "interwoven with primal seduction and maternal passion" (2014, 72). In using the word seduction, she is influenced by Laplanche's idea of the "enigmatic messages" inevitably conveyed to an infant by an adult woman, aware of sexuality and her own sexual responses, handling and interacting with a child who has no awareness of such matters. Presumably, countless enigmatic messages are conveyed to infants by adult behaviours. But sexuality is a particularly important species, so to speak, within the genus of "enigmatic messages," because in later years the management of sexuality will play such a major role in the capacity to form intimate and fruitful relationships. Mary Target (2015, 61) points out that there is also, understandably, a "specific, normal failure of affect mirroring" by parents when confronted with sexual excitement and related feelings in their children, who are left with a sense of mystery and excitement about sex as they grow into adolescence.

The question arising from this piece of theory is whether the idea of "matricial space" offers a way to better understand the nature of an "ethical attitude." Freud's account of the superego, quoted above, allows us to conceive the ethical attitude in terms of a certain sort of depression, a constriction of (what he believed to be) our natural tendency to be aggressive and egoistic without limit. Levinas' "face of the other" brings in a response to the other of an altogether different kind, concerned with, indeed governed by, the needs of the other and not of the self. Levinas' "face of the other" conceives the ethical attitude in a positive direction, putting a brake, certainly, on my selfish desires, but recognising the "transcendent" call of obligation which singles me out and (to borrow Peter Singer's word) gives "meaning" to my life. It's a "transcendent" call, to which I may refuse to listen, but only at a cost to my own humanity.

Eyal Rozmarin, another psychoanalyst who has written perceptively about Levinas, criticised him for the unbridled extremity of this "call," which puts the welfare of the other as my sole concern. It is, says Levinas, "an unlimited responsibility in which I find myself" (1998, 10): a "relation of infinite responsibility to the other person" as the philosopher Simon Critchley puts it (2002, 6). For Rozmarin by contrast – like Judith Butler more recently (2021) – psychoanalysis can only accept that the other may have an equal claim to consideration as myself, but not that I should subordinate myself to his needs: psychoanalysis asserts the ultimate truth of ambivalence, it "cannot put me ahead of the other, nor the other ahead of me" (Rozmarin 2007, 359). Chetrit-Vatine's concept, however, offers us the picture of an "asymmetric" relation, comparable to that described by Levinas himself. Matricial space is offered with an unmistakable purpose: to promote the welfare of a baby who is utterly dependent on others for survival, or, in psychoanalysis, to promote the welfare of a patient who is in need of a safe place in which to risk lowering her adult defences, in hope of finding new possibilities of emotional resource.

Case example: Emily

Matricial space, ethical space, is in a certain sense invisible. It is what, when one trusts another, one "takes for granted." Its failure or its absence, however, can be traumatising. I present here a brief case example, to illustrate not so much its presence as the traumatic impact of its absence.

I received a phone-message one Thursday from a woman who was clearly in an emotional state. She said she had been in an analysis which had broken down "irretrievably"; she felt she had been badly let down by her analyst; she felt a need to talk to another analyst as soon as possible. Something in her tone caused me to ring back immediately and offer her a consultation for the following day.

She arrived for the session in considerable distress. She told me she had been in five-time weekly analysis for several years with a well-known analyst, Dr Q (a woman). Dr Q had initially been very friendly, had seemed very enthusiastic about analysing her patient (whom I will call Emily). Emily described Dr Q in the early days, running energetically up the stairs behind her to reach the consulting room, full of lively interpretations, sometimes making jokes. Emily, a restrained and thoughtful woman in her early 40s, had been somewhat mystified by this reception but also gratified. It had made her feel valued as a patient and contradicted her habitual self-doubt. All had gone reasonably well for two years.

Emily had then gone to a conference in Mexico. Her marriage had ended in divorce some years before; at the conference, she met an attractive man, a Mexican, with whom she began a sexual affair. Returning to London, she corresponded with him warmly, and he seemed keen to continue the relationship. A few months later, he visited her, and they again got on well. She was then in a predicament: what to do? Should she invite him to stay with her in London, or should she end the relationship, sadder-but-wiser? She couldn't decide.

At this delicate moment, Dr Q "pitched in with a suggestion" (Emily's words). She pointed out that the particular work the Mexican could do was currently available on a temporary basis at a certain institution.

Emily by this time was in an intense transference. She was the eldest child of middle-class parents, whose marriage had never recovered after the father had had a brief extra-marital affair shortly after Emily was born. Appearances had been "kept up," but the parents slept in separate bedrooms, and sex and boyfriends could never be spoken of; the mother, a Roman Catholic, retreated into hurt and reproachful piety; the father lived in a state of resentment and deepening depression.

For Emily, to have a relationship with her Mexican boyfriend was both liberating and morally troubling. Her uncertainty about her decision was also a confusion about the basis on which such a decision should be made. In her regressed state, it seemed not simply a difficult, perhaps painful, decision about a personal preference, but also a moral decision, with a bearing on whether she was a good person or a bad person. And so, as she recollected the matter, she heard Dr Q's intervention, presumably intended to merely communicate a possibly helpful piece of information, as a guideline: this was the path Dr Q thought a decent person should take in these circumstances. Instead of wrestling in her own mind to reach her own decision, Emily adopted what she interpreted as Dr Q's advice.

The Mexican boyfriend had lived with her for a period of about six months. Things had not gone well. Emily realised almost immediately that she didn't want the relationship; he had been angry and upset. When he left, she became miserable. And then she became very angry with Dr Q. What was Dr Q doing, giving her that advice; well, OK, information? Emily knew enough about analysis to know that analysts were supposed to know about the transference. Had Dr Q never heard of the transference?

Dr Q, however, seemed unconcerned. From her point of view, something had got sorted out; they'd tested the relationship, it hadn't worked out: a shame, but – time to move on. She, Dr Q, had done nothing wrong and couldn't understand what Emily was so angry about. She talked about Emily's Oedipal difficulties, with a father who had had an affair and spurned his daughter.

This, in brief outline, was Emily's angry story. I felt it was important simply to listen to it. My impression was that, although she had had such a powerful transference to Dr Q, she had not, in Chetrit-Vatine's terms, been able to have a "matricial transference," to meet a safe, ethically reliable openness into which she might then have projected some version of her actual pious, repressed, perhaps profoundly envious mother, whose enigmatic and not-so-enigmatic messages had made sexuality such a difficult area for her. Instead, she had met an analyst whose vigorous presence suppressed the delicate processes by which such enigmatic messages may be re-encountered; she had become "nobody," and, when she had a major and consequential decision to make, had been able to find no resources with which to make it. This experience was a transference too, of course, but not one that could be made therapeutic use of. In fact, it had caused her to act towards her boyfriend with an unthought-out impetuosity that seemed to her now not her own and which caused her painful remorse and guilt. She was also childless; she feared she had lost her last chance to have children. Hence her bitter anger.

This sense that Emily, a competent woman in her profession, had "become nobody" was puzzling. In further meetings, I learned more of her story. I learned that her mother had had several psychotic or near-psychotic episodes at difficult moments in her life (anorexia in adolescence, a manic episode when she first met her husband, an episode of chaos, late in life, when she was diagnosed with advanced cancer). I thought what we glimpsed in the breakdown with Dr Q reflected something of the experience of a baby with a mother who is partly shielded by psychotic defences. The baby meets at moments, not just an "enigmatic" message, but a blank message, something akin to a "still face," which is intolerable, and which has to be filled in, so to speak, with extraneous material – with a fantasy of the child's own badness, perhaps, or the child's goodness as a carer for the damaged parent (what Winnicott described as the origin of the "false self" personality). But behind the false self, there isn't a "true self," there is an incoherent response with many ingredients. In Emily, one ingredient was perhaps envy. One could think that Emily, in identification with an envious mother, had been envious of her confident analyst. She had set Dr Q up to fail, and Dr Q had fallen into the elephant-trap. If so, a triumph for the resentful child, re-creating a "failed parent," but a triumph that came at great cost. But overall her response, which spared her the conflict of real decision-making, and allowed her to escape into a ready-made solution presented from outside, is best seen I think as the product of a void in lived developmental history and experience. Hence the "nobody" that Emily had temporarily become, and her vulnerability then to compliance with an imaginary version of "goodness."

Discussion

In psychoanalysis, matricial space is another way of referencing that element in a psychoanalyst's self-presentation that is both obvious and yet difficult to describe – it used to be called "abstinence" or "neutrality" and is often referenced using Bion's somewhat hyperbolical injunction to "abandon memory and desire." Emily felt she couldn't meet a matricial space in her energetic analyst, either at the start of the analysis when the first transferences became established, or, when things went wrong, when she made her angry complaint. One of the functions of apology in psychoanalysis is to re-set the matricial space when things have gone astray. Dr Q, however, saw no reason to apologise, and Emily's grievance remained unappeased. (I am aware, of course, that I only have Emily's account of what had happened; I had no access to "the facts themselves.")

Earlier too, in relation to her mother, the matricial space seems to have been distorted by the mother's own difficulties: her inability to process her hurt and anger at her husband's infidelity, her inability to discover or retrieve her identity as an adequate, adult sexual woman. There is a feminist adage, "a woman's place is in the wrong," which often came into my mind as I sat with Emily. I think it reflected the fact that she had been unable to find a relationship in childhood in which many of her spontaneous feelings and impulses, perhaps in particular sexual ones, could be given space without a moral marker. When, eventually, I quoted this adage to Emily, she laughed ruefully and said: "Too true!". Safety to be herself, and therefore to develop as a "true self," the fruit of encountering matricial space, had been denied to Emily, both in her childhood setting and in her analysis.

I shall not say more about Emily. I think her story shows the importance of "matricial space" in psychoanalysis. When it is consciously experienced, it creates a certain sort of safety, a feeling which will of course often be inaccessible for many reasons. But matricial space is an objective reality, and its importance is not dependent on its being consciously felt. In its absence, though analysis or development may proceed, the "true self" will not be called into being. In this sense, the offer of "matricial space" may be compared to Winnicott's notion of "holding."

But the idea of matricial space has more positive content than other formulas ("holding"; "neutrality"; the "abandonment of memory and desire"). It isn't just about the absence of something: it includes the presence of "ethics." In contrast to Bion's formula, it clearly involves remembering something. As Chetrit-Vatine emphasises, it's an asymmetrical concept: the analyst is under an (unlimited, Levinasian) obligation in relation to the patient, to maintain an ethical posture; the patient is under no corresponding obligation to the analyst. (If the patient digs an elephant-trap, we have to assume she needs to dig an elephant-trap; it's the task of the analyst to deal with it and, if he falls into it, to appreciate the need to dig it in the first place.) There has been a tendency recently in some analytic circles to emphasise the "equality" of analyst and patient: both are vulnerable, both have large areas of unconsciousness, both act impulsively and make mistakes; all this is undoubtedly correct. But the notion of matricial space emphasises something else: the "asymmetry" of ethical responsibility, and therefore of the analytic encounter.

What both Chetrit-Vatine's account, and Levinas' own thinking, leave to be further examined is the affective dimension of the ethical stance. If an ethical stance is causally efficacious, then it must include affect: it must involve a "motive," an affect or desire that "moves" the subject to action or to adopting matricially relevant postures such as watchfulness, attentiveness, or (Levinas' word) "greeting." Ronald Dworkin, one of the great legal thinkers of his generation, who devoted his career to topics of law and jurisprudence, towards the end of his life turned to a question that had always deeply preoccupied him: what gives matters of law and justice their hold on us? He too found he had to speak about affect. Our convictions about value, he said, are always emotional commitments as well: "Convictions of value are also complex, *sui generis,* emotional experiences" (Dworkin 2013, 20). This in no way implied for him that convictions of value were "merely subjective." "Our felt conviction that cruelty is wrong is a conviction that cruelty is really wrong; we cannot have that conviction without thinking that it is objectively true." Basing himself on the objective reality of value, Dworkin went on to develop a concept of religion that had no need for the idea of a god, that was "deeper than theism." (Deeper because it argued that, if a theist knows that God is good, he can only do so because he has a prior knowledge of what good is.) Dworkin arrived at a profoundly religious attitude that didn't require theistic beliefs but was entirely respectful of them – an atheism, as he said, more akin to theism than to the "science-based" atheisms of Freud or Richard Dawkins. Like Peter Singer, Dworkin was enabled by his theory of objective value to speak of life as having "meaning."

Levinas, emphasising the transcendent nature of the obligation we perceive when we meet the face of the other, emphasises, not the affect evoked in the subject, but the challenge that that obligation places upon "me" to "justify" myself. "This is the question of the meaning of being: not the ontology of the understanding of that extraordinary verb [the verb 'to be'], but the ethics of its justice. The question *par excellence* or the question of philosophy: not, 'why being rather than nothing?' but how being justifies itself" (Levinas 1984, 86). Jacques Derrida, speaking his *Adieu* at Levinas' funeral, told a significant story. He described a conversation with him, in which Levinas said: "You know, they often speak of ethics to describe what I do, but what interests me when all is said and done is not ethics, not only ethics, it's the holy, the holiness of the holy (*la sainteté du saint*)" (Critchley 2002, 27).

This story is very suggestive. Whatever we make of the word *holy*, it indicates that Levinas was aware that something in what he was saying went beyond "ethics" in the ordinary meaning of the word. And if we translate *sainteté* as "saintliness," perhaps we glimpse something more about the affect implicit in Levinas' account of obligation.

I mentioned Dante at the beginning of this chapter. Dante's great poem, the *Divine Comedy*, written in the early fourteenth century, describes a journey through the three realms of the afterlife, Hell, Purgatory and Paradise. This journey is a concentrated ethical education for its protagonist, also called Dante. Dante-the-poet gives Dante-the-protagonist two guides to negotiate these three realms, one of them Virgil, the politically astute Roman epic poet who celebrated the Emperor Augustus, and the other Beatrice, a beautiful Florentine girl whom Dante had known in childhood and young manhood (she died when she and Dante were both age 25). I have written in Chapter 5 about these two guides. They are allegorical figures, and open therefore to many interpretations, but they may be seen centrally as representing two sorts of love, or, better, two different ways in which one can be loved: for one's "doing" (Virgil), and for one's "being" (Beatrice).

Dante was not writing a philosophical treatise, and there are many ways in which each figure does both jobs, but very broadly we see Virgil as Dante's guide through the realm (Hell) in which souls are wholly identified with their damaging motives, and the realm (Purgatory) in which souls have seen the truth of God's love but are still wrestling with their "sins," damaging perversions or excesses of love that prevent them from aligning themselves with the divine. (All motives in Dante's psychology are different configurations of "love"; there is no "death drive" nor, as in some versions of Christianity, is there any innate tendency towards evil.) The suffering of the damned is presented as an inevitable consequence of their state of mind, and in Purgatory "penitence" is of necessity a state of suffering and conflict. Throughout Purgatory, Dante uses metaphors derived from the training of horses: he sees penitence, the experience of learning the lessons of guilt, remorse, and conflict, as a process by which the will is "trained."

There is, however, a quite definite moment, in Canto XXVII of *Purgatorio*, when Virgil tells Dante: "I now have nothing further to teach you." Dante has learned about earthly motives, he has seen them at work in his own feelings, and his will is trained: he is wholly persuaded of the goodness of what, in Dante's allegory, is called divine love, which puts all human motives in proportion. He can now, so to speak, love "correctly."

It is only after this formal statement by Virgil that Dante becomes free to enter the Earthly Paradise, and to re-meet Beatrice. But far from being the joyful encounter that the reader is likely to expect, this experience is profoundly dismaying. She speaks to him severely; Dante is overcome with shame. If we had thought all sorrows had been overcome by the training experiences of Purgatory, we discover we were mistaken.

What I think we see here – to use an entirely different vocabulary – is the transition from "ethics" as we ordinarily understand it – to do with right action in society, to do with being a "good" or "mature" human being, embodying excellent values such as justice, friendship, truthfulness, courage (all things that the non-Christian Virgil is perfectly capable of understanding) – to a quite different sort of evaluation, to do with being the unique person one is, the person only "I" can be, one's "true self" in Winnicott's phrase. Beatrice's severity and Dante's intense shame and then profound grief are to do with his recognition that he has not been true to himself (in the allegory, not been "faithful to Beatrice").

Dante is wrestling with a recognition that is of great significance in psychoanalysis: that one can achieve "maturity" and become (in an ordinary sense of the phrase) ethically responsible and yet fail to live a life that is (to use the word that was crucial to both Singer and Dworkin) "meaningful," and that fulfils one's deepest wishes for one's life. The latter achievement is less about "loving," intensely important though that is, and is more about "being loved," about having been able to receive and respond to the love of another. This is allegorised in Dante's poem as being loved by Beatrice, or "entering Paradise."

Perhaps we may think that the affect that provides the motivational force in Levinas' "transcendence" and Chetrit-Vatine's "matricial space" is not the "love of somebody for what they do" (which gives rise to an appreciation of ethical behaviour in oneself and in others) but is the "love of somebody for who they are," with an unhesitating assumption that they deserve our concern and respect. This may seem ironic in the light of Levinas' insistence that ethical responsibility "transcends" being. It is, however, not incompatible with it if we think that love of this sort is a love, not for "being" in general (a Heideggerian notion), but for a particular being in its uniqueness. Because the love of a unique being can never wholly know the being it loves, it has the quality of being "infinite" that Levinas saw as crucial. The notion of the sacred, which attaches to particular persons or objects in particular religions, does so because in the religion's narratives the quality of infinity is especially perceived in them. Properly, however, as the ecological crisis reminds us, to be infinite is a universal quality of living beings. There is no good reason to confine it, as Levinas appears to do, to human beings.

Chetrit-Vatine's metaphor of a womb gives a vivid way to think of matricial love. We can imagine the womb saying to the foetus: "I offer you a space to grow in; I offer you my intimate processes to use for your own needs; I make no interference with your growth processes to fulfil my own needs or desires." When the baby is born, the "ordinary devoted mother," in Winnicott's phrase, attempts to offer, on the psychological plane, something similar to this. Chetrit-Vatine adopts from Laplanche the phrase "ethical seduction," but the offer in itself is not seductive, though it will of course always be restricted in certain directions by the contingent human and physical reality of the participants. But in itself it can be entirely genuine, and it's the message the baby needs to encounter if she is to develop a "true self," with a proper commitment to her own perceptions, desires and choices of paths of action – and a capacity, too, for the same sort of deeper love that will guide her self-management in relation to the requirements of ordinary ethics in society.

Derrida's story of his conversation with Levinas is very suggestive. Perhaps Levinas had glimpsed that what he was talking about, as he returned again and again throughout his career to the "transcendence" of the command he heard when he encountered "the face of the other," was this deeper ethic, to do with "saintliness," as he put it. He was recognising that the "love of being," intensely ethical in its implications, is something that religious visionaries have always aspired to and is not fully reducible to the issues usually referenced when philosophers speak of ethics. Rozmarin's objection to Levinas' extravagance, in giving "the other" an infinite value in relation to "me," expresses a preference for remaining in the realm of ordinary ethics. That is understandable, and important in practical living if one is to balance the tendency to excess that intense idealism entails. But what these diverse thinkers, Levinas and Chetrit-Vatine, Dante and Dworkin all recognise is the necessity, beyond the good practical judgement of ordinary ethics, of holding on to the ideal as well. Simon Critchley (2002, 28), reflecting on Derrida's story, put it well. He said that Levinas "is seeking to give an account of a basic existential demand, a lived fundamental obligation, that should be at the basis of all moral theory and moral action." Levinas, he said, describes ethical obligation in exorbitant terms: "infinite responsibility, trauma, persecution, hostage, obsession. The ethical demand is impossibly demanding." This is not, however, a fault. It has to retain this quality. Otherwise, "ethics would be reduced to a procedural programming," either utilitarian or merely a compliance with convention. As Nietzsche foresaw, and as Alasdair MacIntyre described in the 1980s, that has increasingly been its fate over the past two centuries.

Conclusion

What I have tried to show in this chapter is that the notion of "transcendence," in Levinas' thought and as adopted in psychoanalytic usage by Viviane Chetrit-Vatine, is a marker for the deeper ethical perspective or orientation that is needed in addition to conventional ethics to be its guide and lode-star. This need has also been recognised by thinkers using quite different vocabularies, like Peter Singer and Ronald Dworkin. But to understand how it can carry effective motivational force, it needs to be linked to an account of affect. I have suggested that it is an expression of the affect that Dante allegorised as "divine" or transcendent love, which in non-religious language may be spoken of as love for a person's "being" and not only for her "doing." Love of this sort for individual "being," despite its apparent extravagance when put into words, is present in many everyday contexts, in the love of parents for babies and for children, in lovers who "fall in love" and in the love of friends and partners, and it is present too in the serious commitment of psychoanalysts and psychotherapists to their patients. The "moments of meeting" described by relational psychoanalysts (Stern et al., 1998) are often moments in which such commitment is glimpsed, and they can be what patients, looking back on their analytic experience, feel most gratitude for. Outside analysis, this "love for being" is present too in the "seriousness" of responses of sympathy for the suffering of others, and in many people's reactions when they hear of the destruction caused by climate-change, and of terrible crimes like genocide and ecocide. No doubt, in the Second World War, it was often the motive of those in occupied Europe who, with outstanding personal courage, protected Jews (including Levinas' wife and daughter) from the Nazis.

The spectacular triumphs of science and materialism in the past two centuries, together with the widespread rejection of religion and "allegorical" ways of thinking, have tended to deprive educated people of any words in which to speak of this "love of being" and this "transcendent" level of ethics. Psychoanalysis too has found it difficult to speak of. The moral chaos of recent public life, the destruction of nature and the rise of populism and authoritarianism all around the globe are perhaps in part a consequence of this failure and absence of vocabulary. It is a matter of considerable importance to rediscover a language in which these issues can be thought about.

References

Butler, J. (2021). *The Force of Non-Violence*. London and New York, NY: Verso.

Chetrit-Vatine, V. (2004). Primal seduction, matricial space and asymmetry in the psycho-analytic encounter. *Int. J. Psychoanal.* 85: 4, 841–56.

Chetrit-Vatine, V. (2014). *The Ethical Seduction of the Analytic Situation: The Feminine-Maternal Origins of Responsibility for the Other*. Trs. A. Weller. London: Karnac.

Critchley, S. (2002). Introduction. In S. Critchley and R. Bernasconi (eds) *The Cambridge Companion to Levinas* 6. Cambridge UP.

Dworkin, R. (2013). *Religion without God*. Cambridge, MA: Harvard UP.

Freud, S. (1895). *Project for a Scientific Psychology* SE I, 295–397.

Freud, S. (1930). *Civilization and Its Discontents* SE XXI, 64–115.

Freud, S. (1933). The Question of a *Weltanschauung*, SE XXII, 158–82.

Levinas, E. (1962). Transcendence and Height. Trs. S. Critchley. In A.T, Peperzak et al. (ed) *Basic Philosophical Writings* 11–32. Bloomington: Indiana UP, 1996.

Levinas, E. (1984). Ethics as First Philosophy. Trs. S. Hand and M. Temple. In S. Hand (ed) *The Levinas Reader* 75–87. Oxford: Blackwell, 1989.

Levinas, E. (1998). *Otherwise than Being, or Beyond Essence*. Trs. A. Lingis. Pittsburgh, PA: Duquesne UP.

MacIntyre, A. (1981). *After Virtue* (3rd ed. 2007). London: Bloomsbury.

McGilchrist, I. (2021). *The Matter with Things* (two vols). London: Perspectiva Press.

Robinson, M. (2010). *Absence of Mind: The Dispelling of Inwardness from the Modern Myth of the Self*. New Haven, CT and London: Yale UP.

Rozmarin, E. (2007). An other in psychoanalysis: Emmanuel Levinas's critique of knowledge and analytic sense. *Contemp. Psychoanal.* 43: 3, 327–60.

Schafer, R. (1976). *A New Language for Psychoanalysis*. New Haven, CT and London: Yale UP.

Singer, P. (1993). *How Are We to Live?* 250. Oxford and New York, NY: Oxford UP.

Stern, D.N., et al. (1998). Non-interpretive mechanisms in psychoanalytic therapy. *Int. J. Psychoanal.* 79, 903–21.

Target, M. (2015). A Developmental Model of Sexual Excitement, Desire and Alienation. In A. Lemma and P.E. Lynch(eds) *Sexualities: Contemporary Psychoanalytic Perspectives* 61, 43–62. London: Routledge.

Chapter 9

Religion as the affirmation of values

This essay starts from the thought that we cannot take for granted that a society's highest values will survive in the long term as effective motivators within that society. By "highest values," I mean values such as justice, concern for members of weak and minority groups, respect for promises and recognition of the importance of speaking truthfully – values that apply at the highest level of generality. If they are to survive and to be effective, two things may be necessary: firstly, unpredictable "epiphanic" moments in which the power of these values is emotionally experienced by individuals, and secondly, institutions and a vocabulary in which these values can be remembered, discussed and affirmed in emotionally and imaginatively impactful ways. In the last two chapters of this book, I shall suggest, referencing in particular the thought of Emmanuel Levinas and Ronald Dworkin, that the *second* of these factors, the remembering and affirmation of values, marks out the crucial, perhaps even the irreplaceable, contribution of a religion to a society. The failure, within psychoanalysis and also more widely, to appreciate the importance of this function in a society over generations may mean that the consequences of "growing out of religion" (to borrow a phrase from Winnicott) have not yet been adequately recognised.

The language here can be confusing, as it's often natural to use some such word as "religious" to describe the epiphanic experiences in which the commandingness of an ethical value is recognised – and Levinas' own account of religion, which I shall outline in the final essay, may seem to point in that direction. But I shall attempt, as he does also, to maintain a distinction between this level of immediate experience and the level at which one might speak of "a religion," a cultural institution with specific teachings and historical reference points.

Introduction

Everyone seems to know what a religion is, but in fact there is no consensus. If we look at a slate of views, taken almost at random from well-known thinkers, we find Marx describing religion as "the heart of a heartless world," Durkheim emphasising that religion unites a "moral community" by means of ceremonial, William James describing it as the feelings of "men in their solitude," Rudolf Otto speaking of it as arising from an encounter with "the numinous," Freud suggesting

DOI: 10.4324/9781003451679-9

it is defined by belief in a Supreme Being and an afterlife (together with a "prohibition against thought" [Freud 1927, 171]), Ninian Smart concerned for it as "activities in a doctrinal context" – and so on. As with the blind sages and the elephant, each grasps something, undoubtedly, but we get little sense of a coherent beast.

Rather than attempt another definition (which I will approach in the next and final chapter), in the present essay I will address the question from a different angle and ask: what would get lost if religion got lost? By "religion" here I mean major developed religious traditions such as Judaism, Christianity, Islam, Hinduism and Buddhism. Many self-consciously scientific thinkers, including T.H. Huxley, Freud and recently Richard Dawkins, have thought that we can simply "grow out of religion" (Winnicott's phrase – see Parker 2011, 1), that religion can simply be replaced by "rational thinking" without serious loss. Are they right?

When I studied philosophy in the 1960s, the prestige of scientific thought was overwhelming. It had arrived, in Anglo-American philosophy, at the beliefs of logical positivism and analytic philosophy, which essentially said there was no meaning in the traditional questions of metaphysics. Ethical values, in particular, were either expressions of personal preference or were calculations of consequence – "utility." The methods of science gave us our only access to reliable knowledge, and the questions philosophers should be asking were questions about language, aimed at clarifying verbal confusion. Many of my teachers in Edinburgh University's philosophy department conveyed a sense of disappointment and anti-climax when they spoke about contemporary philosophy: they preferred to discuss the great thinkers of the past. We focused especially on Plato, Hume and Kant. We barely heard the names of Bergson, Husserl or Heidegger.

After leaving university, like many others at that time, I discovered Buddhism and realised I was meeting something altogether more meaningful than analytic philosophy in terms of my actual experience of life. Later, I didn't lose touch with that realisation, but it went on the back-burner when I embarked on a career in psychotherapy and psychoanalysis.

In psychoanalytic practice, there was no question that ethical values were taken seriously. There was the fundamental value of one's duty to one's patient, and, in Kleinian thought especially, there were the many concerns with value that are summed up in speaking of the oscillation between paranoid-schizoid and depressive positions, the perception of others, in our rather clumsy vocabulary, as "part-objects" or "whole objects." But there was a serious void in psychoanalysis. Aside from the superego, there was no basis in theory for ethical values. They were taken very seriously in practice – the ethical commitment of psychoanalysts was in general very impressive – but there was no way the theory could account for the values that were so clearly embodied in the practice of the best practitioners.

Background: Psychoanalysts on religion

Psychoanalysis, like logical positivism, emerged in the philosophical climate of the late nineteenth and early twentieth centuries. At that time, thanks to the triumphant advances in scientific understanding, which may be summed up by mentioning the names of Darwin, Faraday, Pasteur and others, rationalism and scientific materialism seemed to many to have swept the board. These attitudes are seen with great clarity in Freud's central work on religion, *The Future of an Illusion* (1927), which I shall discuss further in the next chapter. In this, the scientific vision, the causal explanations of natural science, were treated as self-evidently superior to other ways of thinking. Indeed, Freud didn't even trouble to enquire into how more thoughtful religious thinkers conceived their vision. Religion was illusion, he declared with certainty; "our science is no illusion." "Our best hope for the future," he wrote in 1933, "is that intellect – the scientific spirit, reason – may in process of time establish a *dictatorship* in the mental life of man" (1933, 171, emphasis added).

I shall look first at the difficulty psychoanalysis has had in understanding the significance of religion, which is bound up with the difficulty it has had in finding an adequate philosophical basis from which to understand its own functioning. Freud said that psychoanalysis had no world-view, no *Weltanschauung*, different from that of the natural sciences. He defined a *Weltanschauung* as "an intellectual construction which solves all the problems of our existence uniformly on the basis of one overriding hypothesis, which, accordingly, leaves no question unanswered and in which everything that interests us finds its fixed place" (1933, 158). In his disarming way, he went on to acknowledge that science was still far too incomplete to provide such a construction, but he adhered to it nevertheless as the path to reality, and firmly rejected all competitors, including philosophy, as clinging to "illusion" (160–1).

Such a role for science, however, is manifestly unsatisfactory for the reason already indicated, namely, that science by its nature is unable to give any basis for non-instrumental values. It is no disparagement of science to say that it can't provide a basis for "intrinsic" value; it is merely recognising the nature of what science is. Intrinsic ethical values, such as justice, truthfulness, responsibility towards others, personal integrity or the need to find one's life meaningful, are of huge importance to us; the loss of them results in social breakdown, and for individuals in severe depression and anomie, or the many trivial or manic activities that function as defences against those conditions; the recovery of a sense of life as meaningful is, hopefully, among the outcomes of successful psychoanalysis.

Etymologically, the word Freud used to describe religion, *illusion*, is to do with the ludic, with play. As I describe in Chapter 2, it was taken up strongly by Winnicott, a psychoanalyst who emphasised the importance of playing, and by him it was almost inverted from Freud's usage. In a remarkable phrase, Winnicott spoke of the "substance of illusion" ("that which is allowed to the infant, and which in adult life is inherent in art and religion") (1951, 230). With increasing confidence as he grew older, he affirmed the necessity of "illusion" if we are to live fulfilling lives. (For his recognition of the inadequacy of the word "illusion," see footnote on page 60.) He spoke of cultural objects, including religious ones, as existing in a "transitional space" which was of great importance but within which the question of literal truth, and of their basis in reality, could not be raised. "An essential feature of transitional phenomena and objects is a quality in our attitude when we observe them," he said (Winnicott 1974, 113). He was glimpsing here something very different from the "dictatorship" of reason. Winnicott came from an exceptionally devout Methodist background, and he always spoke of religion with respect; the importance of his background has been noted by many thinkers, in most detail perhaps by Stephen Parker who pointed out how strongly, for example, Winnicott's ideas about the "use of an object" echo the Christian understanding of Christ's resurrection (Parker 2011, 128).

Winnicott was not a philosopher, and in his discussion of "illusion" and "transitional objects," he was using traditional psychoanalytic vocabulary to approach more modern philosophical questions to which it was unsuited (see Chapter 2). But his informal use of that language was very adroit; we see its limitations more clearly when one of his followers attempts to spell out the implications further but continues to use the same register of vocabulary: this is, says the French psychoanalyst René Roussillon, "a conception of the mental apparatus which sees it as capable, under certain specific circumstances, of simultaneously hallucinating and perceiving, without becoming confused in the process" (Roussillon 2013, 280). But in fact Winnicott explicitly says that the transitional object is not a hallucination (Winnicott 1951, 233), and surely that is correct: you may not share their understanding, but small children, and religious believers, are not as a rule hallucinating. Winnicott is not describing a pathological state; he is wrestling with an existential fact, much the same existential fact that Martin Heidegger had described 25 years earlier by saying that we are "thrown" from the outset into an "interpreted world." Heidegger didn't mean a world of psychoanalytic interpretations, but a world that "makes sense" to us (including, sometimes, bewildering or frightening senses).

Heidegger was arguing against the sort of philosophical view that says we encounter a world of "sense data," out of which we then construct our familiar world of trees and people and so forth. He is saying that from the outset – "primordially," to use one of his favourite words – we encounter meaning. I cannot live, said Heidegger, in the bare "universe" described by physics, and I deceive myself if I pretend that I do.

Heidegger was acutely aware of the problem for human meanings of the immense explanatory power of science. It's one of the ironies of philosophical history that, more or less as Heidegger was developing his mature thought in Freiburg in the 1920s, in Austria the Vienna Circle of Moritz Schlick, Rudolf Carnap and others, the first logical positivists, basing themselves on Wittgenstein's early writings, were declaring their allegiance to "The Scientific Concept of the World" – to quote the title of their founding manifesto. At the start of the 1930s, with the rise of Hitlerism, Heidegger appalled his admirers by joining the Nazi Party, and the Vienna Circle broke up: most were Jews who left Vienna after the Anschluss and, like Freud, went into exile in the English-speaking countries. The resolute prejudice of Anglo-American philosophy against "continental philosophy," much of it deriving at only one or two removes from Heidegger, dates from this time. This prejudice has been an impoverishment to both traditions. One consequence was what I have described: by the 1950s even the names of the major continental philosophers were barely mentioned in British philosophy departments, or were spoken with such rolled eyes and obvious disdain that it seemed self-evident they were not worth exploring further.

A further consequence of this prejudice was that, certainly in the United Kingdom, the language in which psychoanalysis was done became stuck in the late nineteenth century scientific language of Freud – though the thinking of British analysts such as Fairbairn and Winnicott was already moving towards a different future. (I discuss this in more detail in Chapter 2.) Melanie Klein, with her notion of "unconscious phantasy" which allows the world, by projection, to be found meaningful, spoke of phantasy in ways similar to, and perhaps prefiguring, Winnicott's account of "illusion." Klein and Winnicott, at any rate in British psychoanalysis, were the two most fertile thinkers in the years around, and the decades immediately following, Freud's death in 1939. But essentially, for both of them, lacking the philosophical reference points that would enable them to challenge the primacy of the natural-science view, they could only work with an implicit world-view that was ultimately of a meaningless "objective" material world onto which "subjective" contents – "illusions," "phantasies" – were then pasted or projected. The nature of subjectivity could only be a puzzle to the vision of reductive materialism, as to be an "I" or a "You" is incomprehensible for the consistent materialist. (See, for example, McGinn 1989.) Winnicott's achievement, in escaping the limitations of Freud's thinking without ever directly confronting the fundamental inadequacy of his philosophy, is very remarkable: it was absolutely necessary, but in a sense, philosophically, it didn't have a leg to stand on.

So although in practice psychoanalysis struggled to evade, and was often compelled to ignore, the positivist assumptions of the scientific vision, in its basic theory it had nowhere else to go; and for several decades, the idealisation of Freud contributed to its retention of that vision and made it frightening, and professionally unwise, for psychoanalysts to be seen to depart from it. Wilfred Bion, when he developed his notion of O in the middle 1960s, was influenced by mystical thinkers like Meister Eckhart and St John of the Cross, and by the *Bhagavad Gita*, but felt he had to conceal the fact (Bléandonu 1994). Bion developed this notion late in his career, following his "epistemological phase"; the symbol of O denotes, he wrote, "the ultimate reality represented by terms such as ultimate reality, absolute truth, the godhead, the infinite, the thing-in-itself. O does not fall in the domain of knowledge or learning save incidentally; it can be 'become,' but it cannot be 'known'" (1970, 26). It can, however, "evolve … to a point where it can be known, through knowledge gained by experience" (26). It is related to by F, an "act of faith." Differently from Winnicott's transitionality, about which the question of truth must not be raised, O is undoubtedly real in Bion's account – indeed it is "ultimate reality" – but it cannot be known.

Bion's O, as these quotations may serve to remind us, is a confusing concept, and I am not sure that it tells us much more than the (important) fact that psychological truths can never be fully put into words, from which it follows that psychoanalytic interpretations never give us a final truth. This is a fact about psychological statement that religious mystics have always known; it was emphasised by the Buddha, for example, and also by Meister Eckhart, Ramakrishna, Thomas Merton and

Raimon Panikkar, to name a few mystical thinkers almost at random. The Buddhist image of "teachings" as merely a raft to cross over a river, to be discarded when they cease to be useful, is a popular image to convey this fact. Bion's discussion of O, however, became excessively complicated. It has divided his commentators ever since. Edna O'Shaughnessy spoke of his "mixing and blurring" different categories of discourse (2005). David Taylor (2011) suggested that Bion was in danger of idealising unknowability. Rudi Vermote (2011) argued to the contrary that O valuably names an undifferentiated psychic realm beyond the "caesura" that bounds the use of our ordinary capacity for understanding.

From around 1970, the philosophical climate of psychoanalysis began to alter, influenced by the wider culture of postmodernism and the increasing mistrust of authoritarian attitudes. The American psychoanalyst William Meissner, who was also a Jesuit priest, remains one of the most lucid and well-informed of the psychoanalysts who have discussed religion. In 1984, his *The Psychology of Religious Experience* built very directly on Winnicott's theories of illusion; he said that religion is an "illusion," which can be immensely enriching and help greatly in promoting integrity and wisdom, the fruits of a fulfilled life. But as with Winnicott, the word *illusion*, with its implication of unreality and untruth, was clearly inadequate to the important role Meissner was asking it to occupy. Towards the end of his book, Meissner attempted to find a stabler basis by speaking of faith as validated by the "supernatural" – but unfortunately this word has no useable meaning either for a scientist or for most contemporary philosophers.

Nevertheless, we may respect Meissner for his courage in holding on to his conviction that there was something needing to be spoken of, which the vocabulary of psychoanalysis was unable to reach. What Meissner was courageously recognising was that in order to think seriously about religion, we have to go beyond the vision of science. The word "supernatural" suggests an invisible higher realm of reality; it seems to point to a "spiritual world," distinct from the natural one; it is a metaphor we are no longer able to cash. Nevertheless, it serves as a reminder that the *Weltanschauung* of the natural sciences is not adequate to capture what religions are about.

Emmanuel Levinas

So much for a brief sketch of some of the psychoanalytic background and the philosophical difficulties to which, until at least the 1980s, it gave rise. My own first attempts to write about religion and ethical values date from the 1990s and were also hampered by the wish to remain within the vision and vocabulary of "scientific" psychoanalysis. I had lost touch with the world of philosophy and was unaware that, already back in the 1960s and indeed ever since the 1930s, a philosopher was writing in France, whose name was never mentioned in Edinburgh University's philosophy department, who had seen precisely these problems and had addressed them directly.

This man was Emmanuel Levinas. A Lithuanian Jew, born in 1906, Levinas studied in the late 1920s with Husserl and Heidegger in Freiburg; he was one of the first philosophers to introduce Heidegger's thought into France. He was also influenced by Martin Buber. He became a French citizen, joined the army at the start of the Second World War and spent four years of the war as a prisoner of the German military. His Lithuanian family all died in the Holocaust. (For a summary outline of his life, see Chapter 10.)

A man with such a history was unlikely to be impressed with an argument that ethical values were based on "illusion", or were merely a matter of taste. He took responsibility as his central theme, and his writings, often extremely difficult but always remarkably penetrating, return again and again to the notion of responsibility. One way to approach Levinas is to say that he developed Martin Buber's brilliant and simple insight (Buber 1970) that we encounter the world in two modes, that of the second person, I/You, and that of the third person, I/It. Using psychoanalytic language, we can say that we encounter others in two very different modes, as "objects" and as "subjects." (I have discussed some of the implications of this crucial difference at more length elsewhere, Black 2011, 84–104.)

Around the end of the nineteenth century, many thinkers in Germany were profoundly disturbed by the problem posed for values by the apparent triumph of natural science as giving us our fundamental model for the form knowledge should take. Friedrich Nietzsche, Max Weber and Martin Buber are three examples. The proclamation by the madman, in Nietzsche's fable, that God is dead but the news has not yet reached the ears of men (Nietzsche 1974, 181–2) was a warning that the enormous implications of the loss of religion were still impossible to take in. "Who gave us the sponge to wipe away the entire horizon?" Nietzsche (in his less manic moments) was appalled because he felt that the "death of God" implied the loss of all ultimate ground for meaning and value; there could now be no constraint on the boundless cruelty, violence and despair of which human beings are capable. One might say he accurately foresaw many aspects of the twentieth century. (Freud, an admirer of Nietzsche, was slower to recognise the power of human destructiveness; he finally did so by way of his pseudo-biological theory of the death drive.)

Buber's *I and Thou* was an attempt to move away from this domination by the vision of science. He recognised that we encounter the world in two quite different modes, which he called I/It (essentially the objective, third-person view, entirely compatible with that of science) and I/You, in which we meet another in the second person, as a subject. Buber's account of the encounter of I with You, or "Thou," emphasised the wonderful nature of the experience. When the other is seen as Thou, said Buber, he "fills the firmament" (1970, 59).

Levinas, adapting this notion, converted it from Buber's rather romantic picture into the more sober language of ethical obligation. When I behold You, or, in Levinas' language, when I see the "face of the Other," I recognise the force of the commandment: "Thou shalt not kill." I become aware of responsibility. "In its expression, in its mortality, the face before me summons me," he wrote, "… as if the invisible death that must be faced by the Other … were my business" (1989, 83). And later: "There is a paradox in responsibility in that I am obliged without this obligation having begun in me, as though an order slipped into my consciousness like a thief" (1998, 13).

"The face of the Other" is a technical term in Levinas' philosophy, meaning not the literal face but something more like the human reality of the other; the Other (often given a capital letter) "does not unpack himself as an ensemble of qualities making up an image; the face of the Other destroys at every moment, and exceeds, the plastic image that he leaves me with" (quoted Malka 1989, 22, author's translation); to perceive the "face" of the Other brings with it an inescapable awareness of my responsibility towards him. Like Buber, Levinas resorts sometimes to poetic language to emphasise the power and weight of obligation. The Other compels respect; "he reveals himself in his mastery"; he is (differently from Buber's Thou) not a *Toi* but a *Vous*. (In other words, I view him with respect, not necessarily with intimacy.) At the same time, he is an orphan, a proletarian, a pauper. The power of this recognition of responsibility, which comes with such unarguable force that it seems like a command coming from outside, transcends my ordinary vision. Levinas describes it as an "epiphany." It transcends the world of Buber's I/It, or the world of natural science, in which I might see the literal face of the other and shrug my shoulders; in the world of I/It, or the world of natural science, I might think the other is nothing to do with me; I might see nothing wrong with murder or genocide.

This notion of the "face of the Other," which evokes in me the awareness of my responsibility, is very remarkable. It is not a mythological notion, like the gods or demons of a religion, but nor is it an abstraction like the concepts of traditional philosophy. It is a notion that derives directly from felt experience, not from theory, and theoretical ideas are not allowed a priority from which to criticise, diminish or interpret it. (For the phenomenologist – both Heidegger and Levinas can be included under that heading – experience is the ultimate authority; it trumps theory, which is inevitably reductive and abstract.) The face of the Other, therefore, is a notion that carries both emotion and obligation, and it can occupy the space that is left vacant when philosophers attempt to derive values from empirical facts, and that is also left vacant when one speaks, as philosophers have increasingly found a need to do in the last half-century, of "objective values." To speak of values as "objective," though it's a big step forward from the logical positivist view of them as mere calculations of utility or expressions of personal preference, remains powerless before the person (the depressed person, perhaps, or the cynic) who would say "So what? So what if this value is objective? *I* don't care about it." What ethics needs is a bridge between objective realities, of whatever sort, and a recognition in a subject of the commandingness of the ethical value; this link Levinas' notion supplies.

This foundational ethical experience – and Levinas, true to his phenomenological background, offers no further explanation of it – transcends the world of natural science; it transcends the world that philosophers (including and in particular Heidegger) have called "Being," the world in which ontology has primacy. For Levinas, it is this experience that calls me forth to become someone who "exists," who stands forth (the etymological meaning of "exist") from the field of anonymous causal forces that he terms the "*il y a*," the mere "there is" – that calls me forth into fully human being. To be human, in Levinas' language, is not a biological given, like being a cat or a butterfly, but an achievement.

Levinas' thought, constantly developed through a long lifetime, is extremely powerful, and I shall attempt to convey another aspect of it in the next chapter. His recognition of the "transcendence" of ethical obligation, and its absolute difference from the world recognisable by natural science, is what Meissner was attempting to formulate when he used the word *supernatural*. Meissner was recognising, though he didn't have adequate words for it, something altogether other, altogether more compelling, than the world of empirical fact, and this is what Levinas describes. What in Meissner could only be assertion, made defiantly and courageously in the teeth of the philosophical weather in which he and his psychoanalytic colleagues were working, becomes in Levinas' thought a much calmer and more developed statement, highly individual but nevertheless supported by the larger resource for thinking that phenomenology makes possible.

Developments in analytic philosophy: Objectivity of values

In recent decades, in the world of Anglo-American philosophy, the inadequacy of analytic philosophy has increasingly begun to be recognised, although it probably remains the predominant mode (see, for example, Cottingham 2010). The need to see values as objective, at least in part, and not merely as expressions of personal preference or emotion, has been recognised now by many Anglo-American philosophers, including Charles Taylor, Donald Davidson, Alasdair MacIntyre, Thomas Nagel and Ronald Dworkin. All these are of great interest, but I shall speak here of Dworkin in particular. He is an interesting figure in this connection, as his starting point was not religion but law. An American, born in 1931, he held chairs in the philosophy of law and jurisprudence at both Yale and Oxford, and later at New York University and University College London; most of his professional life was devoted to studying the philosophy of law. Writing in the *New York Review of Books*, he made a notable contribution to understanding the biases and errors in many decisions of the American Supreme Court. It was only towards the end of his life – he died in 2013 – that his insistent enquiry first into the basis of law, which he saw as deriving from ethics, and then into the basis of ethics, brought him to recognise that he had arrived in territory traditionally described as religious. His own cast of mind was rational and scientific, and he had no interest in the idea of a personal God, but he realised, like Levinas, that ethical values, if they are to be finally compelling, must ultimately be their own source of authority; they can't be discovered in the world of science, in which values can only be instrumental. "What matters most fundamentally to the drive to live well," he wrote, is not belief in a god but "the conviction that there is, independently and objectively, a right way to live" (2013, 153).

Dworkin gives a powerful and simple example. He speaks of the need, which many people have as they approach death, to feel that they haven't wasted their life. They have no wish to be fobbed off with consolations. The question has great importance, and the issues involved have an unmistakable reality. Dworkin spoke of this as ultimately a "religious" question, though not one requiring theistic religion, and he coined the phrase "religious atheism" to describe his own position, which he stated with impressive clarity at the start of his book. "Religion" he wrote, "is a deep, distinct and comprehensive world-view: it holds that inherent, objective value permeates everything, that the universe and its creatures are awe-inspiring, that human life has purpose and the universe order. A belief in a god is only one possible manifestation or consequence of that deeper worldview" (2013, 1).

Dworkin's view is of particular interest because "religion" and "belief in a god" are virtually synonymous in the minds of many people in the West. Starting from the issues rather than from the convictions, Dworkin shows that belief in a god is not the heart of the matter. But the "religious atheist," as described by Dworkin, is very much closer to other sorts of religious people, including theists, than to doctrinaire atheists such as Richard Dawkins or Daniel Dennett. Dworkin doesn't discuss Buddhism, but in Buddhism we already have an example of a religion that is non-theistic. Dworkin's thought is important because it opens up a way forward for religious thinking, which so often seems to return its practitioners to a past of ideas that can only be embraced by renouncing some part of what science has taught us.

Of course, a psychoanalyst, confronted with a person who wonders if he has wasted his life, would have many questions to ask – is the person depressed? etc. – but I doubt if any psychoanalyst would dismiss the question as meaningless or would think it made no difference whether the person concerned had contributed positively to human life or had spent his time as the Commandant of Treblinka (Sereny 1974). Dworkin, like Levinas, takes us directly to the territory of intrinsic value; we all immediately recognise the terrain, and it's ironic that the prevailing philosophy of the last two centuries has given little help in getting a purchase on it.

Despite important recent developments, particularly in the United States, I think no Anglo-American thinker, not even Dworkin, has offered so simple and profound a picture as Levinas or has been able to give an account of the space between "ought" and "is" that David Hume famously declared to be unbridgeable. Unless we can move on from Hume, we are unable to do what Levinas does, to look science in the eye and declare the primacy of ethics.

The function of religion

Let me come back now from this wide excursus to the question about religion with which we began. If you have followed the argument, you may be tempted to agree with much of it. OK, you might say, so responsibility arises when I perceive the "face of the Other," a technical term which includes such intangible qualities in the other as his vulnerability and his humanity; or I may perceive the preciousness of human life, or the importance of justice, or truth-telling, or kindness – Dworkin's "objective values" – and all this may then influence my conduct. But why isn't that enough? Why bring in something else, called "religion," that results in so much complication?

That is our key question in this paper. Why isn't it enough just to have whatever values one has, as a result of one's personal epiphanic moments and one's personal history of human relations? How can there be a role for religion in the eyes of an intelligent person who can see, like Freud, or like Richard Dawkins, how often the narratives and "objects" of religion are used by believers to provide false or infantile consolation, or to generate fantasies of specialness, "chosen-ness" and rightness which all too often merely give further justification for attitudes of exclusion and group conflict? Why should we not just stay with our values, recognising now that they are "objective" or even "transcendent," and put all religious baggage behind us?

I will suggest two considerations that are relevant to this question, one empirical, one more speculative. The empirical one is that, where we find a strong commitment to values in someone who is apparently non-religious or even hostile to religion, we may often find that the person carries what psychoanalysts call an "internal object," a conscious or unconscious memory or picture of someone, perhaps a parent or admired teacher, who *was* religious. Many psychoanalysts, for example, are only one or two generations away from religious family members, as was Freud himself. Raymond Tallis recently remarked (2012, 215) that he would rather live in godless Stockholm than devout Baghdad. But it is not accidental that the populations of attractive socialist societies, like that of Sweden at that time, are only one or two generations away from societies powerfully influenced by Protestant Christianity. Even if the individual sincerely believes that she is entirely free of religious attitudes, she may be quite unaware of the unconscious identifications and loyalties that give force to her commitment to her values. This is an empirical matter and could be the object of research. As I've argued in Chapter 8, it's likely that Levinas' "epiphanies," independent of personal biography though they seem in his account, in reality have the sort of depth of emotional and developmental background that psychoanalysis would claim necessarily stands behind all our capacities for emotional experience.

The more speculative consideration is the one indicated in the title of this chapter. We may have moments of epiphany, when we perceive the "face of the other" and experience the compelling sense of transcendent obligation towards him that Levinas speaks of; or we may be moved by the vision of the preciousness of human life and the beauty of the universe that Dworkin describes. I believe we do, and that such moments are extremely important. But moments are by definition transient: the I/You is fated, as Buber said clearly (1970, 68–9), to change back again into the I/It; the Other whom I must not kill becomes the other who is out of sight and will soon enough be out of mind. How am I to remember my values and continue to be influenced by them, even in non-epiphanic moments, even at times when my attention is necessarily elsewhere, or when other motives, like fear or self-preoccupation, may be in the ascendant?

It is to this question that the answer may be a "religion," with its teachings, practices and institutional arrangements. Every religion finds a way to affirm its values by presenting them in connection with stories, with personalities, with rituals and ceremonies, with artworks and music, with "practices" that have the function of reminding the believer of its foundational values, and arousing the emotions that affirm the values. As described in Chapter 4, even Buddhism, technically non-theistic, developed its great celestial Buddhas and bodhisattvas, and in the Buddha Amitābha it generated an impressively loving, quasi-divine figure who brings salvation to his followers by evoking their love and gratitude. In Hinduism, in the *Bhagavad Gita*, the kindly Krishna and the all-powerful Vishnu, embodying two very different versions of God, evoke in Arjuna sharply different emotions that must be reconciled before he can act as duty requires. In the Catholic Mass, the believer takes the body of the incarnate God into himself, giving fleshly form to Saint Paul's metaphor that we are all "members" – limbs – of one another. None of these stories or practices can survive the sceptical scrutiny of Freud's scientific *Weltanschauung*, which esteems facts and logical deduction from facts exclusively. They all necessarily depend for their survival on educational practices, and on organised bodies of people who are committed to upholding them; and they all make understandable sense if one thinks that their function is not to tell the truth about "ontology" but is to affirm central values – values which in virtually every case are more similar across the spectrum of religions than their diverse languages and mythologies suggest.

By "affirmation," I don't mean that the religion creates the values. It doesn't. The values are values because we perceive them as such, in moments of epiphany such as those Levinas described. As Ronald Dworkin points out (and the argument goes back to Plato's *Euthyphro*), we recognise goodness directly: we are moved when we encounter it; we don't deduce it from some third-person statement of God's will or commandments. In fact, on the contrary, we recognise the goodness of God's commandments, if we do, because we see that they are true to our recognition of goodness. (Desmond Tutu once famously remarked: "If God, as they say, is homophobic, I wouldn't worship that God."[1]) Nor do I mean by "affirmation" merely that we affirm our values intellectually. Religions find ways to affirm their values not only intellectually but also emotionally and imaginatively, ways that make them alive and memorable to the believer. Very importantly too, these stories and practices also make them understandable to children at the early ages when fundamental moral and imaginative attitudes to life are established.

These stories even influence unbelievers. Philip Larkin, an unbeliever, describes in his poem "Church Going" his embarrassment when he happened to stray into a church. He took off his cycle-clips awkwardly, against his will feeling obscurely reverent as he recognised the values embodied in his surroundings. Later, when somewhat reluctantly he tried to spell out the significance of the experience, he wrote of the church as being "serious", as having embodied seriousness (Larkin, 1988, 97–8), It was hard for Larkin, with his ingrained depression and cynicism, to say this, but he was absolutely right: religion is about seriousness. I might have entitled this paper: "religion and the affirmation of seriousness." That, I suggest, is what religions are ultimately for: they are for ethical education, for the imprinting on our awareness and our memories of what, in transient moments of acute perception, we recognise to be our commanding values. And if this is right, the initial question here might be reworded in a more nuanced way: without religion, or without some comparably serious form of ethical education, will a society be able, over generations, to retain its hold on its most important values: to keep them as effective motivators in people's conduct and in society's law-making, in the recognition of what makes for a good life, and in what we have become able, after so many centuries of philosophical and religious argument and reflection, to affirm as "universal human rights"?

Note

1 *New York Times*, 23 September 2022: "Church of England stops Desmond Tutu's daughter from officiating at funeral."

References

Bion, W.R. (1970). Attention and Interpretation (Reprinted 1984.) London: Karnac.

Black, D.M. (2011). *Why Things Matter: the Place of Values in Science, Psychoanalysis and Religion*. Hove and New York, NY: Routledge.

Bléandonu, G. (1994). *Wilfred Bion: his Life and Works 1897-1979*. London: Free Association Books.

Buber, M. (1970). *I and Thou* (1923). Trs. W. Kaufmann. Edinburgh: T&T Clark.

Cottingham, J. (2010). Erasmus lecture: YouTube: www.youtube.com/watch?v=0DNGesinV5s

Dworkin, R. (2013). *Religion without God*. Cambridge and London: Harvard University Press.

Freud, S. (1927). *The Future of an Illusion.*

Freud, S. (1933). The Question of a Weltanschauung. In *New Introductory Lectures*, no XXXV. SE 22, pp. 158–82.

Larkin, P. (1988). *Collected Poems*. London: Marvell Press with Faber and Faber.

Levinas, E. (1989). Ethics as First Philosophy (1984). Trs. S. Hand and M. Temple. In S. Hand (ed) *The Levinas Reader*. Oxford and Malden, MA: Blackwell, pp. 75–87.

Levinas, E. (1998). *Otherwise than Being, or Beyond Essence* (1974). Trs. A. Lingis. Pittsburgh, PA: Duquesne University Press.

Malka, S. (1989). *Lire Lévinas*. Paris: Editions du Cerf.

McGinn, C. (1989). Can We Solve the Mind-Body Problem? Mind 98: 391, 349–366.

Nietzsche, F. (1974). *The Gay Science* (1887). Trs. W. Kaufmann. New York, NY: Vintage Books.

O'Shaughnessy, E. (2005). Whose Bion? *Int J. Psychoanal.* 86: 1523–28.

Parker, S. (2011). *Winnicott and Religion*. Lanham, MD: Jason Aronson.

Roussillon, R. (2013). Winnicott's Deconstruction of Primary Narcissism. In Abram (ed) *Donald Winnicott Today*. London and New York, NY: Routledge, pp. 270–90.

Sereny, G. (1974). *Into that Darkness: an Examination of Conscience*. London: Pan Books.

Tallis, R. (2012). *Defence of Wonder and Other Philosophical Reflections*. Durham: Acumen.

Taylor, D. (2011). Commentary on Vermote's 'on the value of "late Bion" to analytic theory and practice'. *Int. J. Psychoanal.* 92: 1099–1112.

Vermote, R. (2011). On the value of "late Bion" to analytic theory and practice. *Int. J. Psychoanal.* 92: 1089–98.

Winnicott, D.W. (1951). Transitional Objects and Transitional Phenomena. In *Through Paediatrics to Psychoanalysis* (1982) 229–42. London: Hogarth Press.

Winnicott, D.W. (1974). The Location of Cultural Experience. In *Playing and Reality* 112–21. Harmondsworth: Penguin.

Chapter 10

Levinas' re-basing of religion

Introduction

I want in this final essay to address an issue that underlies most of the earlier chapters: what is being spoken of when religion is spoken of? Freud straightforwardly called religion an illusion, and most educated readers will have little difficulty in agreeing that many statements by religionists are illusory: the notion that God is a "good father" who will protect the believer from physical danger, for example. Such beliefs have been contradicted too often in human history; they can be reinstated only if so heavily interpreted that they largely cease to represent the meaning they have at first sight.

At the same time, there has been a persistent current of thought, in the psychoanalytic world as elsewhere, that to dismiss religion entirely because many of its claims, taken literally, are illusory, risks throwing out an important baby along with the bathwater. In the past two centuries, no one has thought more insightfully about the role of religion than Emmanuel Levinas. His writing is profound but exceptionally difficult, and in this essay I shall set myself as a main task to outline what he understood a religion to be. I shall follow mainly his argument in *Totality and Infinity* (1961), a work of his maturity – he was in his 50s when he wrote it – and although he continued to develop his thought in his later work, he never repudiated the fundamental picture he developed there.

To make the connection with psychoanalysis, I shall then contrast his picture with Freud's understanding in *The Future of an Illusion* (1927), in which we see not only a different estimate of the value of religion, but a quite different conception of what a religion essentially is. Freud's work too is the fruit of maturity – he was over 70 when he published it – and he too never repudiated the broad lines of the picture he gives here, though later, in *Moses and Monotheism* (1939), he recognised that the psychological impact of religious belief may be very much greater and more consequential than he had earlier realised.

But first – Emmanuel Levinas. I shall begin with a brief outline of Levinas' life, which is relevant to understanding the extreme seriousness he brought to the issues of ethics.

DOI: 10.4324/9781003451679-10

Emmanuel Levinas: A brief outline of his life

Emmanuel Levinas (1906–95) was born in Kaunas, Lithuania, the eldest of three sons of a Jewish book-seller and stationer. The family spoke Russian as their first language. Levinas' mother is credited with awakening his love of literature, particularly for classical Russian authors such as Pushkin and Turgenev. Later, in his religious writings, he referenced in particular Dostoievski. These Russians were of course Christian writers and it's notable that, although himself a practising religious Jew and later a considerable scholar of the Talmud, Levinas' thought has always appealed to people beyond the boundaries of Judaism. He used to say, jokingly, that his ambition was to translate the Bible into Greek – meaning, to find ways to formulate the insights of Judaism in the universal language of philosophy. He never doubted that, if there were truth in religion, it must be true for everybody, not solely for a single ethnic community.

During the First World War, the Levinas family escaped the German occupation by moving to Russia and then Ukraine; they returned to Lithuania in 1920. In 1923, aged 18, Levinas moved to France, to study philosophy at the University of Strasbourg. There he met many people who would be influential in his thinking, including Maurice Blanchot who became a life-long friend. In 1928–1929, he spent two semesters across the German border in Freiburg. He later said: "I came to see Husserl, and what I saw was Heidegger."

But he saw Husserl as well and clearly impressed him. Rather astonishingly, in 1929, when Husserl gave the series of lectures that became his *Cartesian Meditations*, it was the youthful Levinas who was invited to translate them into French. With his customary energy, he translated them immediately, and they appeared in French some 20 years before they were published in their initial German. Levinas first came to attention in the 1930s as a pioneer in introducing the French intellectual world, including Sartre, to the importance of phenomenology.

But for Levinas himself, the most dramatic event of his time in Freiburg was attending lectures given by Heidegger, whose great work, *Sein und Zeit (Being and Time)* had been published in 1927, when Heidegger was only 37 (Heidegger 1927). Heidegger's work and teaching attracted a cult-like devotion from many young philosophers, many of them Jewish. Levinas was one of these, and like the others, he was appalled in 1933 when Heidegger joined the Nazi party. But Levinas never renounced his conviction that Heidegger's thought was of supreme importance. Heidegger's fundamental conviction, that we awaken to an "always already" interpreted world, would be foundational for Levinas also. Another thing he may have seen in Heidegger was the determination to follow the track of one's own thinking, regardless of alleged "authorities. While this characteristic eventually took Heidegger in some very unpleasant directions indeed, in Levinas, deeply loyal to the Jewish tradition, it allowed an important freedom. One might add: including the freedom to enquire where authority really resides.

In 1932, he became a French citizen, and in the same year he married Raissa Levy, whom he had known since childhood in Kaunas where her family and the

Levinas' had been near neighbours. Raissa, musically very gifted, had come to Paris to study at the Conservatory; here the two re-met and fell in love. Their first child, a daughter named Simone, was born in 1935. Raissa's unfailingly supportive and reliable presence was of incalculable importance to Levinas, all the more so when they were re-united as Holocaust survivors after prolonged separation in the Second World War.

In addition to his work in philosophy, Levinas also became known in the 1930s in French Jewish circles. He worked for a Jewish educational agency, the Alliance Israélite Universelle, where he spoke out very directly against the barbarism that threatened Europe. Initially, he looked to Christians to support the Jews against the dangers of Hitlerism. His biographer Salomon Malka quotes an article he published early in 1939: "In an increasingly hostile world that is being covered in swastikas, it is to the cross with its straight and pure limbs that we often raise our eyes" (Malka, 2006, 61). When war broke out, his knowledge of German allowed him to join the French army as an interpreter; he was taken prisoner on 18 June 1940, four days before the fall of France.

He spent the next four years as a prisoner of war in Germany, working in humiliating conditions as a lumberjack and, as a Jew, expecting daily to be handed over to the SS. Meanwhile Raissa and Simone, living in occupied France, also survived, protected initially through the good offices of Maurice Blanchot and later by a community of courageous Christian nuns. Their families were not so fortunate. Back in Kaunas, Levinas' parents and his two younger brothers were all murdered by the Nazis by machine-gun fire (the "Holocaust of bullets"); Levinas learned of their deaths only when he emerged from captivity in 1945. Raissa's parents, living in Paris, were deported to Drancy and thence also to their deaths in the Nazi camps.

Levinas virtually never spoke of his loss. Once, when he wrote a sketch of his biography, he made no mention of it until the concluding sentence: this life, he wrote, "was dominated by the presentiment and the memory of the Nazi horror" (Malka, 2006, xiv). We need have no doubt that that was the case. He refused ever again to set foot in Germany. His enormous energy after the war, his obsessive hard work, his loving and irascible personality, and above all his intense and unceasing preoccupation with the theme of ethics, of the "infinite" importance of the Other, of the imperative of responsibility towards the other – all these features are comprehensible as a highly organised response both to his appalling loss and to his gratitude to those who had survived and to those who, often at great personal risk, had enabled their survival. All this in turn was in the context of his enduring personal loyalties: to Judaism, to the European philosophical tradition and to the Russian authors of his childhood.

After the war, Raissa gave birth to a second daughter, Andree Eliane, who died soon afterwards, and then in 1949 to a son, Michael, who inherited his mother's talent for music and is now a well-known pianist and composer.

Levinas' original work also began after the war. In 1947, he published *De l'existence à l'existant* (*Existence and Existents* [Levinas 1947]), based partly on notes written while he was still a prisoner; in 1961, *Totality and Infinity*; in 1974,

Otherwise than Being (Levinas 1974) These latter two books are usually described as his major works. In between, and subsequently, there were a multitude of other books and papers. His reputation spread only slowly, partly because of the sheer difficulty of his writing, partly because after the war he returned to the world of Jewish education as principal of the Ecole Normale Israélite Oriental. Not until 1961 did he acquire a post at a university, in Poitiers. In 1973, he became a Professor at the Sorbonne. By the time he died in 1995, he was widely recognised as one of the major French thinkers of the twentieth century.

Levinas' account of religion

In the first of his major books, *Totality and Infinity*, Levinas made a resonant claim: *"Totality and the embrace of being, or ontology, do not contain the final secret of being. Religion ... is the ultimate structure"* (1961, 80).

What did he mean by this?

Essentially, he believed that any rationally coherent philosophy, such as an account of reality in which evidence-based natural science gives us our model of truth, or the sort of idealist picture in which non-material concepts (such as Plato's forms) give rise to an understandable, unified picture, can only at the end of the day describe a closed and finite universe – a "totality," in his favoured word (with its overtone of "totalitarian").

But human beings, in addition to their finite and graspable characteristics, are also "psychisms": they come with an indeterminable cloud of interior experiences, to which no one else has direct access: these might include aspirations, wishes, fears, revulsions, delights, hopes, many of which are in no way manifest from the outside, and some of which are not known even to the person him- or herself. The story told by the biographer or the historian is a story told from outside and in a shared language: it will never include the interiority of the person and it cannot do so. The person therefore is, in Levinas' phrase, a "separated being." "Separation designates the possibility of an *existent* being set up and having its own destiny to itself, that is, being born and dying without the place of this birth and this death in the time of universal history being the measure of its reality" (1961, 55, italics in original).

Human persons, therefore, are never fully described by the accounts we can give of them. What Levinas says of "history" is true of every sort of verbal description (including, we may add, the psychoanalytic). "The thesis of the primacy of history constitutes an option for the comprehension of being in which interiority is sacrificed .... Cronos, thinking he swallows a god, swallows but a stone" (57–8).[1]

Attempting to say more about this never fully describable thing, the "psychism," Levinas gives a sequential account. There is first what he calls "participation," then the "break with participation" and finally, when the liberated psychism encounters the other, "Desire." None of these notions is immediately self-explanatory. Participation precedes separation. It is a state characterised by entanglement with another, or with others, and is perhaps related to what psychoanalysis calls narcissism, a psychological state in which the self is entangled with others by different sorts of identification, both projective and introjective. The "break with participation" therefore is a separation out of the self, or in Levinas' word the psychism, from its projections and introjections; it is an attempt to stand on one's own base. The separation out from participation gives rise to the psychism as a "separated being."

For psychoanalysis, this attempt has been a goal in its own right: to be as autonomous as possible, to be aware of one's desires and to be the conscious "slave of three masters," id, superego and external world – making one's decisions about one's own welfare on as large a base of information as one can contact – such things were virtually the definition of Freud's initial account of psychic health. Later, with the increasing recognition of the importance of individual relationships, things became more complicated. Levinas describes this achievement as "the being autonomous in separation," or "the I endowed with personal life," and he speaks of this version of the psychism rather surprisingly as "happy" and as "having no wants." The point is that such an "I" feels complete in itself. It has of course desires and sadnesses in the ordinary way, but it has no reason to be disconcerted by them: they are "my" desires, "my" sadnesses, etc.: they do not alter the fundamental truth of "my autonomy" as a separate being.

But this happy, separated I does seek the truth. "To seek and to obtain truth," says Levinas, "is to be in a relation not because one is defined by something other than oneself, but because in a certain sense one lacks nothing" (61). His meaning seems to be that when one "participates" in others one can't seek truth because truth depends on separation. One can only see something when one is apart from it. Only when I am separate from the world can I look at it appraisingly and decide what is true and what is false. And when I am in this state, "happily" using my intelligence to understand the world in the objective, rational terms of philosophy, science or history, I perceive the world as a closed universe, a totality in which everything is ultimately "the same" and can be added together to make a single picture, a "theory of everything," so to speak.

But in becoming a separated being, I may have uprooted myself from "participation," but I have not in fact distanced myself from others. They are still there, still playing roles in my life. And now, as I appraise them, as I seek to know the truth about this homogenous universe that includes me and yet may apparently be understood as if it were something external to me, something new happens. Something new is awakened in me, something that originates not from me, but from the other, namely, Desire. "Desire is an aspiration that the Desirable animates: it originates from its 'object'" (62). In terms of a familiar conundrum of philosophical ethics (is the good good because we desire it, or do we desire it because it is good?), Levinas opts clearly for the latter.

This desire is not any ordinary sort of appetite, like the appetite for sex or for food. It is not for anything for "me"; it is for something for the other. "It is absolutely non-egoist; its name is justice" (63). It involves essentially the notion of otherness. This has been very hard for psychoanalysis to understand, as the model of desire, as conceived by Freud, is "libido," the wish for drive-satisfaction, and even when extended by empathy, identification, projection, etc., it can only be "my" desire that I aspire to satisfy. – That is not Levinas' picture. For him, that would give rise at best to "politics": the demand for reciprocal recognition, or the avoidance of envy by the acceptance of equality[2]. He wants to emphasise something altogether different: the otherness of the other; my Desire is insatiable because it is a response to otherness, to the "manifestation of a face" over and beyond form (66). "Face," for Levinas, is not the "plastic form" of eyes, nose, mouth etc.; it is "the living presence"; it is expression; it is the revelation of the other in his complete otherness from "me."

This notion of the complete otherness of the Other is the key to the whole of Levinas' thought. It is in one sense a glimpse of what he has already spoken of as the indescribability of the interiority of the psychism (I can't get my perception of the Other into words); but it goes beyond it when I have the "epiphanic" experience (1961, 171) of seeing the "face of the Other" and recognising that the face commands me; it carries the command "Thou shalt not kill" – a call to responsibility which transcends anything that I can understand or control. At this point, I perceive the "infinity" of the other. He can no longer be adequately seen in the objective terms of science or of idealist philosophy; he can no longer be grasped by any of my sets of categories: "this being is nowise an object" (70). "It is not the insufficiency of the I that prevents totalisation, but the Infinity of the Other" (80). As he would write later:

> The negativity of the *in* of the Infinite – otherwise than being, divine comedy – hollows out a desire which cannot be filled, nourishes itself with its very augmentation, and is exalted as a desire, withdraws from its satisfaction in the measure that it approaches the desirable. It is a desire that is beyond satisfaction, and, unlike a need, does not identify a term or an end. This endless desire for what is beyond being is dis-interestedness, transcendence – desire for the Good.
>
> (Levinas 1975, 139)

It's important to recognise that what Levinas is describing is not a mysticism, or not the sort of mysticism that goes beyond ordinary experience to perceive the self as "united" or merged with something larger than itself – with God, or with Being, or with the universe. Levinas was always opposed to such mysticisms, and to the emotions of ecstasy or rapture that often accompany them. When I maintain an ethical relation, he wrote, "I refuse to figure in a drama of salvation or of damnation that would be enacted in spite of me" (79). Both I and the Other are individual beings, "existents" in Levinas' term, never Being in general, a notion found in Heidegger from which Levinas clearly distinguished his own view. Despite the apparent extravagance of some of his language when he speaks of Otherness or of Infinity, Levinas' stance in relation to these things is always ethical, rational and down to earth. "Only an I," he says, "can respond to the injunction of a face" (305). He remains a "separated being."

But, though never a "mystic" in this sense, he does want to retain the notion of religion. "Totality" is achieved by systems of thought that perceive the other as "the same," as "like me," an *alter ego*, comprehensible in the same terms in which everything else can be comprehended – systems which add up to and give rise to a whole. To perceive the otherness of the Other, to perceive his "Infinity," is to perceive a system which it is impossible to totalise in this way.

And yet, he says, we do want to name this co-existence of same and other: "The conjuncture of the same and the other, in which even their verbal proximity is maintained, is the *direct* and *full face* welcome of the other by me. This conjuncture is irreducible to totality; the 'face to face' position is not a modification of the 'alongside of ....' Even when I shall have linked the Other to myself with the conjunction 'and', the Other continues to face me, to reveal himself in his face. *Religion* subtends this formal totality .... The face to face remains an ultimate situation" (1961, 80–1, italics in original). (At this point Levinas comes close to another great Jewish thinker, Martin Buber, whom he discussed in a paper originally published in German (Levinas, 1963).)

This, then, is Levinas' definition of religion. It is a way of speaking that doesn't totalise the universe but recognises the ethical realities of separation, Infinity, and transcendent command. Religion is about human relating. "Everything that cannot be reduced to an interhuman relation represents not the superior form but the forever primitive form of religion" (79). I shall come back to this later.

Discussion

I have been following the argument presented by Levinas, in his customary dense and arresting prose, in *Totality and Infinity*. It is worth pausing for a moment to consider the highly original definition of religion to which this argument has brought us.

It is a claim essentially that religion is about perceiving the power of ethical obligation, and about *experiencing* that power. Religious allegorical stories are a help, if they are helpful at all, towards that end. The power of ethical obligation is a reality, experienced when we perceive the face of the Other. This is not an empirical reality, although it arises within the awareness of the subject as a result of an experience – the experience of contemplating the Other, a particular object. It transcends the ordinary reality of "ontologies," including the knowledge we have of the world from science. This is what is meant by saying that "ethics is first philosophy," a phrase that became the title of an important later paper (Levinas, 1984).

He does not say, but it seems inescapably entailed by his argument, that to perceive the call to responsibility carried by the face of the Other also has its own ontological implications. It shows us that the world we live in is not closed into a finite "totality" but is "plural." Its living constituents have the quality he calls Infinity, derived from an interiority (perhaps we might say a subjectivity) which can never be captured by third-person description. Levinas points in the direction of this pluralist philosophy when he looks back to the conception of "the only analogical unity of being" in Aristotle, or to Plato's idea of "the transcendence of the Good with respect to being" (1961, 80). These ideas, he says, should have been the source of "a pluralist philosophy in which the plurality of being would not disappear into the unity of number nor be integrated into a totality" (80). (In his phrase "the plurality of being," we glimpse how difficult it is to *really* put "ontology" into a subordinate place.)

The word *religion* serves to name this plural vision, this continual recognition and call of value as we survey the world of our responsibilities and perceive the faces of the many Others who make it up. How we choose among them, what we choose to actually *do*, in given circumstances, is in Levinas' term "politics": we are influenced by countless factors, including proximity (perhaps but not necessarily) and by our own practical skills and capacities. But the fact that it is this world of infinity, plurality and obligation that we most deeply live in is what is meant by "religion" in Levinas' understanding. It is a highly original conception.

From a psychoanalytic perspective, it is of particular interest because it defines religion without reference to religious "objects." When Freud, who was not religious, examined religion in *The Future of an Illusion* (1927), his understanding of religion was primarily that it was the solution to a problem. He described eloquently the unsatisfactoriness of human life, whether in "the state of nature" or in "civilisation." The resulting task, he said, was "a manifold one. Man's self-regard, seriously menaced, calls for consolation; life and the universe must be robbed of their terrors; moreover his curiosity ... demands an answer" (SE XXI, 16). Man's response was to assimilate his condition of helplessness to its "infantile prototype," and as in infancy he had learned to discover in the frightening and powerful adults around him the characteristics of a father, so he turned the frightening forces of nature into gods. Gradually "a store of ideas is created, born from man's need to make his helplessness tolerable and built up from... memories of the helplessness of his own childhood and the childhood of the human race" (18). The comforting fantasies of a benevolent Providence, life that continues after death, a superior wisdom which directs the course of history – all these emerged in response to the true predicament of helplessness and uncertainty. Finally, man discovered "the father who had all along been hidden behind every divine figure as its nucleus" (19) – this was the idea of the monotheistic God, from whom, as with a human father, one could have the hope of reward, or at least the feeling or the belief that one was his beloved child.

Freud defined religious ideas as "teachings and assertions about facts and conditions of external (or internal) reality which tell one something one has not discovered for oneself and which lay claim to one's *belief*" (25, italics added). It was on this matter of belief that Freud based his argument. If we look for the ground of these beliefs, he said, we discover only that these teachings were believed by our ancestors, that their proofs had been handed down from primeval times, and that it was forbidden to question them (26). Given the obvious insufficiency of these grounds, he dismissed religious beliefs as "fairytales" (29)[3].

Freud's account of religion therefore – to use a slightly later psychoanalytic language – is one of religious "objects": God or gods, angels, demons, bodhisattvas and the emotional responses appropriate to such objects: love, fear, gratitude, the wish to propitiate and so forth. This is probably the ordinary view of religion that most educated people hold, and it is strongly supported by the use of the word *belief* in many religious teachings: to "believe in God" is at least plausibly understood as meaning to believe in the existence of a religious object named God, to whom then as to other "objects" can be ascribed familiar attributes: loving, judging, condemning, intending, creating, approving, and so forth.

This is a view of religion seen from the outside, in the third person, though it is no doubt also very common in religious believers themselves. It is the sort of view Levinas discusses and attributes to the ontologist – in this case the historian – who sacrifices the interiority of the psychism to the facts of a universal historical time: "Cronos, thinking he swallows a god, swallows but a stone."[4] Freud, looking with the eyes of the historian and the scientist, discovers the stone and says much that is acute about it. But his scientific, objective standpoint makes it impossible for him to see the "god," the entirely different picture of the "other" that Levinas' phenomenological starting point makes possible.

How are these two pictures related? We needn't dismiss either of them as simply mistaken; both have an entirely intelligible validity. But Levinas' view makes room for Freud's, as Freud's does not for Levinas'.

It is of the essence of a phenomenological point of view that different starting points give rise to a different view of the world. In a fascinating discussion of internalisation, the psychoanalyst Hans Loewald compared Freud's account of the death drive (Freud 1920) – based on a picture of the ego as governed by Fechner's constancy principle and the wish to protect itself from change – with Loewald's own picture of the psyche as achieving higher order organisation as a result of accepting change and allowing the internalisation of new content (Loewald, 1973). These two pictures are, says Loewald, the result of a shift of standpoint. Freud's standpoint was that of the ego, Loewald's that of psychic life. "What from the viewpoint of psychic life is higher and richer organisation, from the viewpoint of the constancy principle is a further complication and delay on the return road to the state of rest" (74). It was for this reason that Loewald came to say that the great innovation in *Beyond the Pleasure Principle* (Freud 1920) was not the introduction of the idea of the death drive – a new version of the familiar constancy principle – but the subsuming of libido into Eros, a force making for integration.

It was his fidelity to the "standpoint of the ego" that caused Freud to see "civilisation" in terms of its "discontents" – the frustrations imposed on the individual by the requirements of civilised society (Freud, 1930). This is of course a perfectly valid viewpoint, and it illuminates a lot, but Loewald's argument enables us to see that it is only one viewpoint and there are others. The same is true of Freud's account of religion. He sees it from the standpoint of an ego that is defending itself against disturbance: I am frightened by the recognition of my helplessness in a big world, by the world's unpredictability, and by the fact of my own inescapable death and the deaths of those I love and depend on. Religion is compellingly attractive, therefore, because it gives me a way to think I don't have to fear these things. They may be realities in "this world," but the fairytales of religion allow me to believe there is another, truer world in which they are not realities. The ego need not be so disturbed; it can return to its state of rest.

From this standpoint, religion is indeed delusive, and to mature, to accept the dictates of the reality principle, requires facing the fact that these things, my helplessness, the world's unpredictability and so forth, are all part of "grim reality," part of the inevitable "discontents" of every human existence. This is sometimes called the tragic view of life, and it has an unmistakable validity.

It had particular force for Freud because it was also the view of objective science. The purely objective view of human life, whereby human beings like all other organisms are the product of millions of years of natural selection, of a meaningless interplay between random mutations in living matter and an ever-changing physical environment, offered no alternative: human beings might have their poignant quality of subjectivity, which Levinas described as interiority, but it too was without meaning; indeed it was even, as the logical positivists would insist, meaningless to raise the question of meaning, or of values other than instrumental ones. Something might be of value to me if it enabled me to feed, to sleep or to mate (the intelligible goals of the Darwinian organism), but any "intrinsic" value could only be delusive and distracting, at best an idiosyncratic personal preference. As Thomas Nagel has said: "The pursuit of objectivity with respect to value runs the risk of leaving value behind altogether. We may reach a standpoint so removed from the perspective of human life that all we can do is to observe" (Nagel, 1986, 209). That is necessarily the standpoint of a purely "scientific" psychoanalysis.

Levinas' phenomenological account, like Loewald's, but unlike Freud's, makes room for different viewpoints, all of which have their potential validity. Freud's vision was the totalising homogenous vision of natural science; it saw certain things with great clarity – religion does indeed often provide false consolations to its followers – but could not see what is shown from the viewpoint of what Levinas meant by "religion," which perceives a plural, non-homogenous world in which the face of the Other opens a path to "Infinity" and to the transcendent command of responsibility. To say "ethics is first philosophy" is to set aside the objective priority of natural science and base one's world-view on something systematically invisible to science, something accessible solely from within the realm of "my" experience as a subject.

Levinas does not, however, in *Totality and Infinity*, call his vision "ethics": he calls it "religion." This is confusing. Religions, particularly the so-called Abrahamic religions, do indeed present themselves in the form of the sorts of stories involving religious objects that Freud describes. We hear for instance that God bargained with Abraham before the destruction of Sodom, spoke to Moses out of the burning bush and so forth. The Christian creeds, the formal statements of what Christians "believe," are about precisely such stories and objects; they have the air of making ontological claims entirely analogous to the claims put forward by science or history. The Indian religions, Hinduism and Buddhism, have traditionally been more cautious about making summary statements about what religionists commit themselves to, but they too relate to central figures and narratives, largely legendary if not altogether fictitious. Freud was probably right to say that ordinary adherents of all these religions believe many of their stories to be literally true, even if all the developed religions also have more thoughtful thinkers who emphasise the symbolic nature of these stories and the inadequacy of verbal formulations to express religious truth.

Faced with this complicated array of considerations, it's tempting to say that Freud and Levinas are speaking of two quite different things, both confusingly called religion, and the simplest solution would be to give them two different names – perhaps to say that Freud was talking about religion and Levinas about ethics. But this would overlook the fact that Freud's objective perspective on religious beliefs and religious objects (in which they seem like fairytales) is not the only one possible. In other perspectives, which ignore the issue of their historical truth, the telling of a religious narrative can be heard somewhat as one would hear the account of a dream in a psychoanalytic session – not as a narrative of literal fact but as a starting point for free association and reflection. In the case of the dream, we are confident that it has an importance because it has been dreamed and brought by the patient; in the case of the religious story, we discover its importance because it illuminates the "infinite" perspective – and the experience of receiving a command – that Levinas describes when he speaks of encountering the face of the Other. Just as we can see the actual physical face of another person without having the epiphanic experience Levinas describes, so too we can encounter the statements or ceremonies of religion without being moved by them. But if the religionist is moved by them, their tendency is to awaken her to the ethical dimension of her relations to the world and to others.

It was a weakness in Freud's psychoanalysis that it could give no account of intrinsic ethical value. The theory of the superego, of values imported into the psyche by introjecting the attitudes of others, can give no account of a person recognising her own ethical values and accepting them as having authority. Levinas' picture provides exactly this. Levinas, in addition to being a philosopher, was also a practising Jew and a Talmud scholar; in his own mind the connection between ethics and religious texts was never broken, though as a philosopher he felt it important to use a secular language. He believed that the language of philosophy could make the truths of his religion universally accessible – and if something was true it was not a Jewish truth or a Christian truth, it was a universal truth. It was important therefore to make the philosophical statement "in Greek," as he put it, meaning in the universal language of philosophy, not in the local language of a particular religious tradition. "At no moment," he said to Philippe Nemo, "did the western philosophical tradition in my eyes lose its right to the last word; everything must indeed be expressed in its tongue" (1982, 24).

The implication of Levinas' understanding is potentially far-reaching. It seems to shift the balance between religion and ethics, and where in the past religion has usually been presented as the senior partner, in the light of this deepening understanding ethics may come to seem the heart of the matter, and the function of religion to be ancillary, to provide one of the avenues to recognising efficacious ethical values. It is a striking fact that all the developed religious traditions, insofar as they have remained thoughtful and not collapsed into a fundamentalist reading of idealised ancient texts, have arrived at remarkably similar ethical values: justice, truthtelling, the foundational importance of love and kindness – such values are taught in all the world's major religions. What Levinas' "universal" formulation suggests in addition is that such values arise spontaneously in human beings, with or without the guidance of religious belief, when we perceive "the face of the Other." This arising is essentially a psychological event, a discovery of a changed perspective. "Moral consciousness is not invoked here as a particularly commendable variety of consciousness, but as the concrete form taken by a movement within the Same in the face of the Other, a movement that is more fundamental than freedom but that returns us to neither violence nor fatality" (Levinas 1962, 20).

Psychoanalysis can add something further, however. Levinas' picture of an epiphanic experience is of something taking place in the present; he doesn't give a picture of the psychological formation of the person in whom this experience takes place. But a psychoanalyst is bound to enquire into this background: why does one person have this experience and act upon it, perhaps changing his or her entire life in the light of it – and another person has no such experience, or has some version of the experience but shrugs it off and remains ungoverned by it? It may well be that we would find, as in Levinas himself, that the person whom the experience affects most profoundly is someone who has been educated by the stories of religion, or in whose life someone has been of great importance who had been educated by the stories of religion. In other words, the person for whom the epiphanic experience is most powerful is perhaps someone who has been predisposed towards it by the sort of developmental history, the sort of play of internal objects, that psychoanalysis finds when it looks into other formative emotional experiences in the present tense.

To use the word "religion" to describe the picture of a plural world that we discover when we take the epiphanic experience with full seriousness is also to imply something further. It is in the nature of experience to be transient: we may see something, be moved, and pass on to the next experience, leaving the first behind. Religion, as Levinas uses the term, counteracts this tendency by emphasising that this particular experience, the encounter with the face of the Other, has a peculiar importance. It tells us that we live in a world of "infinity," not of "totality," a world (as Levinas would emphasise in his later writings) that singles me out, that "chooses" "me" to carry unique responsibility. (Levinas came to link this idea with the "chosen-ness" of the Jews – but now it was generalised: *every* human being is "chosen" by the face of the Other to be an agent of obligation and responsibility.) The epiphanic experience tells me, but then religion helps me to hold in mind, and discusses further, that I as a subject am not judged by history alone, but by another standard that is uniquely my own.

I said I would come back to Levinas' strong statement: "Everything that cannot be reduced to interhuman relation represents not the superior form but the forever primitive form of religion" (1961, 79). Climate change and the crisis of extinctions and ecocide remind us that our ethical obligation extends beyond the human. It is a limitation in Levinas' thought that he failed to see that the face of the Other need not only be a human face: we may perceive it in nature, in other species, and perhaps even in Gaia herself.

Conclusion

If we accept that Levinas' understanding, with its recognition of different viewpoints of which Freud's historical and factual position is one, gives a profounder insight into what is lastingly important about religion, then we may think as well that the mythological elements of religion are not the heart of the matter. What is at the heart of religion is its ethical understanding. Philosophically, this is not perceivable from the standpoint of science and requires the sort of phenomenological standpoint that Levinas speaks from.

Levinas was by no means alone in discovering this standpoint, though no one else I think has described it in so much detail and with so much subtlety. Even within anglophone analytic philosophy, Elizabeth Anscombe (1958) and Alasdair MacIntyre (1981, 1988) recognised how prioritising the methods of empirical science as giving the only model for reliable knowledge had resulted in the hollowing out of ethical language, causing words that once had great power, like truth, justice, or goodness, to become mere labels set on personal preference, or on complicated and always questionable calculations of consequence (such as the various forms of utilitarianism). Both Anscombe and MacIntyre took this recognition extremely seriously, and both in their personal lives dealt with it by turning to Catholicism and reinstating the earlier meaning of such words in Christian history. But their essentially historical account of what had been lost offered nothing comparable to Levinas' radical critique of the Western philosophical tradition, and his reformulation of the base on which ethics and religion stand.

One anglophone thinker who came closer to Levinas was Ronald Dworkin – rather surprisingly as his very distinguished career was as a specialist in law and jurisprudence. But he was always concerned with the question of what it was that caused matters of justice to be of such commanding importance, and towards the end of his life, he addressed this question in two books, *Justice for Hedgehogs* (2011) and *Religion without God* (2013). In the latter book in particular, he develops with great simplicity and eloquence his thesis that we recognise ethical values directly, "objectively" as he put it. We recognise, he said, "that inherent, objective value permeates everything, that the universe and its creatures are awe-inspiring, that human life has purpose and the universe order" (2013, 1). There was no need for the sort of mythology that speaks of God, or gods, though Dworkin acknowledged that his "religious atheism" is closer to religious theism than it is to the sort of atheism represented by scientists such as Richard Dawkins (whose position in this matter is much like Freud's). Dworkin writes: "The religious attitude ... insists on the full independence of value: the world of value is self-contained and self-certifying" (16). He compares it to the world of mathematics. Even if the human race ceased to be able to do mathematics, it would remain true that seven plus five equals twelve, and there could be no good reason to doubt it. Similarly, "if value is objective, then consensus about a particular value judgement is irrelevant to its truth" (18).

In Dworkin's argument, the claim that values are "objective" takes the place of Levinas' more psychological account of the recognition of obligation arising from the perception of the face of the Other. The phrase "objective value," though widely used in philosophy, is not in itself satisfactory. Values may be objectively true, but a value can only be powerful, can only truly be a value (the root of the word *value* is the Latin *valere*, to be strong) when it affects a subjectivity; to speak of objective value necessarily implies also the existence of a subject who can be moved by that value. But, such considerations aside, the place at which each of these thinkers arrives has an important similarity: both Levinas and Dworkin believe that ethical values are recognised directly and have an immediate (unmediated) power for us. I shall use the phrase "ethical seriousness" to describe this position. Full ethical seriousness requires an essentially phenomenological understanding: the alternatives, the viewpoints either of objective science or of religious "belief," interpose a middle term (the complicated consequentialist discussions or the stories about religious objects), which interferes with the simplicity of the commanding experience that both Levinas and Dworkin insist on.

Levinas' argument, that ethics is not only immediately apprehended but also has "priority" over ontology, is not I think quite satisfactory. In perceiving others, we surely perceive "being" as well as obligation. The argument permits of a both/and as well as an either/or. But what it does show is that we are mistaken if we give priority instead to the ontology of science. Any approach such as Freud's, that gives priority to empirical natural science, necessarily abolishes ethical seriousness. That is a logical consequence: full ethical seriousness requires that subjective experience be given a central place in the picture.

If all this is correct, then narratives involving religious objects – which are often thought to be fundamental components of religion, and which Freud rightly criticised as objectively untrue or unprovable – can best be understood as "allegorical," meaning that while they may not be true on a factual level (they don't require to be "believed in"), they may offer imaginative paths to discovering, remembering and discussing more deeply the values that it is the ultimate function of the religion to affirm. Because of the nature of the human imagination, as we see also in dreams, art, poetry and so on, it may continue to be very natural for us to approach issues of value and decision by way of remembered or imagined narratives involving "objects," real or imagined. And even if in the course of growing up such stories are eventually abandoned, they may continue to have an important role to play in ethical education and earlier training.

This then is Levinasian religion. It isn't about believing "six impossible things before breakfast." It is about perceiving the "infinity" of the Other, and about hearing the call to responsibility that emanates from it. The stories told by religion may be fictional, but religion is not adequately described as illusion. Historically, it has played a fundamental role in preserving the language of ethical seriousness, which is essential if individuals are to find their lives meaningful and if the cardinal institutions of civil society, including the affirmation of human rights, the rule of law, and respect for nature and the world's ecosystems are to be maintained over long periods of time. This role is ultimately the reason for religion's importance. Levinas' argument singles out this role; it does not answer the many further questions of how ethical seriousness will be expressed in practice, in terms of actual decisions and actions. Such questions involve practical knowledge, self-management, and the wisdom born of experience. In the metaphor I have used in earlier chapters, discussing Dante, they are the province of Virgil and not of Beatrice. But at this point the discussion moves into different territory, the territory of "politics" and practical ethics, which is beyond the scope of this book.

Notes

1 Levinas' brilliant metaphor references the Greek myth of Cronos, god of time, who feared being usurped by his children and therefore ate each child as it was born. After he had eaten five of his children, his wife, Rhea, substituted a stone for the sixth, Zeus. Cronos duly swallowed the stone. Zeus, raised on the island of Crete, subsequently overthrew his father.
2 In later writings, Levinas tended to avoid the word "justice," used here, in order to further separate his concept from "politics".
3 Levinas would have agreed with Freud at least in part of this analysis. Once, discussing the "innocent" Jews who lost their faith in Auschwitz, Levinas spoke of their conception of God as "childish" – "a God of rewards and punishments" (see Morgan, 2007, 341).
4 See endnote 2 on p. 60.

References

Anscombe, G.E.M. (1958). Modern moral philosophy. *Philosophy* 33: 124.
Dworkin, R. (2011). *Justice for Hedgehogs*. Cambridge, MA and London: Harvard UP.
Dworkin, R. (2013). *Religion Without God*. Cambridge, MA and London: Harvard UP.
Freud, S. (1920). *Beyond the Pleasure Principle*. SE 18, 1–64. London: Hogarth.
Freud, S. (1927). *The Future of an Illusion*. SE 21, 1–56. London: Hogarth.
Freud, S. (1930). *Civilization and its Discontents*. SE 21, 57–145. London: Hogarth.
Heidegger, M. (1927). *Sein und Zeit*. In English *Being* and *Time*, trs. J. Macquarrie and E. Robinson. New York, Harper and Row, 1962.
Levinas, E. (1947). *Existence and Existents*. Trs. A. Lingis. The Hague: Nijhoff, 1978.
Levinas, E. (1961). *Totality and Infinity*. Trs. A. Lingis. Pittsburgh, PA: Duquesne UP, 1969.
Levinas, E. (1962). Transcendence and Height. Trs. A.T. Peperzak. In A. Peperzak, S. Critchley, R. Bernasconi (eds) *Basic Philosophical Writings*, 11–31. Bloomington, IN: Indiana UP, 1996.
Levinas, E. (1963). Martin Buber and the Theory of Knowledge. Trs. S. Richmond. In S. Hand (ed) *The Levinas Reader*. Oxford: Blackwell, 1989. 59–74.
Levinas, E. (1974). *Otherwise than Being or Beyond Essence*. Trs A. Lingis. The Hague: Nijhoff, 1981.
Levinas, E. (1975). God and Philosophy. Trs. A. Lingis et al. In A. Peperzak, S. Critchley, R. Bernasconi (eds) *Basic Philosophical Writings* 79–96. Bloomington, IN: Indiana UP, 1996.

Levinas, E. (1982). *Ethics and Infinity: Conversations with Philippe Nemo*. Trs. A. Lingis. Pittsburgh: Duquesne UP, 1985.

Levinas, E. (1984). Ethics as First Philosophy. Trs. S. Hand and M. Temple. In S. Hand (ed.) *The Levinas Reader*. Oxford: Blackwell, 1989, 75–87.

Loewald, H. (1973). On Internalization. In *Papers on Psychoanalysis*. New Haven, CT and London: Yale UP, 1980.

MacIntyre, A. (1981). *After Virtue*. London and. New York, NY: Bloomsbury.

MacIntyre, A. (1988). *Whose Justice? Which Rationality?* London: Duckworth and Co.

Malka, S. (2006). *Emmanuel Levinas: His Life and Legacy*. Trs. M. Kigel and S.M. Embree. Pittsburgh: Duquesne UP.

Morgan, M.L. (2007). *Discovering Levinas*. Cambridge: Cambridge UP.

Nagel, T. (1986). *The View from Nowhere*. Oxford: Oxford UP.

Index

Page numbers followed by 'n' refer to notes.